Problem-based
Learning
Online

Problem-based Learning Online

Maggi Savin-Baden and
Kay Wilkie

Open University Press

Open University Press
McGraw-Hill Education
McGraw-Hill House
Shoppenhangers Road
Maidenhead
Berkshire
England
SL6 2QL

email: enquiries@openup.co.uk
world wide web: www.openup.co.uk

and Two Penn Plaza, New York, NY 10121-2289, USA

First published 2006

A catalogue record of this book is available from the British Library

ISBN-10: 0335 22006 1 (pb)   0335 22007 X (hb)
ISBN-13: 978 0335 22006 9 (pb)   978 0335 22007 6 (hb)

Library of Congress Cataloging-in-Publication Data
CIP data applied for

Typeset by RefineCatch Limited, Bungay, Suffolk
Printed in Poland EU by OZGraf. S.A www.polskabook.pl

For . . .

Katherine Bowes

and

David and Edith Cormack

'Guts' is grace under pressure (Hemingway, 1929)

Contents

List of figures   ix
List of tables   xi
Acknowledgements   xii
Contributors   xiii

Introduction   xix
  Maggi Savin-Baden and Kay Wilkie

Part 1 Possibilities and challenges   1

  1   The challenge of using problem-based learning online   3
      Maggi Savin-Baden

  2   Issues in cyberspace education   14
      Ray Land and Siân Bayne

  3   Institutional perspectives: making PBLonline possible and
      sustainable   24
      Frances Deepwell and Andy Syson

Part 2 Facilitation and mediation   39

  4   Tracing the tutor role in problem-based learning
      and PBLonline   45
      Kirsten Hofgaard Lycke, Helge I. Strømsø and Per Grøttum

  5   From face-to-face to online participation: tensions in
      facilitating problem-based learning   61
      Cindy E. Hmelo-Silver, Anandi Nagarajan and Sharon J. Derry

  6   The academic developer as tutor in PBLonline in
      higher education   79
      Roisin Donnelly

Part 3   Technopedagogy   99

7   PBLonline: a framework for collaborative e-learning   105
   David Jennings

8   Online learning and problem-based learning: complementary
   or colliding approaches?   126
   Maggi Savin-Baden and Carolyn Gibbon

9   Developing expertise in professional practice, online,
   at a distance   140
   Karen Lee

Part 4   Developing technology   155

10   Digital support for a constructivist approach to education:
    the case of a problem-based psychology curriculum   159
    Wilco te Winkel, Remy Rikers and Henk Schmidt

11   Tools to empower problem-based learning: a principled and
    empirical approach to the design of problem-based
    learning online   174
    Frans Ronteltap

12   Analysing the use of communication tools for collaboration
    in PBLonline   191
    Chris Beaumont and Chew Swee Cheng

Epilogue   210
Glossary   212
References   216
Index   239

List of figures

5.1   Problem-based learning activity system   63
5.2   Videocase with links to case-related concepts in
      Knowledge Web   64
5.3   eSTEP roadmap   65
5.4   Tensions in eSTEP   68
5.5   LBD assessment example   69
5.6   Excerpt of whiteboard discussion assessment proposal
      of foreign language case   73
6.1   Blended problem-based learning module   83
6.2   Tutor roles in a blended PBL module   91
6.3   Continuum of blended communication strategies:
      e-moderating and PBL   93
6.4   Avoiding pitfalls in tutoring blended PBL   95
7.1   The move towards inclusive, collaborative and constructive
      domains of sharing knowledge within an
      online environment   111
7.2   A model for collaborative interactions in an online
      PBL environment   112
7.3   Schematic of PBLonline scenario within the VLE Blackboard   125
10.1 The problem ' "ASHAMED FOR HUMANITY"(?)' together
      with its suggested resources   166
10.2 Example of a personal favourites folder, in which students
      can collect and organise all personally relevant
      learning resources   168
10.3 Example of a personal note-taking system   169
10.4 Example of how students can add a rating, a review or their
      own learning materials   172
11.1 Steps in design research   175
11.2 Communication patterns   178
11.3 Analysis of group learning and design of a learning
      situation for productive interactions   180

11.4	Model of affordances for productive learning interactions	182
11.5	Knowledge Builder (group environment)	186
11.6	Knowledge Manager (personal environment)	187
11.7	Example of message in POLARIS	188
12.1	PBL scenario for first cycle	194
12.2	Tool preferences in early stages of problem-based learning cycle	199
12.3	Tool preferences in later stages of problem-based learning cycle (1)	200
12.4	Tool preferences in later stages of problem-based learning cycle (2)	201
12.5	Induction workshop as an activity system	204
12.6	Initial meeting as an activity system	205
12.7	Programme as an activity system	206

List of tables

5.1   eSTEP activities   66
8.1   Types of knowledge and types of problem   135
        Source: Adapted from Schmidt and Moust, 2000: 68
9.1   Results of questionnaire on use of Blackboard   147
9.2   Design considerations for e-learning   152
        Source: Hung and Chen, 2001
11.1 Interaction differences related to space of time   185
11.2 Functions available in POLARIS   189
12.1 Problem-based learning activities   198

Acknowledgements

Thanks are due to a number of people: Gilly Salmon, Mike Prosser and Glynis Cousin for their endorsements of the book and Shona Mullen, Managing Director, McGraw-Hill Education, for her support and guidance during this project.

Our thanks are also due to John Savin-Baden for his support, critique, proof reading and indexing and to David and Neil Wilkie for their patient explanations about the way technology actually works.

The views expressed here and any errors are ours.

Contributors

Siân Bayne is based in the Department of Higher and Community Education at the University of Edinburgh, where she is lecturer in learning and teaching in digital environments. Her particular research interests focus on digital pedagogies, online identity and the cultural impact of the digital on learning and teaching.

Chris Beaumont is Senior Lecturer, Department of Computing, Liverpool Hope University. He is currently pathway leader for internet technology where he teaches on undergraduate and MSc computing programmes and is a member of the Learning Technology and Pedagogic Action Research Groups. After graduating as a senior scholar in computer science from Trinity College, Cambridge, he worked in industry with GEC-Marconi and Digital Equipment Corporation for a number of years before returning to higher education. He is a member of the Higher Education Academy and has also held a number of external examiner posts within the UK. He has been practising and researching problem-based learning for a number of years and has published and presented several papers in this area.

Chew Swee Cheng is a lecturer at the Learning Academy, Temasek Polytechnic, Singapore. She was a school facilitator for problem-based learning and associate consultant to the Temasek Centre for Problem-based Learning for a number of years before joining the Academy. She is involved in designing and conducting induction workshops for tutors and students in problem-based learning, collaborative and inquiry-based learning. She has been engaged in consultancy work with local secondary schools in these areas since 2001. Her current research interests include collaborative learning, especially in the analysis of student interactions in a collaborative setting. She was also the leader of a project investigating the use of ICT in supporting distributed problem-based learning, funded by the British Council using a purpose-built portal that she created with students.

Frances Deepwell, works in the Centre for Higher Education Development at Coventry University. She is course leader for the postgraduate certificate in learning and teaching in higher education and also works to provide academic and evaluation support to the institution-wide delivery of WebCT. Her research interests lie in evaluation and associated educational developments, in particular with regard to institutional change and learning technologies and she is currently working towards a PhD in this area.

Sharon J. Derry, Professor of Educational Psychology at the University of Wisconsin-Madison U.S.A. received her PhD in educational psychology with specialties in quantitative methods and cognition and instruction from the University of Illinois at Urbana-Champaign. Derry's recent projects have created conceptual frameworks and learning environments that are grounded in the learning sciences and that support the professional development of STEM teachers at both graduate and undergraduate levels. Her most recent work is focusing on helping STEM teachers, including university faculty, acquire transdisciplinary competencies for teaching, living and working in an increasingly multicultural and sociotechnical world. Derry has published in the *American Educational Research Journal, International Journal of Human–Computer Studies, Journal of AI in Education, Journal of Educational Psychology, Review of Educational Research* and numerous other journals and has edited books and conference proceedings. She has also edited books on learning technology and interdisciplinary collaboration and has received local and national awards for distinction in research.

Roisin Donnelly has been working for the past six years in the Learning and Teaching Centre in the Dublin Institute of Technology, where she has been involved in designing and delivering continuous professional development opportunities (both short courses and accredited programmes) for academic staff in e-learning and problem-based learning. She continues to deliver e-learning pedagogy workshops and consultations as part of the institute's e-learning training programme. She has a range of publications to date reflecting her teaching and research interests, including *Blended Problem-based Learning, Design, Tutoring and Evaluation* and *E-Learning Pedagogy*. She is continuing her research in higher education through a doctorate of education degree (EdD) where her research thesis is 'Exploring strategies for sustainable best practice in academic development: a case study of the tutor's role in propagating a blended problem-based learning in higher education'.

Carolyn Gibbon has worked with problem-based learning and pre-registration nursing students since 1996 in two higher education institutions. Formerly project manager for the FDTL4 Students Online in Nursing Integrated Curricula project, she is currently Principal Lecturer for learning and teaching in the Department of Nursing at the University of Central Lancashire. Carolyn was instrumental in developing and implementing problem-based learning at Liverpool John Moores University and continues that work at the University of Central Lancashire. She has presented at national and international problem-based learning conferences and is developing staff in facilitation of problem-based learning.

Per Grøttum, MD PhD, is Professor of Medical Informatics at the Faculty of Medicine, University of Oslo, Norway, in charge of ICT at the Faculty of Medicine, including e-learning activities as distance education in clinical placement of students and in specialist education, development of web-based e-learning programmes and development of a web-based 'mycourses' portal. Research interests are computer-assisted education and mathematical modelling of biological systems.

Cindy E. Hmelo-Silver is an Associate Professor of Educational Psychology at Rutgers University, U.S.A. She received a PhD in cognitive studies from Vanderbilt University and served postdoctoral fellowships at the Georgia Institute of Technology and the University of Pittsburgh's Learning Research and Development Center. Her research interests include problem-based learning, knowledge construction, particularly in the area of complex systems, collaborative learning and software-based scaffolding. She is incoming Associate Editor of the *Journal of Research in Science Teaching* and serves on the editorial boards of the *International Journal of Computer-Supported Collaborative Learning, Journal of Experimental Education* and *Journal of the Learning Sciences*. She has written numerous articles and has co-edited books entitled *Problem-based Learning: A Research Perspective on Learning Interactions* (2000) with Dorothy Evensen and *Collaborative Learning, Reasoning, and Technology* (in press) with Angela O'Donnell and Gijsbert Erkens. She received awards for Best Paper by a New Investigator, from the AERA Division I, an NSF Early CAREER award and a National Academy of Education post-doctoral fellowship.

David Jennings is a lecturer in educational development at the Centre for Teaching and Learning, in the School of Education and Lifelong Learning, University College Dublin. He brings a wealth of experience to his current role, originating as a researcher in the Irish Archaeological Wetland survey, where the effective use of technology formed an integral part of the project, to becoming the educational technology officer for University College Dublin, where he promoted the use of technology in teaching and learning across the university. His research interests include interactive teaching technologies and the impact of reusable learning resources, collaborative techniques in teaching online and the role of e-moderating in student support.

Ray Land is Professor of Higher Education at the University of Strathclyde in Glasgow and Director of the University's Centre for Academic Practice and Learning Enhancement (CAPLE). His current research interests include the theory and practice of educational development, threshold concepts and troublesome knowledge, and theoretical aspects of education in cyberspace.

Karen Lee was a clinical nurse specialist in infection control and then joined the University of Dundee to deliver a degree/specialist practitioner qualification in infection control. This was initially delivered face to face then translated into distance learning. As a result of this she has become increasingly interested in e-learning, has completed an MA in online and distance education and now spends 50% of her time facilitating the use of e-learning within the School of Nursing and Midwifery. Her particular interests are in using collaborative learning with students at a distance to enable learning of expert clinical practice, particularly situated within communities of practice.

Kirsten Hofgaard Lycke is Professor at the Institute for Educational Research, University of Oslo, Norway, where she is engaged in educational innovations on policy and implementation levels. Her research is focused on the quality of studies and learning environments in academia and in the workplace. Recent publications include *PBL goes ICT: Problem-based Learning in Face-to-face and Distributed Groups in Medical Education at the University of Oslo, Perspectives on Quality Assurance in Higher Education in Norway* and *Students as Journeymen between Communities of Higher Education and Work*, written in collaboration with colleagues in Norway and abroad.

Anandi Nagarajan is a doctoral candidate at Rutgers University, U.S.A. She is interested in facilitation and scaffolding in technology-based learning environments.

Remy Rikers received his PhD in experimental cognitive psychology from Maastricht University, Holland. He is currently Associate Professor in the Department of Psychology and Director of the Higher Education Research Center (HERC), Erasmus University, Rotterdam. Dr Rikers has researched and published in a variety of domains including the development of (medical) expertise, instructional design (cognitive load theory) and spacing effects in free recall tasks.

Frans Ronteltap is Managing Director of the Learning Lab, centre of expertise for ICT and education, which provides support for University of Maastricht faculties with the deployment of ICT in the education process. His doctoral thesis is exploring the use of knowledge in problem solving. At the Faculty of Medicine, he fulfilled an executive function for the team of media and technology with regards to computer-supported education and other media in the medical curriculum. After carrying out this position, he was asked by UM to set up an experiment to investigate the possible stimulating effects of ICT for the quality of the Maastricht problem-based learning system. This became the POLARIS project, the results of which provided a basis for the establishment of the Learning Lab.

Maggi Savin-Baden is Professor of Higher Education Research and Head of Research in the Centre for Higher Education Development, Coventry

University. She first began using problem-based learning in 1986 and commenced research into it in 1987. Over the last 10 years Maggi has researched and consulted widely on problem-based learning. Her current research is exploring threshold concepts and troublesome knowledge in the context of problem-based learning. To date she has published four books on problem-based learning, a fifth entitled *Leading in a Fractured World* and two new books that can be found on the internet: *Foundations of Problem-based Learning* (www.mcgraw-hill.co.uk/html/0335215319.html) and *Challenging Research in Problem-based Learning* (www.mcgraw-hill.co.uk/html/0335210554.html).

Henk Schmidt is a Professor of Psychology in the Faculty of Social Sciences at Erasmus University, Holland, and founding dean of its problem-based psychology curriculum. His areas of interest are learning and memory and he has published extensively on problem-based learning, long-term memory, and the development of expertise in professional domains.

Helge I. Strømsø is Associate Professor at the Institute for Educational Research, University of Oslo, Norway, where he is coordinator for the Group for Faculty and Curriculum Development. His research interests include reading comprehension, self-regulated learning and the use of information and communications technology in higher education.

Andy Syson is Head of Learning Technology, Coventry University. His role is to coordinate the work of the learning technology team that assists the staff of the university to provide the students with a rich online learning environment. In particular, he works closely with the Computing Services Department to ensure that the system is working efficiently, on and off campus, and that it integrates fully with the university's online network. He also works closely with members of the Teaching and Learning Taskforce and the schools' teaching fellows in planning any changes or upgrades to the online learning environment so that it closely matches their needs.

Kay Wilkie is Director of Learning and Teaching at the School of Nursing and Midwifery, University of Dundee. She coordinated the implementation of problem-based learning in the pre-registration nursing and midwifery diploma programmes within the school. Her research focused on the lived experience of nursing lecturers making the transition to becoming problem-based learning facilitators. She is currently exploring the effectiveness of combining problem-based learning with other learning and teaching strategies.

Wilco te Winkel is an Assistant Professor at Erasmus University, Rotterdam, Holland. From the start of the psychology programme he was involved in the development of an electronic learning environment tailored to the problem-based curriculum. His research interests involve problem-based learning in relation to technology.

Introduction

Maggi Savin-Baden and Kay Wilkie

The purpose of this book is to provide research-based information about the realities of setting up and running problem-based learning programmes using technology and to demonstrate the diverse uses of technology with problem-based learning across disciplines and countries. Additionally, it is designed to address some of the more complex issues regarding learning online, such as addressivity, identity, issues of power and control, constructions of text and notions of positioning and voice.

The book is not discipline specific, but, rather, aims to present a medley of experiences and to transcend disciplines and cultures, while also engaging with the interfaces between disciplines. We have aimed to bring together issues and debates about problem-based learning online in one volume, while also presenting or exploring a range and diversity of applications of problem-based learning online. Thus the chapters across this volume engage with readers' questions – not only the everyday questions such as 'how do I go about problem-based learning online?', but also questions about how course design and issues of power influence learning.

The book is presented in four parts, each designed to deal with different issues, namely: the possibilities and challenges presented by combining problem-based learning with computer technology; the debate surrounding the role of the online facilitator/mediator; the pedagogy related to technology in learning; and, finally, the exploration of developments in technology which assist in understanding the nature of student interactions in problem-based learning online.

Each part has an introduction written by the editors that draws on wider pedagogical concerns related to problem-based learning and online learning, thus locating each chapter in the wider literature.

In this text, we use the term PBLonline as a generic term because it captures that vast variety of ways in which problem-based learning is being used synchronously and asynchronously, on campus, or at a distance. Further, it represents the idea that students learn through web-based materials including text, simulations, videos and demonstrations, and resources such as chatrooms, message boards and environments that have been purpose built for problem-based learning. The book also contains a glossary to assist understanding of terms. While many of the terms have no single universally accepted definition, we have defined them as they are used by the chapter authors.

The increasing adoption of problem-based learning and the growth in online learning both reflect the shift away from teaching as a means of transmitting information towards supporting learning as a student-generated activity. This is not to imply that teachers are not required in PBLonline, but rather that their role is altered; existing skills need to be adapted and new skills adopted to support students in learning in virtual environments. As mentioned earlier, problem-based learning exists in many guises. Salmon (2002) refers to the increasing web of evermore sophisticated networked technologies. Combining the two approaches squares the number of possibilities. This plethora of combinations offers an all too real potential for confusion. We hope that by sharing their experiences of problem-based learning in an online environment, the authors in this book will help to avoid or resolve some of this confusion. The book unfolds as follows.

Part 1: Possibilities and challenges

The challenges associated with uniting problem-based learning and online learning are manyfold and, as yet, poorly explained. In Chapter 1, Savin-Baden examines the relationship between them; presenting the relevant literature and examining the extent to which the pedagogies associated with both approaches either complement each other or collide. Here an analysis is offered of what might count as problem-based learning, arguing that there are several perspectives on problem-based learning and ways in which it might and might not be used in online learning. This chapter will also address the 'state of play' and challenges associated with research in this area, including possible future research agenda.

Challenges arise from the nature of problem-based learning, the model chosen for online design and the engagement of learners with online material. Space in which to learn, examine practice or develop concepts is a recurring theme in the web-based learning literature (for example Clarke, 2004; Collison *et al.*, 2000; Dupuis, 2003). Land and Bayne explore this concept in Chapter 2. Online spaces can be viewed as less ordered than embodied spaces and this tendency towards the 'chaotic' is apparent in notions of digital identity and epistemology as well as in the ways in which we engage with digital textuality. In some cases, the perceived risk inherent within the online space renders it subject to modes of technological surveillance and control and establishes the need for an 'ordering' strategy, such as a virtual learning environment (VLE). Hence, paradoxically, cybertechnology is viewed simultaneously as both a source of, and means of controlling, risk.

The institutions in which PBLonline is situated and the people engaged in developing and sustaining problem-based learning in an online format may also create challenges. Deepwell and Syson in Chapter 3 consider issues such as academic and technical staff working together in teams across organisational boundaries and the challenges of using different virtual learning environments. Ways in which quality assurance systems and academic development issues may be brought together are also raised for discussion.

Part 2: Facilitation and mediation

Enhancement of learning through the use of an electronic forum is now a routine constituent of most degree programmes. There is a wide range of online learning technologies that match the more traditional teaching and learning/instructional strategies. Facilitation and mediation of such a forum can be time consuming and of limited effectiveness (McLuckie and Topping, 2004). Facilitation of problem-based learning is in itself a source of concern for many teachers. The combination of the two focuses attention on the skills required by those who would guide online students through the processes of problem-based learning.

Wood (2001) suggests that skills acquired from face-to-face tutoring experiences can be usefully adapted to form the basis of computer-based tutoring. In Chapter 4, Lycke *et al.* identify similarities and differences between the tutor role in PBLonline and face-to-face problem-based learning. Their research indicates that approaches to facilitation, whether face to face or online, are related to tutors' individual skills, attitudes and role conceptions.

In addition to providing students with an interactive asynchronous means of sharing meanings, online technology offers opportunities for computer program to be designed to take on some of the activities of the facilitator, thus dealing with some of the concerns voiced by institutions who quickly realised that 'going online' did not necessarily lead to savings in staff time. In Chapter 5, Hmelo-Silver *et al.* argue that technology can provide opportunities to deploy a skilled facilitator across several groups. The online activity structure helps to offload some facilitation functions onto the computerised environment, allowing less experienced individuals to facilitate. However, there are a number of differences between online and face-to-face modes of facilitation and there are tensions that need to be resolved. Hmelo-Silver *et al.* examine the role of the facilitator in online and face-to-face environments and consider the special challenges that arise in online facilitation as well as approaches to dealing with these challenges.

In developing online teaching and learning strategies it is vital to adopt support approaches that are sustainable. Donnelly's research, reported in Chapter 6, explored the tutor's cognitive, social and managerial role in a blended problem-based learning module, specifically in relation to building a sustainable model of educational development. Through exploration of the experience of developing and implementing an online problem-based staff development module, Donnelly addresses issues related to the tutor's role in sustaining/propagating the best features of online learning and problem-based learning and the replicability of this model of best practice in educational development.

Part 3: Technopedagogy

The literature tends to suggest that the development of PBLonline has been haphazard. In some situations, such as the SONIC project reported by Gibbon and Savin-Baden in Chapter 8, the online move is developed by tutors already well versed in running face-to-face problem-based learning programmes; the online development being an extension of the established problem-based pedagogy. In other situations, problem-based learning was adopted by developers of online programmes such as Jennings (author of Chapter 7), who recognised its potential for stimulating and focusing discussion among online learners. The potential for discussion to focus on social and practical, procedural issues is well documented (Rourke and Anderson, 2002). This difficulty is seldom reported in problem-based learning online, possibly because of the increased focus provided by the 'trigger' or by the recognition of facilitators that 'frame factors', such as practical, procedural and social issues also occur in face-to-face problem-based learning (Jacobsen, 1997, 2004; Wilkie, 2004).

Several authors (see Atack and Rankin, 2002; Bachman and Panzarine, 1998) report that acquiring the skills for learning online can interfere with participation in online discussion. Atack (2003) reported that her learners spent 'half the module' learning how to operate the VLE. However, Dix *et al.* (2004) claim that users develop their skills very quickly. Lee, in Chapter 9, working with a group similar to Atack's registered nurses, reports few problems, with learners quickly engaging in online discussion. Where PBLonline is used as part of a wider course, information technology (IT) skills are increasingly provided at the commencement of or as a prerequisite for web-based programmes. For example, Dennis (2003) states that her group were provided with the skills prior to commencing PBLonline.

Part 4: Developing technology

The use of electronic learning environments with problem-based learning is not restricted to mechanisms for displaying information and promoting and recording discussion. Technology permits online discussion to be mapped, monitored and analysed to an extent far beyond that which is possible in the face-to-face situation. Online environments have been accused of being restrictive and limiting of learners' skills, often being perceived as little more that a vast collection of material, presented in a readily accessible form. The argument goes that the superficiality of the material (in terms of access) leads learners to adopt a surface approach to learning. If this were indeed the case, the fit of problem-based learning and virtual learning environments would be very poor. We hope that this book goes some way to demonstrating the opposite. Part 4 explores the use of technology to demonstrate that online learners *do* develop critical thinking skills.

In Chapter 10, te Winkel *et al.* provide an overview of a number of electronic tools that have been developed to support and enhance problem-based learning curricula. They continue by describing a learning content management system that handles all curricular content and supports students' learning activities during their self-study, concluding with a critical reflection on the benefits and drawbacks of the system. Koschmann *et al.* (1996) introduced the principled approach in the analysis of the role that technology might have in innovations of problem-based learning. Principles such as interdisciplinarity, self-directed learning and ownership can be used as a framework in the prevention of unwanted consequences of a technology push. In Chapter 11, Ronteltap uses Koschmann's approach to explore some of the questions related to the increasing use of technology and problem-based learning; in particular questions about the role of technology and its impact on problem-based pedagogies.

Analysis of the use of one computer system for PBLonline, the INT-SCL Portal, is reported in Chapter 12. The INT-SCL portal (student-centred learning portal for school of IT), which houses instruments and materials that tutors could use in their implementation of problem-based learning programmes, is the focus of research by Beaumont and Cheng. To understand the dynamics between the participants (students and tutors), the mediation tools and the different parts of the problem-based learning programme, the researchers used the activity theory to identify three major activity systems and the contradictions that exist within them. Of particular interest were the ways by which the participants resolved these contradictions, thereby establishing for themselves problem-solving strategies that helped them to progress as a team.

The range and type of tools used not only for implementation of PBL-online, but also adopted to explore what is happening in terms of learning through student–student interaction via computer, serves to highlight the complexities of combining problem-based learning and online learning. The fluidity and flexibility apparent in the development of face-to-face problem-based learning have continued into its transition to technology, as educationists, and indeed students themselves, continue to mould the strategy to meet the needs of learners.

Conclusion

The storage, access and utilisation of knowledge has been profoundly affected by the introduction of technology (Dix *et al.*, 2004). The effect on organisations and work environments, and we would argue, higher education, has also been significant. Further, Kerrey *et al.* (2001) called for 'expanded, revitalised and reconfigured educational research, development and innovation program . . . built on a deeper understanding of how people learn, and how new tools support and assess learning gains'. This book presents research into and development of PBLonline. It explores ways in which technology can be used not only to support and assessing problem-based learning in an online format, but also to improve understandings of how students learn through PBLonline.

Part 1

Possibilities and challenges

The challenges associated with uniting problem-based learning and online learning are many and remain poorly explained. This part begins by examining the relationship between the two, presenting relevant literature and examining the extent to which the pedagogies associated with both approaches may complement one another or collide. An analysis is offered of what we might consider to be problem-based learning, suggesting that there are several perspectives on problem-based learning and ways in which it may and, possibly, may not be used in online learning. The 'state of play' is examined, as are challenges associated with research in this area, including possible future research agenda.

Challenges arise from the nature of problem-based learning, the model chosen for online design and learners' engagement with online material. Space in which to learn, examine practice or develop concepts is a recurring theme in the web-based learning literature that is explored further in Chapter 2. Online spaces can be viewed as less ordered than embodied spaces, this tendency towards the 'chaotic' being apparent in notions of digital identity and epistemology as well as in the ways in which we engage with digital textuality. In some cases, the perceived risk inherent within the online space renders it subject to modes of technological surveillance and control and establishes the need for an 'ordering' strategy, such as a virtual learning environment (VLE). Hence, paradoxically, cybertechnology may be regarded simultaneously as both source of risk and a means of controlling it.

The institutions in which PBLonline is situated and the people engaged in developing and sustaining problem-based learning in an online format may create further challenges. The final chapter in this part considers issues of academic and technical staff working together in teams across organisational boundaries and the challenges of using different virtual learning environments. Ways in which quality assurance systems and academic development issues may be aligned are also put under the spotlight.

1

The challenge of using problem-based learning online

Maggi Savin-Baden

Introduction

This chapter explores a number of concerns that relate to adopting PBL-online. The argument of this chapter centres on the notion of unrealised complexity; which is that we do not really know or understand fully what it is we have created in PBLonline. PBLonline is an approach to learning that is both varied and flexible and which introduces questions about what it means to be a problem-based learner in an online setting. This chapter begins by exploring why people have begun to develop PBLonline, moving to examine some of the models, media and environments in use. The second segment of the chapter examines the interrelationship of technology and pedagogy and suggests that this relationship still requires considerable exploration. The final section examines issues related to facilitation and learning in teams and suggests that PBLonline creates new kinds of learning space that prompt dialogic learning.

The nature and processes of online learning have changed considerably over the last few years. Britain and Liber have noted that considerable effort has been expended on the development of managed learning environments rather than the pedagogy of such development (Britain and Liber, 2004: 8). There also continues to be debate at both local and global levels about what counts as problem-based learning and what does not. In comparison with many other pedagogical approaches, problem-based learning has emerged relatively recently, being popularised by Barrows and Tamblyn (1980) following their research into the reasoning abilities of medical students at McMaster Medical School in Canada. Problem-based learning is an approach to learning where curricula are designed with problem scenarios central to student learning in each curricular component (modules/units). Students working in small teams examine a problem situation and, through this exploration, are expected to locate the gaps in their own knowledge and skills in order to decide what information they need to acquire in order to resolve or manage the situation. Lectures, seminars, workshops or laboratories support the inquiry process rather than transmit subject-based knowledge. The starting point should be a set of problem scenarios regardless of whether a module or a whole programme is being designed. The scenarios enable students to become independent inquirers and help them to see learning and knowledge as flexible entities. Problem-based learning has expanded worldwide since the 1960s and, as it has spread, the concepts associated with it have changed and become more flexible and fluid.

Why use problem-based learning online?

The objective of combining problem-based learning and online learning is in itself complex. Terms such as 'computer-mediated problem-based learning' and 'online problem-based learning' have been used to define forms of problem-based learning that utilise computers in some way. This terminology is problematic since it offers little indication about the ways in which computers are being used, areas where students interact, which tools are used, how learning materials are selected and applied and the extent to which any of these fit with problem-based learning (see for example Barrow's (2002) discussion of distributed problem-based learning).

As mentioned in the Introduction, we have agreed with the authors across this volume to adopt PBLonline as a generic term since it captures the vast array of ways in which problem-based learning is being used synchronously and asynchronously, on campus or at a distance. Further, it represents the idea that students learn through web-based materials, including text, simulations, videos, demonstrations and resources, chat, whiteboards and environments that have been purpose built for problem-based learning. Yet at the same time PBLonline has many of the hallmarks of the original problem-based learning models developed in the 1960s. It is more than a linear approach to problem solving where problem scenarios or case studies are used as prompts for learning in online environments.

Despite this, many of the concerns raised by delegates at problem-based learning conferences around the world include whether PBLonline will:

- affect the existence of face-to-face problem-based learning since PBLonline will be seen as being more cost effective
- destroy some of the original aims of problem-based learning since some forms of online problem-based learning tend to focus on solving narrowly defined problems that fail to encourage students to be independent inquirers who own their learning
- reduce the impact of learning in teams, in terms of students learning to work through team difficulties and conflicts in the way required by face-to-face problem-based learning.

At the outset it is important to realise that PBLonline is an approach that does not focus on replacing one form of learning with another, but is about complementing and developing what is already in existence. In terms of queries about the original aims of problem-based learning there are already a number of variations – both face to face and online. For example, since the popularisation of problem-based learning, many have continued the attempt to define it in some way and thus the early approaches developed by Barrows and progressed by Boud and Feletti (1997) have been both supported and superseded by others (for example, Duch *et al.*, 2001; Evensen and Hmelo, 2000; Savin-Baden, 2000). However, there is still confusion about the models, media and environments being used to support various kinds of problem-based learning that use technology in some way. A summary is offered in the following section.

Models, media and environments

Some forms of online learning are difficult to marry with types of problem-based learning that seek to provide opportunities for the students to challenge, evaluate and interrogate models of action, knowledge, reasoning and reflection, such as problem-based learning for critical contestability (Savin-Baden, 2000). In such models, tutors seek to provide higher education that offers, within the curriculum, multiple models of action, knowledge, reasoning and reflection, along with opportunities for the students to challenge, evaluate and interrogate them. Students therefore will be expected to examine the underlying structures and belief systems implicit within a discipline or profession itself, in order to understand not only the disciplinary area but also its credence. Knowledge is thus seen as being constructed by the students, who begin to see themselves as creators of knowledge and who become able to build on and integrate previously learned knowledge and skills with material that is currently being learned. Difficulties in attempting to marry diverse types of problem-based learning and online learning tend to occur because some approaches are overly managed through the online environments. Thus, in some cases, undertaking PBLonline is more about managing knowledge and information and developing a virtual space to deposit such knowledge, than actually engaging students in a collaborative online process.

Computer simulation in problem-based learning

There are a number of computer simulations that have been developed for use with problem-based learning, some of which are being used in blended forms of problem-based learning. For example, Rendas *et al.* (1999) introduced a computer simulation that was designed for problem-based learning in order to motivate learning, structure knowledge in a clinical context and develop learning skills for medical students, at a stage in the programme when they had had little contact with patients. It was also designed to evaluate how students reasoned and learned in each session. The problem situation provided all the information about a patient in a predetermined sequence and students, working three to a computer, were expected to find out further information by asking one question at a time, seeking justification for the hypothesis they had put forward and being encouraged to identify learning issues. The answers provided by the students were logged and later analysed with a tutor. The difficulty with this particular model of computer simulation is that it offers students little opportunity for creativity and personal responsibility and in many ways resembles some of the earlier forms of guided discovery. What is really occurring here is that problem-solving learning is being used to guide students to the right answer or diagnosis.

To promote problem-based learning it would seem better to locate simulations within problem-based learning rather than using them as a mechanism or strategy.

Multimedia resources for problem-based learning

Multimedia resources in problem-based learning tend to mirror the Content + Support model of online education (Mason, 1998), in which course content is, in general, separate from tutorial support. Content is provided for the students either on the web or as a package of material, whereas tutorial support is given via email or computer conferencing and usually represents no more than 20% of the students' study time. This is a result of using multimedia resources largely to support existing course material. In some virtual learning environments (VLE) resources are accessed as an integral part of a learning package but to date the inclusion of videos, small-scale simulations and lectures is primarily the extent of what has been done. Although there have been many developments in recent years, the relationship between pedagogy and technology still seems to be lacking in this area. Furthermore, off-campus access for students, although growing, can be problematic with material that takes time to download causing students to view it as both costly and time consuming.

Virtual learning environments in problem-based learning

VLEs are learning management software systems that are not intended merely to replace the classroom online, but rather to offer learners a variety of options for learning. Many advocates of these environments see in them the potential for allowing student-centred learning to be incorporated into teaching in new and innovative ways. The use of terminology relating to these environments tends to be predominantly pedagogically driven, but the term 'virtual learning environment' is used here to include learning management systems and online learning environments. Thus VLEs are learning management software systems that synthesise computer-mediated communications software, such as email and online course materials.

While the number of systems available is large, many of them have similar features and although they are, in general, designed to promote varied and effective teaching styles there are a number of limitations that apply to collaborative forms of learning. Most systems are capable of supporting content-driven online education, but there are few data that indicate which systems can support problem-based learning effectively. This is why new environments, such as eSTEP and POLARIS described in this volume, have been designed specifically to support problem-based learning.

Blended PBL

The term 'blended PBL' tends to be used to reflect the idea that students learn through the combination of online and face-to-face instruction (Graham, 2004). For example, students learn through web-based materials that include text, simulations, videos, demonstrations and resources. This type of blended PBL tends to focus around a particular site through which students are guided by the use of strategy problems, online material and specific links to core material. While at one level the use of the site is student led, the materials provided necessarily support the learning they undertake in face-to-face problem-based learning groups. An example of such a site is the SONIC project (Savin-Baden and Gibbon, this volume).

PBLonline

This conception of problem-based learning places it pedagogically in a collaborative online environment and thus it has a number of advantages over models mentioned earlier. While many of the current models of online education focus on teacher-centred learning, PBLonline needs to be focused on team-oriented knowledge-building discourse.

PBLonline is defined here as students working in teams numbering 8 to 10 on a series of problem scenarios that combine to make up a module. Students are expected to work collaboratively to solve or manage the problem. Students will work in real time or asynchronously, but what is important is that they work together. Synchronous collaboration tools are vital for the effective use of PBLonline because tools such as chat, shared whiteboards, video conferencing and group browsing are central to ensuring collaboration within the problem-based learning team. Students may be working at a distance or on campus, but they will begin by working out what they need to learn to engage with the problem situation. This may take place through a shared whiteboard, conferring or an email discussion group. What is also important is that students have both access to the objectives of the module and the ability to negotiate their own learning needs in the context of the given outcomes. Facilitation occurs through the tutor having access to the ongoing discussions without necessarily participating in all of them.

It is important to realise, however, that the forms of environments on offer, whether created specifically for problem-based learning or adapted to be used with it, all seem to have a strong management genre in terms of the forms of authorship used. The design of such digital spaces could be seen as being authored (in both the sense of authorial design behind the web and the authors of the written text in front). While the authoring of text (whether inked or virtual) and the authoring of design can be seen as very different functions, it seems that both could be seen to 'impede the free circulation, the free manipulation, the free composition, decomposition, and recomposition of fiction' (Foucault, 1988: 209). This would seem to introduce questions about the extent to which constructive approaches to learning can be authored and managed. Further, as Ravenscroft (2005: 139) has argued: 'We need to investigate, examine and where possible, design appropriate learning communities if we want to support effective e-learning discourse.'

Technology and pedagogy

There has been much criticism in recent years about blended learning environments that fail to create effective settings for learning (Noble, 2001; Oliver and Herrington, 2003; Reeves, 2002). One reason for this has been that the focus in blended learning environments has been on technological rather than pedagogical design. There have been suggestions that there is a need for a reengineering of the concept of learning design rather than just a simplistic repackaging of the course content into blended learning formats (see for example Collis, 1997; Mason, 1998). Yet Cousin (2005) has argued that the 'pedagogy must lead the technology' perspective has become something of a mantra, a mantra that she argues against. Conversely, Cousin suggests the medium *is* the pedagogy. While this appears to be a convincing argument, she risks denying the difficulties inherent in putting technology in the lead. It seems that many of the difficulties about the relationship between pedagogy and technology stem from a failure to ask what might appear to be some fairly straightforward questions, such as:

- What do we mean by pedagogy in online learning?
- What is the technology to be used for?
- What is the relationship between the type of pedagogy to be adopted and the type of pedagogy currently being used?

In PBLonline it seems that, in most cases, the pedagogy *did* emerge first. The result has been the development of a number of innovative approaches designed to match the pedagogical challenges of problem-based learning (see for example those cited by te Winkel *et al.*, this volume). While there are those (such as Cousin) who rail against statements made by funding bodies who suggest, for example, 'that the technology should follow the learning and teaching objectives' (HEFCE, 2003: 11), there is a sense that the difficulty connected with the philosophy of 'learning and teaching objectives' has been forgotten along the way. The use of such language is problematic; whether or not that particular funding council meant 'objectives' in the narrowly defined way in which they are used worldwide in curricula, or whether they meant 'objectives' to be used in a much looser sense is unclear. Stenhouse suggested that we must be wary of believing that the objective model of education was the solution to larger curricular problems and argued: 'We do not *have* objectives: we choose to conceptualize our behaviour in terms of objectives – or we choose not to' (Stenhouse, 1975: 71). Stenhouse's work is interesting in that many of the important points he made about designing curricula have been discounted. The result has been an increasing move toward outcome measures and performance, so that students must behave and learn in particular ways rather than be seen as people who live and work in context and in relation to one another. Furthermore, it seems that in many undergraduate programmes, and particularly with the increasing use of benchmarking standards, the issues of the morality of such educational practice come into question: 'From a moral point of view, the emphasis on behavioural goals, despite all of the protestations to the contrary, still borders on brain washing or at least indoctrination rather than education' (Kliebard, 1968: 246). The issue then is how we can develop curricula that allow for the moral initiation of students into the appropriate culture of the profession or discipline, while also inducting them into knowledge in ways that avoid indoctrination and promote democracy and creativity. The suggestion that 'education as induction into knowledge is successful to the extent that it makes the behavioural outcome of the students unpredictable' (Stenhouse, 1975: 82), will be uncomfortable for many course leaders and managers in the current higher education system and yet, to a large extent, this is precisely what does occur in many problem-based curricula.

It is important to remember, as Cousin (2005) points out, that technology is not just lying there waiting for pedagogues to put it to good use. The chapters across this volume indicate the need for strong and effective interaction between pedagogy and technology to ensure that both are used to best effect in implementing and enacting PBLonline. Many of the authors here imply an underlying argument that suggests that there is little point in designing PBLonline if, like with a box of chocolates, no one is prepared to either open it or consume it. Additionally, narrowly defined pedagogies, whether virtual or face to face, can prevent students from engaging in meaningful learning.

Yet there are a number of contradictions between the arguments occurring about the nature and process of the pedagogy and technology in PBLonline. For some tutors there are concerns that there is a danger that PBLonline could become increasingly instrumental. It might be that, as facilitators become more familiar with the approach, they become more teacher centred than learner centred and PBLonline falls into the performativity trap. Nonetheless there are other hidden similarities between the pedagogy of problem-based learning and the increasing use of the internet for learning. Problem-based learning and surfing the internet share similar qualities, for example the process of learning in problem-based learning teams is interactive, non-sequential, random and often seems rather chaotic. Students of the net generation who are observed surfing and using the 'fast click' to access information (Savin-Baden and Gibbon, this volume) seem equally non-sequential and chaotic; yet in both cases this does not mean that learning is not occurring (although it must be acknowledged that there are nomadic learners who wander across the problem-based and internet desert losing themselves in the sandstorm of available information). Such mirroring of interaction between technology and pedagogy in new and emerging forms of PBLonline would seem to represent 'a new "learning ecology" '. This is not just another addon, but a technology that is 'transforming our educational institutions and how we conceptualise and experience teaching and learning' (Garrison and Anderson, 2003: 123). It is an ecology that is also transforming our online and face-to-face pedagogic identities.

Facilitation, dialogic learning and online teams

There have been increasing debates over the years about whether facilitation is just one form of good teaching or whether in fact it is something else. Facilitating problem-based learning face to face is a complex activity which requires that tutors are equipped to be facilitators. For tutors engaged in problem-based learning the transition from lecturer to facilitator demands revising their assumptions about what it means to be a teacher in higher education. This is a challenge to many, since it invariably demands recognition of a loss of power and control when moving towards being a facilitator. Becoming a facilitator can be a daunting experience because, although lecturers may have taught students through workshops and small group sessions, their role as a facilitator in problem-based learning often requires more of them than in these other forms of teaching. For many tutors, this involves letting go of decisions about what students should learn, trusting students to acquire knowledge for themselves and accepting that students will learn even if they have not been supplied with a lecture or handout by their tutor. The conflict for many tutors is in allowing students freedom to manage knowledge, rather than keeping their previous roles and relationships with students as the controllers and patrollers of knowledge.

Yet whether it is in face-to-face problem-based learning, PBLonline or e-moderating, there appears to be an assumption that there are specific roles, attributes and ways of being that characterise some facilitators as being 'good' or 'better' than others. PBLonline does require that tutors are supported. An electronic moderator is someone who 'presides over an electronic online meeting or conference' (Salmon, 2000: 3). In her comprehensive guide to e-moderating, Salmon draws on research from tutor and student perspectives, offers guidance on training e-moderators and suggests a useful model for teaching. However, it is not yet clear whether facilitating PBL-online is the same as e-moderating. It might be that PBLonline requires more of a silent presence by the facilitator, along with appropriate hinting and prompting, rather than some of the direction and intervention that seems to be evident in much e-moderating. What is clear though is that the skills of face-to-face facilitation in problem-based learning do overlap with those required for facilitating PBLonline. Furthermore, as with students undertaking face-to-face problem-based learning, those students doing PBLonline seem to need less facilitator support and guidance as they become more familiar and skilled with managing the learning approach.

Yet it does seem to be the case that effective face-to-face facilitators do not necessarily make effective online ones. This might be because of the absence of non-verbal cues in PBLonline compared with face-to-face problem-based learning. Rosenberg and Sillince (2000) found that nonverbal cues affected activities such as requesting help and information, getting commitment and recognising the effort of others. The findings of their study indicated that learning media such as computer-mediated communication may make successful collaboration difficult because of the absence of nonverbal cues. In terms of interventions made by facilitators, Wegerif and Mercer (1996) have suggested that successful exchanges in collaborative forms of learning that use problems are more likely to include moves such as 'exploratory dialogue'. Such dialogue would include explaining, clarifying, challenging and justifying. However, the idea that facilitation is a specific kind of 'role' remains problematic. It appears that there is a need for some tutors to construct a false identity in order to prevent themselves from becoming too subjective and too involved with students and their learning. Bayne's work to some extent illustrates such perspectives. Bayne (2005a) found that tutors in online environments (although not problem-based ones) tended to construct for themselves a teacher identity, so as to both feel and be in control; to be an authority figure in the online space.

While there is a growing body of research exploring what occurs in problem-based learning seminars (for example Barrett, 2007; Wilkie, 2004) it is interesting to note that there is still relatively little research that has explored what it is that students *do* when they go online. There are accounts of tutors' and students' experiences of engaging with particular online environments (Bayne, 2005a, 2005b; Donnelly, 2004; Salmon, 2000), and with discussions about tutor interventions, yet there is still little understanding of what goes on in the minds of tutors and students engaged in PBLonline. Concerns about what and how students learn in teams is an area that has still not been particularly well resolved in online or face-to-face problem-based learning contexts. Work by Ravenscroft (2004, 2005) explored a number of concerns about learning in online communities and McConnell (2000) has researched collaborative e-learning, some of it relating to a loose type of problem-based learning. Facilitators and students influence one another in a whole variety of ways, such as their views about what counts as knowledge, the interplay of content and process and the ways in which they do and do not deal with conflict in the team. Conflict may emerge because a team member feels a peer is not participating or alternatively if the team perceive that the online facilitator is interrupting rather than interacting. Again, while conflict in teams has been researched in face-to-face settings, the management of virtual conflict is still largely under-researched.

The way dialogue occurs in PBLonline may affect the nature and process of learning that occurs. For example, asynchronous discussion seems to create a reflective learning space whereby the learner is able to respond in a way that is both a reply and a reflection. Extended written commentary such as this rarely occurs in face-to-face problem-based learning where conversation flow is characterised by fast exchanges of short sentences. In asynchronous PBLonline, the students (the authors of the commentary) often seem to be in the process of 'sense making' as they speak. Such 'sense making' would be likely to affect the quality of the dialogic learning in the team and result in more meta-commenting than would occur in face-to-face problem-based learning.

Dialogic learning (following Mezirow, 1981) is learning that occurs when insights and understandings emerge through dialogue in a learning environment. It is a form of learning where students draw on their own experience to explain the concepts and ideas with which they are presented and then use that experience to make sense for themselves and to explore further issues. This kind of learning, learning with and through others, can encourage students to critique and challenge the structures and boundaries within higher education and industry, whether virtual or face to face. Learning through dialogue brings to the fore, for students and tutors, the value of prior experience to current learning and thus can engage them in explorations of and (re)constructions of their identity. However, synchronous PBLonline seems to reduce the possibility for both dialogic learning and meta-commenting and in some cases would seem to be much more complex an activity through which to learn than face-to-face problem-based learning (see for example the complexities raised by Lycke *et al.*, this volume).

Conclusion: future learning spaces?

The language used in online learning, such as desktops, virtual classrooms and even the names of VLEs, Blackboard, First Class, has similarities with the language used in face-to-face learning. Yet the uses of face-to-face and virtual spaces are quite different. Online learning still seems to be a largely uncomfortable learning space for many students. This may be because there is a sense that in online learning, identities are seen as more boundless and flexible that in face-to-face contexts. However, there do seem to be some enlightening similarities between face-to-face problem-based learning and PBLonline from the students' perspectives. For example, in face-to-face problem-based learning students have often reported feeling out of control, fragmented and ill at ease because the experience of learning through problem-based learning is markedly different from prior learning experiences (see for example Savin-Baden, 2000). Problem-based learning can offer students greater autonomy to learn for themselves and opportunities to develop independence in inquiry, opportunities many of them may not have encountered in lecture-based learning. Similarly, students in PBLonline (and in online learning in general) often speak of feelings of loss of control and also of a sense of danger. In online learning, such loss of control and danger seem to relate more to the presentation of identity than to issues about the control of knowledge, something that is so often at the forefront of student concerns in face-to-face problem-based learning. Perhaps it is the case that online learning brings to the fore and prompts students to confront their contradictory identities (Hall, 1992) earlier than in face-to-face learning, where they feel able to hide such contradictions more easily behind the need to acquire and manage knowledge.

Many of the questions and queries raised by those concerned about using PBLonline would seem to relate to wider concerns connected with the relationship between diverse forms of technology and the pedagogies of problem-based learning. For example, Barrows has asked:

> Can a communication technology be developed that will mediate PBL yet avoid distorting the PBL process as it is used in face-to-face small group work? It would have to be able to present an ill-structured problem verbally, visually and auditorially as appropriate. It should allow for both synchronous and synchronous discussion. There should be a whiteboard, operated by a member of the group, to facilitate and record the group's progress, recording ideas generated, data acquired, and learning issues to be pursued. I am waiting with baited breath.
>
> (Barrows, 2002: 122)

Perhaps Barrows has missed the point of PBLonline. PBLonline is *necessarily* different from face-to-face problem-based learning at a whole variety of levels: the nature and type of dialogue has changed, the means of giving and receiving information is largely through hyperlinks and facilitation is often about indicating presence and using hinting and prompting exploration than some kind of embodied notion of presence. However, there are still questions that need to be explored about the way in which problem scenarios are designed for PBLonline and the extent to which digital environments can be learner centred and learner driven. Perhaps, too, we need to be asking whether students are allowed to recreate the problems wiki style? Further, if they did, how would this then affect the perceived authenticity and authorship of the problem? Yet despite the fears and concerns about the notions of a disembodied identity raised by both tutors and students, in a number of studies, PBLonline does seem to offer a new learning space for identity (re)construction and formation, with technology that can support new and innovative forms of interactive learning.

2

Issues in cyberspace education

Ray Land and Siân Bayne

Introduction

The increasingly global use of digital environments in education has introduced fundamental challenges to the ways in which we understand notions of identity, community and knowledge itself. Theoretical analyses of cyberspace have provided useful insights into the changes we are experiencing culturally, socially and politically as a result of our shift online. This chapter draws on these insights to explore issues of which educators might need to be aware if they are to design and implement problem-based learning in this radically different context and richly complex space. The chapter explores the premise that, owing to altered notions of time, presence, boundedness and stability, online spaces can be viewed both as less authentic and less ordered than embodied spaces and that a tendency towards multiplicity, instability and disorder is manifest in the nature of digital textualities, identities and epistemologies.

From this perspective, the risk perceived as inherent within the online space establishes the need for an 'ordering strategy' such as a virtual learning environment (VLE) and renders it subject to modes of technological surveillance and control. Hence, paradoxically, digital technology is viewed simultaneously as both a source of, and means of controlling, risk. In turn this gives rise to the question of whether the challenging pedagogical paradigms of problem-based learning are uniquely suited to the new spaces of the digital realm or, alternatively, need to shift yet again when undertaken in the contexts of cyberspace. Issues of reconfigured subjectivity and identity construction arise both in the context of problem-based learning and in the context of cyberspace. The degree of congruence in these separate processes is a further issue that merits consideration.

Authenticity and presence

Now that we are well into the second decade of systematically organised learning within the digital domain, it is increasingly accepted that it has much to offer – freedom from the constraints of timetables, freedom of location, opportunities for collaborative, cooperative approaches to learning, formation of new online learning communities and new media spaces in which alternative forms of literacy and knowledge construction can be nurtured. Nonetheless the preferred mode of teaching and learning for many academics and students remains the traditional, 'face-to-face' or 'embodied' mode, characterised by synchronicity and embodied presence. Learning within the digital domain is frequently felt to offer a lesser experience, one that is less authentic, less 'real'.

Explanatory accounts of this sense of inadequacy or inauthenticity range from those founded on the pedagogical and technological practicalities of teaching using technology, through social presence theory and the concern with reduced social cues, to the more determinist social learning approaches that suggest that we are hardwired for specific types of social interaction. Feenberg (1989: 22) points to the embodied presence of the learner and teacher as providing a sense of immediacy that validates the experience as 'real':

> In our culture the face-to-face encounter is the ideal paradigm of the meeting of minds. Communication seems most complete and successful where the person is physically present 'in' the message. This physical presence is supposed to be the guarantor of authenticity: you can look your interlocutor in the eye and search for tacit signs of truthfulness or falsehood, where context and tone permit a subtler interpretation of the spoken word.
>
> (Feenberg, 1989: 22)

As PC ownership increases and the digital domain becomes the routine location for social and recreational activity among the upcoming generations of 'digital natives' (Prensky, 2001), there is a sense in which the digital environment is becoming normalised in some domains of activity. Yet in education, the privileging of the face-to-face encounter to which Feenberg referred almost 20 years ago still, often, holds (Bayne, 2005a).

One angle on the pervasiveness of this view of online learning is offered by the post-structuralist perspectives that draw attention to this mode's primarily textual mode of communication. Learning online does not, in most of its forms, involve unmediated speech and is characterised in most instances of its use by its other distinctive aspect – asynchronicity. In the conceptual hierarchies prevalent within current higher education practice, asynchronicity takes a secondary position to synchronicity and presence, while the written remains subordinate to the spoken:

Traditionally speech is favoured as the concept which best represents the semantic relationship of language to thought in virtue of its own essential and immediate causal proximity both to the thoughts which give it its meaning and to the thinker having those thoughts, expressing these meanings.

(Parker, 1997: 76)

Speech, as Feenberg, too, has revealed, appears to emanate directly from its 'author' and involves a requirement for the presence of the speaker. In post-structuralism, the notion of presence offers the possibility of foundational meaning which cannot be questioned. Notions of god, self and nature can all be seen as rooted in the 'logocentrism' which, for Derrida (1978 [1967]) is closely bound up with what he calls the 'metaphysics of presence':

Presence appears as the things we see; as the immediacy of the ideas and representations we have; as substance, essence and existence; as the temporal present, the now of the moment, as the self-presence of consciousness, of subjectivity, as one's own inner experiences and ideas etc. . . . Presence constitutes the essential truth of reality; hidden from our sight possibly, but present in its entirety to some divine mind.

(Parker, 1997: 77)

This notion of presence underpins traditional western ideologies and value structures (humanism, positivism, foundationalism) in that it enables the construction of a network of conceptual hierarchies dependent on the function of binary oppositions rooted in that of presence–absence. The relationship between each set of terms is hierarchical – in each of these oppositions, the former term is dominant, while the latter is seen as a deviance from or perversion of it. The key point is that the dominant term is always that which 'belongs to presence and the logos'; it is that which has the status of 'truth', of 'rightness' (Culler, 1983). Hence presence, in the sense of physical presence, requires synchronicity, and, from a 'logocentric' perspective, the asynchronous activity of much education in cyberspace undermines such truth at a glance. Writing is by definition asynchronous in nature, traditionally seen as being a step removed from the 'author' in a way that speech is not. Learning within digital environments is, of course, heavily and obviously mediated both through written text and computer technology. Face-to-face learning, in comparison, appears to approximate far more closely to reality, to 'here-ness' or presence. The digital nature of online learning is duly rendered inauthentic. The basis of such perception is rarely articulated – instead we get the intuitive sense that face-to-face just *feels* better.

In a similar fashion problem-based learning can also be seen to transgress dominant hierarchical binaries of traditional learning. It challenges the teacher's knowledge by privileging the status of the collaborative learner group, as well as disrupting the traditional dominance of the discipline by emphasising the negotiability and interrelatedness of the knowledge required in specific contexts. A similar complaint of inauthenticity is often reported by commentators as an initial student response, often leading to a temporarily confusing and frustrating liminal state characterised by Savin-Baden (2006) as 'disjunction'.

Disorder, disjunction and disquietude

The decentred and seemingly disordered nature of the knowledge domain that is the initial impression of many problem-based learning students has resonance with the boundariless and unstable nature of knowledge within cyberspace. Computer technology fosters a culture of simulation, of collaboration, of playful experimentation and navigation over surfaces, which often seems to contrast with our understanding of that which comprises authentic learning. The web in particular, sprawling, limitless, consisting of endless, unstable, changing elements, each one potentially linked to each other and therefore bearing within it infinite traces or connective possibilities, offers particular challenges to the notions of textual stability and authority that have been fundamental to traditional learning media.

These fluid, flowing spaces would seem to find resonance with the concepts of 'flow' (Csikszentmihalyi, 1991) and 'hard fun' identified by Papert (2002) which Barrett (2005a, 2005b) has identified as characteristic of, and requisite to, problem-based learning spaces. Perhaps it is unsurprising that when asked to learn within a problem-based learning environment that emphasises a negotiated, exploratory and socially co-constructed route to understanding, there is a strong sense of disquietude among learners. This sense of 'riskiness' and disorientation is likely to be even more accentuated when this activity is located in the unstable textual domain of cyberspace.

As the media through which learning activity is conducted move from the printed text and face-to-face dialogue to the digital forms enabled by internet-based media, learners are implicitly asked to confront some quite fundamental notions of textual stability and the nature of academic knowledge. By 'destabilising' and seemingly disordering the academic text, the new educational media enable new forms of academic discourse, literacy and knowing to emerge (Gee, 2004; Ingraham, 2005; Kress, 2003; Landow, 2004; Privateer, 1999). In doing so, however, they alter, potentially quite fundamentally, traditional roles of teacher and learner and, by extension, the nature of the academic institution itself.

It is no longer possible, Spender (1995) argues, for teachers to appear as experts in digital learning environments as there is just too much information for any one individual to master. Within the print-based university – the society of the closed, static text – knowledge was in short supply, a special commodity. This empowered the gatekeepers, the initiators into disciplines, to determine intellectual boundaries, to regulate entry to the next level of information. Lyman (1994) talks of an 'ecology of knowledge' in which, when knowledge is scarce, centralisation and conservation take precedence. In an information-saturated environment, however, selection as much as conservation is the distinctive information problem. Whether problem-based learning activities are uniquely suited to go with the 'flow' of this disruptive, fluid space or whether the seeming disorder of the digital environment will merely intensify potentially problematic aspects of problem-based learning is an interesting question for future debate.

The problem-based learning student within cyberspace

At the textual level, cyberspace appears to offer the potential of a shift to openness, inconclusivity, fluidity and learner centredness. In his pioneering work on hypertext and academic discourse, Landow (1997) outlined some of the possibilities such environments offer for the transformation of the student learning experience. Within digital space, students gain both information and habits of thinking critically in terms of 'multiple approaches or causes'. The online environment, therefore, can be seen to orient students towards developing a habit of 'making connections'. This fosters 'a participatory reading-and-writing environment' which empowers the student 'by placing them within – rather than outside – the world of research and scholarly debate'. It thus enables students to explore and create new modes of discourse suited to the ways of reading, writing and collaborating that are increasingly used in digital space. The new forms of digital textuality that have emerged since Landow first published on hypertext – weblogs, wikis and their variants – serve to further reinforce these characteristics of online academic work (Augar *et al.*, 2004; Efimova, 2005; Oravec, 2003; Sauer *et al.*, 2005).

The emphasis on connectivity, multiple approaches and causation would seem highly congruent with the problem formulation and collaborative analysis of complex scenarios required of many problem-based learning settings. The digital environment affords excellent opportunity for collaborative learning, whereas such activity, as Ede and Lunsford (1990) demonstrate, tends to be mistrusted in closed-text environments, where a relatively unquestioned assumption is that writing is mainly a solitary and individual act.

A clear implication for the role of the problem-based learning student in such environments is the requirement that they adopt an active approach. The hypertextual systems on which digital learning environments are predicated, argue Jonassen and Grabinger (1990), require the learner to take more responsibility for accessing, sequencing and deriving meaning from the information. In this regard the digital space is probably best considered as a learning rather than teaching environment in which an exploratory, research-minded approach to learning may flourish. By predisposing students towards multilinear and multisequential patterns of thinking, and immersing them in environments of multivocality, digital environments may also stimulate processes of 'integration and contextualisation' – higher order cognitive skills – in ways not achievable by linear presentation techniques (Mayes *et al.*, 1990). This accords with Landow's interpretation of conceptual skill as 'chiefly making connections' and would seem to be a capacity eminently appropriate to the demands of problem-based learning situations.

Such shifts imply a transfer of responsibility to learners, which imposes on them a duty for autonomy, critical judgement and a higher degree of tolerance of complexity and ambiguity. This, in turn, might ultimately relieve the problem-based learning tutor from the traditional status-oriented informative, didactic and confrontational interventions of traditional practice in favour of more supportive and guidance-oriented interventions. The transition, however, might initially prove as disjunctive to the tutor as to the problem-based learning class.

Learner identities in the digital domain

One effect of working within digital environments that problem-based learning students are likely to encounter is the disconcerting realisation that, within a heavily textually mediated digital environment, their representation of self, and that of others, is subject to construction and reconstruction through language. As Turkle (1996) has revealed: 'In my computer-mediated worlds, the self is multiple, fluid, and constituted in interaction with machine connections; it is made and transformed by language; . . . and understanding follows from navigation and tinkering rather than analysis' (Turkle, 1996: 15).

Gergen (1991) reiterates the notion of the self as a social construct in his idea of 'the saturated self'. He sees personal identity as a complex interweaving of social relationships. Through communication technology we are saturated with the 'many voices of humankind':

> We realise increasingly that who and what we are is not so much the result of our 'personal essence' but of how we are constructed in various social groups . . . Previous possessions of the individual self – autobiography, emotions, and morality – become possessions of relationships. We appear to stand alone, but we are manifestations of relatedness.
>
> (Gergen, 1991: 113)

The fluidity and inter-connectedness of selfhood is often foregrounded when we work online and this can form another front on which the shift into cyberspace can be disconcerting. That, at some level, learning to engage in communication online will involve students in a questioning of their own identity, can perhaps help us to understand why many find it to be a disorienting experience, one which might seem alienating and 'cold'. In the context of online problem-based learning, such disquietude may accentuate the disjunctive effects (Savin-Baden, 2006) reported when learners encounter the methodology for the first time. Engagement in what are not only novel learning environments but also unfamiliar modes of experiencing selfhood requires a tolerance of ambiguity and complexity and an acceptance of uncertainty, which present challenging demands on students to cultivate both reflexivity and critical openness in approaching what is already an often challenging and novel way of learning.

It is important, however, to stress that it is likely that learners will develop strategies to deal with these troublesome properties of technology-assisted learning environments. Rushkoff (1997) in his study of the 'children of chaos' – or 'screenagers' – described how a younger generation of students have found, through their engagement with new digital technologies, a means of thriving in environments of uncertainty and complexity: 'Our children, ironically, have already made their move. They are leading us in our evolution past linear thinking, duality, holistic, animistic, weightless and recaptured culture. Chaos is their natural environment' (Rushkoff, 1997: 269).

The argument is not dissimilar to more recent claims made for the 'net-generation' (Oblinger and Oblinger, 2005; Prensky, 2001). It will be interesting to see whether these learners who have 'grown up digital' (Seely Brown, 2000) will prove less anxious in or resistant to the seeming disorder of the digital domain or, indeed, experience less disjunction when encountering the similarly disconcerting boundarilessness of problem-based learning environments. Only by being aware of some of the fundamental cultural and ontological issues at stake as we move further into the digital age are we able to support not only learners experiencing transitional anxiety, but also those future generations who have already fully come to terms with the new ways of working and knowing.

VLEs as ordering strategies within cyberspace

Cyberspace, we have seen, is as an unbounded environment, a space replete for learners with both anxiety and promise. It also poses daunting dilemmas for the university as a managerial space. As Bergquist (1995) argues, in modern organisations 'boundaries (and identities defined by roles and rules) serve as "containers" of anxiety'. We can envisage disciplines, modularisation, academic management and reward structures serving such a function. However, in the postmodern condition these boundaries are eroded and there is a 'spilling out of anxiety', a 'sense of living on the edge' (Bergquist, 1995: 11).

Deleuze has used the term 'enclosed environments' to describe territories that are circumscribed within organisations 'to concentrate; to distribute space; to order time; to compose a productive force within the dimension of space–time whose effect will be greater than the sum of its component forces' (Deleuze, 1992: 3). Taylor meanwhile suggests that terms such as 'boundaries' and 'sites of enclosure' are used 'to describe attempts by institutions to create contexts – enclosed territories – in which only the occupants define the particular rules and practices which govern internal operations' (Taylor, 1999: 11). Faced with the protean boundarylessness of the digital domain, an 'ordering strategy' is required if managerialist efficiency is to be maintained and performative agendas to be achieved. In one interpretation, the web portal (Coyne *et al.*, 2003) and virtual learning environment (Cousin, 2005) seem to have emerged to fit this particular bill, involving us in a perception of digital space as simultaneously both a location for, and means of limiting, risk.

There would appear to be a paradigmatic contradiction operating here. Although the technologies on which the VLE is predicated (web-based learning environments and relational databases) involve us in practices that constitute the subject as multifaceted, heterogeneous and dispersed, nonetheless the ethos of the VLE – the online space in which, in higher education, problem-based learning is increasingly likely to be organized and conducted – can be viewed as both managerialist and performative. It is about order, efficiency, identified outcomes and control. The attraction to course organisers of the inbuilt databases and surveillance tools of VLEs is not just their retrieval speed but their relational abilities and totalising nature. In its institutional orientation, and its concern for control and managerial efficiency, the VLE reveals the assumption of a quite different subjectivity, that of the individualised and 'containable' learner.

Visibility and surveillance: screen as monitor

A final set of issues we would like to consider are the surveillance aspects of the new learning technologies and, in particular, those of the virtual learning environment. Although the discourse of problem-based learning might position the tutor as 'moderator' or 'facilitator', the forms of agency involved when these practices take place within a VLE might include the more problematic roles of monitoring, recording, interpreting and forwarding online data. In this particular formation of the digital environment tutors become 'seers' of their students, and are also 'seen' by their managers. Both learners and tutors are drawn into a more visible, and hence more calculable, space (Land, in press). The visibility of this space has prompted several commentators to bring a Foucauldian reading to bear on the intersection of education with technology (for example Kitto, 2003; Provenzo, 1992), seeing the digital as offering a highly technologised location for the panoptic (or 'superpanoptic' (Poster, 1996)) gaze.

The surveillance tools of VLEs – their access statistics and hit counters – represent far more than the electronic equivalent of the attendance sheet. As in so many arenas, computers have enabled us to do things that were previously impossible or very difficult. VLE surveillance tools record every move a student makes within the learning space and provide intimate details of every student's working hours and patterns of study. Where a VLE is integrated with wider institutional information systems, anyone wishing to generate a student record walks through an even richer information landscape. System administrators have always been able to extract information at a similar level of detail from almost any networked activity, whether undertaken by students or staff. However, where to track activity within a web-based learning environment previously would have involved the deliberate, rather complex analysis of log files and server statistics (something for which the majority of teachers would be likely to have neither the time nor the inclination), within VLEs surveillance is a casual act – sophisticated and detailed reports on individual students can be obtained with a couple of mouse clicks. While such tracking tools are included in learning environments as an integral element of their *pedagogical* functioning – they are promoted with the promise that they will enhance teachers' ability to offer students high-quality learning experiences (for example Goldberg, 2000) – in their worst instances they can manifest in what Mullen has called a 'pedagogy of suspicion' (Mullen, 2002).

From this perspective, we can see disciplinary apparatuses or 'technologies of power' (of which the VLE is an example) as being about creating a *certain type of subject*; in using these technologies we are therefore also involved in creating a certain type of learner. For Lyotard, predicting, back in 1979, the impact of technology on education, the kind of learner being produced would be one who, in the name of enhanced performativity, would be an efficient, skilled user of information (Lyotard 1979: 51). In the current discourse of learning technology, and of problem-based learning, as we have seen earlier, we might describe the kind of learner we are trying to produce as active, autonomous, resourceful, collaborative and enquiring. The Foucauldian approach, however, might problematise the notion that it is possible to place the problem-based learning student at the centre of the learning process. Instead, it would see the subjectivity of the learner as constituted through and by the learning environment and the discourses/ practices located within it.

We should, perhaps, not underestimate the extent to which this power to constitute and disperse the subject can be applied in virtual learning environments. While humanist ways of knowing might resist the idea that identity formation can take place outside the skin of the individual, we need to consider the possibility that the online problem-based learning student may be starkly objectified in his or her virtual construction, that 'the learner' may be, as far as our systems are concerned, to some extent constituted by records of her first login, last login, frequency of login, number of discussion board submissions, pattern of page visitation across the site, and so on. Such an identity might exist not only beyond the control of the individual learner, but its very existence – and the possibility of 'judgement' being applied to it either wittingly or not – might remain unknown to them. The literature is full of claims to the emancipatory potential of online communication in educational and other contexts, particularly in the way it enables us to reformulate ourselves and experiment with new identities. In our focus on the way in which we are able to 'make ourselves' in cyberspace, however, we should not neglect the ways in which cyberspace technologies might also make us.

Conclusion: problem-based learning within cyberspace

Interesting implications arise from the issues we have discussed here in relation to the organisation of problem-based learning within cyberspace. What was to some extent private and interiorised within traditional disciplinary culture becomes exteriorised with the increased visibility and ordering strategies of the VLE. VLEs might be characterised as a device complicit with the managerialist disaggregation of research and teaching – a formerly somewhat intractable nexus in the collegial or disciplinary spaces of higher education – in order to effect their separation as two more distinctly manageable spaces. A case perhaps of divide and rule. However, insofar as problem-based learning can be seen to some extent as a radical departure from more traditional discipline-based pedagogy, it might be seen as being potentially unperturbed by such disaggregation.

We have also seen, however, that problem-based learning is about constructing a new identity for the learner, as problem formulator and actor within complex, volatile, unpredictable and conflicted environments. Problem-based learning, as a number of scholarly analyses (including those within this volume) have indicated, is a risky enterprise. The encountering of new ways of understanding both self and knowledge is perhaps what gives rise to the phenomenon of disjunction identified by Savin-Baden (2006). In that sense perhaps the subject position required of the problem-based learner has resonances with that of the learner subjectivities constructed within cyberspace environments. However, those subjectivities would seem to sit uncomfortably within the ordering strategies represented by VLEs, with their processes of standardisation and risk minimisation serving, apparently, to render teaching and learning transactions and spaces more predictable and, hence, safer. The apparent messiness and disjunctive nature experienced within much problem-based learning, its strongly liminal and somewhat unpredictable rhythm and direction does not sit easily with the calculable and performative modes we have touched on. Unless, of course, successful coping within these complex and seemingly boundariless informational environments is exactly the kind of performativity required for the practices of a globalised neo-liberal economy?

Acknowledgement

Some material used on visibility and surveillance in this chapter has been adapted from a more extensive treatment of the topic which first appeared as Land, R. and Bayne, S. (2002) Screen or monitor? Issues of surveillance and disciplinary power in online learning environments in C. Rust (ed.), *Improving Student Learning Using Learning Technologies.* Oxford: OCSLD. Our thanks are due to the Oxford Centre for Staff and Learning Development for permission to reuse this material here.

3

Institutional perspectives: making PBLonline possible and sustainable

Frances Deepwell and Andy Syson

Introduction

This chapter is concerned with the educational context in which problem-based learning occurs and wider issues surrounding the online tools to support it. Problem-based learning is often discussed at the level of the classroom encounter with a focus on the experiences of participants (students and tutors) or the intricacies of the curriculum. The chapter will explore the arena beyond this, looking at wider, contextual issues that are a prerequisite for sustainable use of online problem-based learning, such as the institutional setting, the availability of technologies and the support and resources for them, professional development, quality assurance and quality enhancement. We will weave into the narrative our own experiences of the development of online learning in one higher education institution, since they represent a familiar experience of the recent expansion of online provision in the UK. While much of the chapter can be seen to have relevance for a range of pedagogical approaches to learning and teaching, we have sought to highlight the dimensions that relate most specifically to PBLonline. We will therefore explore the enabling factors of online learning in upholding the principles of ownership, self-directed learning, interdisciplinarity and collaboration. Irrespective of the educational merits of an online approach to problem-based learning, we argue that its survival in an institutional setting is dependent on the external conditions present in that environment. The chapter is written from a UK perspective by two educational developers/ learning technologists based in a modern university, that is, one of the former polytechnics that gained university status in 1992.

Introducing technology into higher education

We start this chapter by offering a brief analysis of how innovations in technology have come into learning and teaching in higher education in the UK to explain how we have reached today's situation where technology is so deeply embedded into university life. Learners have come to expect online support for their learning in most disciplines in higher education. Email, online access to library resources, web browsing, discussion boards and personal course pages are now commonplace. The reason behind this change in expectations of online learning availability in higher education comes not only from the general increase in the use of technology in our personal lives, but also from the political and cultural changes that have swept through higher education across the world. These may be summarised under the headline terms of visualisation, lifelong learning, personalisation for the individual client and globalisation and internationalisation (Collis and Moonen, 2001).

University education has transformed into a commodity; the learners (or their parents) become the consumers. In this newly emerging climate, the learner requires patterns of learning that meet their varied needs. 'Flexibility is seen as the key idea, and flexibility requires technology' (Collis and Moonen, 2001: 31). This newly developing reality places a burden on technology to deliver the expected gains for the institution, both in terms of opening up new markets through distance or distributed teaching and by reducing the unit of resource (the tutor:student ratio) through shifts away from classroom delivery to resource-based support for learning.

It also requires that learners, now positioned as consumers, should be able to account for what they have learnt since universities are in what Barnett describes as a 'performative slide' (cited in Savin-Baden, 2000: 15), where: 'Higher education is sliding towards encouraging students to perform rather than to necessarily think and do' (Savin-Baden, 2000: 15). That is to say, the expansion in the use of technology has coincided with the increasing pressure in undergraduate programmes for students to demonstrate acquisition of skills through proven attainment of the very specific objectives or learning outcomes of the course.

Set against this political backdrop is another dimension to the use of technologies in education, namely the personal drive from individuals or teams of teachers. Since the early computing days of the personal computer in the 1980s, teachers in HE have been 'pushing the envelope' in relation to innovations in learning technology. The pioneers in learning technology were, and remain, mainly tutors who would characterise themselves as innovators. Although these innovators may want to experiment with new technical possibilities out of personal curiosity, a strong motivation lies in exploring how technology can enhance the learner experience. It is from this motivation that some of the more interesting pedagogical advances and new understandings about the processes of learning emerge:

It appears that the more successful uses of the online learning environment were linked to a constructivist approach to its deployment. Students' motivation was higher when students were actively involved in the creation of the learning environment, and in the negotiation of the 'new electronic literacy'.

(Orsini-Jones and Davidson, 2002: 83)

This sense of exploration into new literacies and learning activities has generated significant action research into learner experiences of technology and has also led to the establishment of networks, professional communities and membership organisations, such as the Association for Learning Technology in the UK in the early 1990s. Increasingly, the possibilities of the technology for particular pedagogical approaches are being investigated in relation to their relevance to the ways of teaching within a particular discipline.

Possibilities before the era of online learning

Learning technology often seems an amnesiac field, reluctant to cite anything 'out of date'; it is only recently that there has been a move to review previous practice, setting current developments within an historical context.

(Oliver, 2003: 148)

In these times of ubiquitous technology, it is hard to imagine the constraints imposed on earlier innovations in learning technology. The rhetoric of A4 learning (any time, any place, any pace, any subject (Stiles and Orsmond, 2002: 48)) is to some extent realised and can be found in mainstream higher education as well as in other educational settings, such as schools, community and corporate learning and professional development. While there are still a number of very live issues, such as access and accessibility, interoperability and reuse, training and development, and course designs for blended or online learning, the availability of technology and case studies of its use are widespread.

Throughout the 1980s and 1990s, in contrast, the situation was very different. Innovations in learning technologies were largely time and place bound and available only in limited subject areas. A plethora of technologies emerged with little compatibility between them; their operating systems, the software or the hardware. Each computer lab was rarely configured in the same way as another. This greatly restricted the likelihood of technology-based learning scenarios being recreated in other departments or institutions. The technological barriers were high and perhaps equalled by the obstacle of the cultural and emotional phenomena widely known within the learning technology community as the 'not-invented-here' syndrome (Stoner, 1996; Strang, 1995). This syndrome is used as an explanation of why teachers prefer to expend great energy on building their own setups rather than adopting the materials, methods or techniques of others.

Added to these barriers was the significant constraint of using fixed media, such as CD-ROM, laserdisk, videodisk and floppy disk, to distribute the learning material. This meant that students would see the material only when it was completed or at a considerable stage along the way to completion. Any amendments would accumulate until the next publication of the entire media. Most of the tools and experience came from a corporate training background and normally the material or tool was used individually. Where feedback was provided to the user, it was in the form of pre-loaded responses. Software such as this was described as 'interactive': using the term in a highly restrictive sense. With this software, there was no communication between students or between students and the tutors. There was furthermore no possibility of the tutor modifying the material as a result of any feedback from the students and there was no facility for students themselves to contribute to the content of the learning package.

The fixed nature of the media also meant that, with each new phase of hardware or software development, the material became obsolete and had to be laboriously transferred into the next setup. Investment in courseware production grew enormously during the early 1990s, with some notable major initiatives such as the first phases of the Teaching and Learning Technology Programme (TLTP), which was set up to 'make teaching and learning more productive and efficient by harnessing modern technology, creating computer-based learning materials in a wide range of subjects' (Haywood *et al.*, 1999: 8). However, many of the developments with technology in higher education were limited by 'constraints on student access to hardware or user support, or staff feeling that this was a limitation on their freedom to innovate' (Haywood *et al.*, 1999: 23). This was reflected in perceptions of low uptake of these materials, particularly once the lifetime of the specific initiative had passed. The successes of these funded technology projects often related 'to process rather than outcome . . . Whether or not the outcomes of the project are achieved, it is a positive experience if the collaboration has been good along the way' (Dempster and Deepwell, 2003: 52).

Web possibilities and realities

Into this environment of innovation, which was beginning to be stifled by its own inbuilt obsolescence and frustrations at the efforts required to re-version material for different platforms, came the opportunities presented by the world wide web. The global network of computers and graphic interface opened up enormous possibilities for learning technology. It made possible all manner of communications and collaborations that had not been conceivable before. Issues of compatibility for those working in large institutions dwindled once the common language of HTML and hypermedia was appropriated.

The introduction of the web brought about a step change in the way computers could be used to enhance learning. No longer was it necessary to wait until the material was 'finished' or 'perfect' before releasing it to students. Modifications could be made to a learning package, even while it was open to students and results were instantly visible. The two-way communication completely transformed the paradigm of learning techno-logy, thereby making collaborative learning, and by extension PBLonline for example, a realistic possibility.

Along with the networking of students came moves to encourage collabor-ations between departments and across different universities, exemplified by the third and final phase of the TLTP initiative, which carried a strong mes-sage of embedding learning technologies into teaching rather than creating more new materials. The initiative's first aim was to 'encourage the take-up and integration of TLTP materials and other technology-based materials into mainstream teaching and learning'. The other aims related to collaborations between institutions, dissemination and network building.

Within our experience, the appeal of using an *online* environment for learning was high, but the institutional constraints of student access, tech-nical support, sustainability and quality assurance often outweighed indi-vidual capacity to employ such technologies. Without institutional support, the cases where there was innovative practice were not sustainable over time or transferable to similar settings.

Pressures to adopt technologies

The use of technology in teaching, therefore, carries a certain weight of ambiguity. On the one hand, it is an instrument to achieve the organisational goals for flexibility of provision and sustainable growth in student numbers. On the other, it is an enabler for pedagogical advances. The ambiguity mani-fests itself in the differing approaches to implementation and change in complex organisations that are often characterised as 'top down' or 'bottom up' (Trowler *et al.*, 2003: 4). The top-down approaches are the realm of university leaders, institutional strategies and government policies. The bottom-up approaches come through local or national user groups, discip-linary communities and a wide range of practitioner networks, some of which won national financial support through initiatives such as the Com-puters in Teaching Initiative and later the Learning and Teaching Support Network (now the Subject Centres of the Higher Education Academy) for 24 discipline areas in higher education. Further ambiguity emerges if we acknowledge the wealth of hybrid approaches to technological implementa-tion, with top-down, bottom-up and middle-out strategies vying for position in a complex and unstable environment. This is the realm of educational development, which remains a fluid, sometimes fluent, sometimes stilted, mover between all the players.

Our own experience of implementing online learning across an institu-tion is one of these hybrid approaches. The decision to adopt an institutional online learning environment on a large scale was made at the top, with active encouragement from one pro vice-chancellor in particular. At the same time, pushing from the bottom was considerable desire from tutors and students across the discipline spectrum to have easy access to web-based technologies. The final pressure came from an educational development community that designed and promoted the online environment and worked to facilitate and monitor its adoption within teaching and learning.

Ownership and consultation in technology implementation in higher education

> If we did a sociogram of what happens, and which [learning and teaching] projects work and which don't, the ones that have very little effect is when we do a one-off, when those people in the room have got no other connection to us, and where we have a big effect is where somebody in that room has more connection to us.
>
> (a head of educational development, cited by Cousin *et al.*, 2004: 6)

In this section, we start to explore concepts of processes of ownership, collaboration and interdisciplinarity in problem-based learning and how they relate to the processes of implementation in an online environment. When the decision is made to embed a new technology, the process of change is as important as the change itself. To use our university as an example, the implementation occurred within the context of a change management initiative called the 'teaching, learning and assessment taskforce' (Beaty and Cousin, 2002: 144–147), which sought to enhance teaching and learning developments by bringing together some 20 or so examples of good pedagogical practice and encouraging tutors to share and develop their ideas collaboratively. One of the early processes under the taskforce initiative was to encourage sharing and interlinking of ideas. The members of the initiative also worked together to identify blocks to the development of better teaching practice. From this it quickly became apparent that more could be achieved with easy access to and control of online facilities. There was an early decision to embrace a large-scale implementation plan that would put online learning at the heart of technological developments. The plan for implementation was devised and its operation led by an academic development team whose primary concerns were to ease the adoption of technology by those who teach and to facilitate a range of pedagogical approaches rather than to favour one particular course design.

Elsewhere, we have reported on the collaborative and consultative process towards selecting which online learning environment best fitted our purposes against a self-generated quality indicator (Deepwell and Beaty, 2004). At that time the concept of online learning was relatively unknown. The detailed list of criteria was produced from discussions and feedback from tutors who were willing to experiment with a variety of systems in order to gain improved understanding of what opportunities were possible. Deepwell and Beaty (2004) report the complete set of criteria, but a sample includes: ease of use by both students and staff; online discussion and assessment facility; direct updating by tutors; viewable using industry standard browsers without additional software; access only to students registered on the module concerned.

It is worth outlining just one of the more technical criteria in order to explain its importance to the teaching and learning context. The requirement for the online environment to be supported by current, industry standard browsers, without a need for client-based software to be downloaded and installed, was *fundamental* to the principle of ease of use. It was envisaged that the online learning environment would be accessible to all, including those who were not familiar with technology and who would not necessarily have the benefit of technical support, for example students off campus in their own homes or in a workplace, potentially anywhere in the world. It therefore needed to run on as wide a range of browsers as possible and via a low-speed connection to the internet. The online environment has since been upgraded and we have come full circle as there is now virtually no software running on the web without additional plugins or other addins. Installation and any other necessary modifications are now, however, considerably simpler for most users. Issues do arise, however, if, in the name of network security, users have not been granted sufficient administrative rights to make the necessary adjustments.

Off-site access to the online environment is critical to its success. In the first year of our implementation of the virtual learning environment (1999), we monitored nearly 20% of usage off campus. This has risen steadily year on year, to over 65% off-campus access in activities that support self-directed and autonomous learning.

The development of a common template simplified the new concepts of 'the virtual classroom' and enabled lecturing staff to envision the online reality that was approaching. The template was based on patterns of usage, discussion and negotiations with experienced innovators in the pilot phase (Deepwell and Beaty, 2004). The template was easy to learn and flexible enough to support a number of pedagogies, all in the tutor's control. The inclination is towards communication and student collaboration being at the heart of the learning environment. This approach, rather than a resource-based approach, has facilitated uptake among teachers who want to apply teaching strategies that are problem oriented.

Collaboration and competition over resources

The modern university environment is fiercely competitive for both internal and external resources. Under a modularised system, such as our own, internally funded models are based largely on student recruitment to particular departments or modules owned by the departments. This mitigates against collaborations that involve the sharing of resources and technologies, since there is little local economic benefit to be had from improving the student experience of those who are counted elsewhere for cost purposes.

Additionally, there are central units that operate independently, where resources are allocated in pursuit of particular institutional strategies rather than departmental or interdepartmental concerns. These include, for example, information services, libraries, student support centres, academic registry, finance and quality enhancement units. With the introduction of a central online learning environment, there had to be some shared interactions and joined-up thinking for all students at the university (Boys, 2002). In order for accurate information about usernames, module registrations and programmes of study to be passed into the online learning environment, there needed to be lines of communication between this and the administrative record system. This was not simply a technical challenge; it is a political and cultural challenge to established practice. Boys (2002) identified that seamless access tended to be concentrated where the student and the managed learning environment (MLE) met, at the portal. The 'seamless' integration of the MLE into the everyday workings of the institution, or as part of a wider set of outcomes concerned with improving teaching and learning practices, organisational performance and collaborative working, received little or no attention. In our case, the lines of power were initially quite clear cut and led directly to the top-level support for this university-wide initiative.

Nonetheless, some support departments were resistant to changing the existing practices and processes that had been perfected over many years and were working well. Wherever possible the implementation process involved adapting the online learning environment rather than changing existing procedures. However, the pan-university nature of the online environment brought home to administrative support departments the importance of the accuracy and timeliness of their data input; this previously had not mattered until registration for examinations. Accurate information was now needed immediately for the online registration process at the start of the year. In order to simplify the processes of establishing the online spaces and to reinforce the top-down priority of using online learning, the implementation was rolled out across the entire university. Every module, every course is given a pre-set starting website, based on a common template, and student accounts are generated automatically from information stored in the university student record system.

This represents an unanticipated consequence of the implementation for students. For the first time, students can see precisely which course and which modules they are registered for in the student record system. Any errors are immediately apparent and the student can get them corrected. This feedback loop dramatically improves the accuracy of the student record system's data. Previously errors might not have been detected until coursework or examination marks needed to be input. This increased accuracy has a further positive consequence: because the class lists within the online environment are accurate, tutors are more inclined to use the system.

Exploring the costs of online learning

> But [integrating online learning] takes a lot of time; it is fortunate that I enjoy it, because I have spent holidays, weekends and entire evenings working at this.
>
> (a tutor, cited in Deepwell, 2004: 9)

For those choosing to adopt online learning approaches within their course delivery, one of the primary concerns is around the concept of cost. Cost is multifaceted and in the context of online learning implementation it means different things to different players or stakeholders in the process. Under a JISC-funded project, Ash and Bacsich (2002) reviewed cost models for networked (and blended) learning and came up with a broad framework for institutions to calculate the costs for the course lifecycle. Their three phases were: planning and development; production and delivery; evaluation and maintenance. This model enables a comparison with costing other forms of teaching, where online learning approaches are so often viewed independently of any other learning and teaching development. This phased model draws together research into costing online development and delivery of an isolated course, while our concern is for a less bounded change that extends beyond individual developments. Indeed, as Ash and Bacsich themselves acknowledge, the calculation of cost of online learning must also regard the institution as an open system rather than a closed one (Ash and Bacsich, 2002: 40), involving changes in the financial relationship within and beyond the institution. For problem-based learning, this is most relevant, since it 'sits at the interface of industry (public and private sector) and higher education' (Savin-Baden, 2000: 157). The systems and people involved are culturally and geographically disparate and yet work together to make a whole course experience. For the tutor, the move to online learning signifies personal cost in terms of time, effort to redesign an existing or new course, negotiations of additional technical or administrative support and ensuring student access. It can also mean a cost to individual academic practice, as creating a learning space online may expose practice to wider scrutiny and possibly challenge by co-tutors, practitioners working in the field or managers. There is a fine line between sharing practice, peer observing and surveillance. By the same token, the move towards online learning has provided extensive scope for improvements and developments in pedagogical practice through reflection with colleagues and students (Orsini-Jones and Davidson, 1999).

There is also the recurrent notion of opportunity cost, namely, by innovating with technology, what losses are you incurring? How might your face-to-face delivery have improved if you had put an equivalent amount of effort into the non-technology-based aspects of the next iteration of the course?

For the institution, the cost can be regarded as a similarly broad, but different matrix of factors that affect the costs of provision, both human and technical, such as:

- information services – server configurations, software upgrades, licence fees, security measures and containment of risk
- physical campus – reconfiguring computer labs and classroom spaces; provision and maintenance of compatible hardware
- technical support – central support extended to cover 24/7/365 for password and access queries; local support for tutors and student computing needs
- training – needs analysis, ICT skills, specific skills for the online learning environment (e-moderating, content preparation, online assessment, online administration); plagiarism prevention
- human resource management – academic workload accounting (finding suitable measures to account for online teaching versus the established measures of hours of face-to-face teaching contact); emergence of new roles for technicians/demonstrators, learning technologists, tutors
- learner satisfaction – student satisfaction surveys; national ratings and reputation; complaints; retention and progression.

It can be seen from this list that these costs to the institution are extensive and far reaching, which is why they cannot realistically be borne by one individual or a course team. Those who do bear the costs, namely the central administration, may be tempted to coerce the implementation process because of the high level of commitment required centrally. However, our experience has shown the benefits of a facilitative approach over a transformative one. The strategy 'seeks to *manage* rather than *control* change in our institution' (Deepwell and Beaty, 2004: 21). In our case, the facilities are made available, training is provided, teaching rooms are redesigned and new roles are defined to support learners in using technology. The message from the top is encouraging, but not prescriptive. Gradually, over a number of years, experience has grown and systems have been adapted in response to staff and student pressure, such that many of the early barriers of access and integration have been overcome and the environment is conducive to new developments in online learning. The benefits of moving online, although not to be viewed as 'return on investment', can be counted in improvements in individual and group learning and administrative efficiency, as well as opportunities for new student markets. It is therefore these systemic changes in the institution that have made online methods not only possible, but also sustainable in the medium- or long-term climate of higher education.

Who can you turn to? Support and training infrastructure for online learning

Our experiences, based in a central support and development unit, indicate that a training programme in online learning is most effective when it is supplemented with local, over-the-shoulder support. Ideally, this is provided by others who have taught the students or who are familiar with the discipline area or pedagogical approach. We have been able to draw on the dispersed educational development resource of members of the taskforce initiative, many of whom have been supportive 'buddies' to their colleagues locally as they try to adopt online elements into their teaching practice. Additionally, the provision of online guides and advice is a useful reference. The centralised template made it easy to produce guides centrally, with visual (screenshot or multimedia) reinforcement of the instructions (Syson, 2005), which have made them exceptionally user friendly even for novice computer users among both tutors and students.

In a recent survey of support models for e-learning in higher education within the educational development community in the UK (Deepwell, 2005), it emerged that there was a range of setups currently in existence. Some institutions depended on a central educational support department, others on IT services, other institutions combined this provision with local or faculty-based support with the smallest number relying solely on localised support. These results show the wide variation in the nature of support needed to support online learning. For some, the IT skills are paramount, for others it is the educational dimensions – which can also be considered enhanced by disciplinary-based support. In the case of our university, much of the formal support has come from a central unit, but this unit works extensively with locally based teaching fellows and other experienced tutors who enrich the understanding of any local application within all faculties and departments of the university. The support offered includes guides and documentation; individual or group advice and consultations; training courses and drop-in surgeries; materials development; trouble shooting and administration; user networking and community building.

Gaining skills in online facilitation

Problem-based learning appears to fit well with online learning methods. The opportunities in online media for student-to-student communication, tracking of progress and group work are the unique selling points for any problem-based or problem-oriented learning design. In order to be able to work effectively with the online environment in learning and teaching, tutors need to have knowledge and skills in both pedagogy and technology. Professional development and training provision go hand in hand. When tutors are exploring *how* to use specific tools within the online environment (e.g. discussion, assessment, content building), they also need to consider *why* they want to employ them. Similarly, tutors investigating teaching and learning techniques (e.g. groupwork, peer assessment, use of triggers in problem-based learning) might usefully consider the use of relevant online tools. Online resources have a threefold function within the online environment, namely: (a) ingredients for writing problems, (b) inspiration for problem design, and (c) information for solving problems (Watson, 2002).

The role of the tutor is crucial to the dynamics of online learning, which draws on constructivist and conversational models of learning (Laurillard, 2002; Orsini-Jones and Davidson, 1999; Salmon, 2000) and even more so in relation to online problem-based learning (Donnelly, 2004). The 'import-ance of dialogue and communication in internalizing knowledge and developing understanding' (Wilkie, 2004: 90) is central to the role of the facilitator in problem-based learning. Facilitating this online requires not only great attention to the detail of the written word but also close monitor-ing of virtual presence, while at the same time guarding against the trap that Donnelly identified in her research of seeming too 'authoritarian' through the online medium (Donnelly, 2004), and thus running counter to the principles of problem-based learning.

Another fundamental aspect of learning to tutor online is acquiring a threshold skills base in information technology. Competency in word pro-cessing, email, web browsing and file management now form the expected skill set of tutors in higher education. At a university such as ours, which has made such substantial investment in online learning, there is a further expectation that all tutors can operate effectively within the online learning environment. The Higher Education Academy accredited postgraduate course in learning and teaching, for example, operates as a blended learning course, with opportunities for participants, largely university tutors, not only to have the experience of being an online learner, but also a chance to present their online learning innovations to their peers on the course. For the purposes of running an online course, the tutor role normally incorpor-ates elements of e-moderator, instructional designer, technologist and IT trainer. In order to deliver these skills most effectively, the training needs to be provided 'just in time' of need, pay good attention to the tutor's stated needs, support peer learning of these skills and be appreciative of the tutor's desire to learn the minimum to get by, while achieving immediate payoff in their tutoring practice.

Upholding quality and managing risk

The processes of implementation of technological innovations at insti-tutional or departmental level are often presented as a series of steps or stages in a process, with various permutations on pre-initiation, implementa-tion and institutionalisation (Bates, 2000; Bonamy *et al.*, 2002; Collis and Moonen, 2001; IVETTE, 2002). In reality, for the individuals or groups con-cerned, the situation is far less compartmentalised. Recent narrative inquiry into individual perspectives on the implementation of online learning across a range of European universities found that progress is often fraught with setbacks, as personal, political or cultural as well as organisational factors such as quality assurance and risk aversion come into play:

> [T]he collection of stories of implementation that have been gathered, reveal far more complex and recursive processes at play. The

implementation processes, however well resourced, planned and championed, are subject to push and pull factors, many of them unanticipated.

(Deepwell, 2004: 6–7)

So how is this implementation managed from a quality perspective? Quality can be neatly defined as 'fitness for purpose' and raises questions such as: does the use of the online learning environment fit with the stated teaching philosophy? Do the available learning resources enable learners to achieve the stated learning outcomes? Do the online tools allow for small group communication and knowledge construction? Is there induction into the online learning environment for all who are required to use it? Quality assurance at this level is embedded into the planning processes at local, departmental and institutional levels. However, there is a division of opinion in the quality debate. There are those who believe that the online elements should be absorbed into the existing procedures for quality assurance, while others believe that these elements are so substantially different to monitor and reflect on that a different set of quality procedures should apply. In part this comes down to the segregation of online learning at some universities into peripheral departments of computing specialists rather than more mainstream educational or subject-specific departments.

Another aspect of quality that has come to the fore in the recent years of the commodification of higher education is the management of risk. Universities and their funding councils generally adopt a risk-averse strategy for implementing change. This makes it very hard to initiate a large-scale deployment of online learning, mainly for the cost implications outlined here. However, as time goes on, there is an ever greater cost implication of *not* moving online which has been recognised and acted on by the majority of UK higher education institutions. Our university took a big risk early on in the cycle of online development by investing in the largest scale implementation of an online learning environment outside the USA. Every annual cycle, however, there are new risks that need to be managed, for example the transition to newer versions of software. Each transition is a high-risk manoeuvre and there needs to be sufficient impetus behind the change for it to be successful. In our experience, there have been major upgrades to the software available almost annually, but we have restricted our institutional upgrades in order to maintain the confidence of the tutor and student population as long as possible. Moreover, each upgrade has required a coordinated training programme. While this decision has proved unpopular to some, since we have periodically been running a version of the software that is out of date in the national or international user community, it has benefited others who have appreciated the comfort factors of continuing to use a software product that is known to them.

Conclusion: looking to the future

There is no time for complacency in the arena of learning technologies. As the higher education sector gradually becomes used to the concepts of participative online learning, the next technologies are pushing in at the door and with them come a host of new possibilities for pedagogical development. The next major challenges are already on us and include: blogs, wikis, e-portfolios and how to match these technologies to the new emerging hybrid pedagogies of online learning that cut across subject areas and curriculum models. The aspects we have explored in this chapter have sought to elaborate how the development of problem-based learning as an online pedagogy requires a high level of institutional readiness. Online developments draw on resources outside those of the course team and therefore require changes in quality assurance processes, enhancement and funding models. Embedding the technologies into the fabric of an institution enables sustainable advances in educational practice for the benefit of our learners.

Part 2

Facilitation and mediation

Facilitation is established as an essential element of face-to-face problem-based learning. Accounts of attempts to capture the essence of facilitation in problem-based learning through exploration of what facilitators ought to do, what students want them to do and what they actually do is prevalent in the literature (Barrows, 1988; Dolmans *et al.*, 2002; Savin-Baden, 2003; Schmidt and Moust, 1995; Wilkie, 2004).

Technology developed with the intention of promoting learning, rather than simply as a superfast information resource, also requires some form of learner support or moderation (Collison *et al.*, 2000; Salmon, 2000). With the growth of e-learning and the recognition that problem-based learning pedagogy may have something to offer online learners, the focus of concern about the transferability of facilitation skills to problem-based learning has shifted from other face-to-face learning contexts such as seminars (for example, Haith-Cooper, 2000; Oliffe, 2000), to the degree of transferability of face-to-face facilitation skills to PBLonline. As with so much in life the central issue is one of balance; of resolving tensions created by combining problem-based learning with technology and dealing with the paradoxes of web use. In particular, the balance between freedoms and constraints, techno-logical and pedagogical elements and the equilibrium of human and computer are explored by the authors of Part 2.

Freedoms and constraints

Use of virtual learning environments (VLE) offers educators and their students certain freedoms; however, as discussed by Land and Bayne in Part 1 of this book, use of VLEs also brings constraints, in facilitation as in other aspects. Facilitation in face-to-face PBL is recognised as being resource intensive, particularly in early stages until students become familiar with the problem-based learning processes. The optimal number of students in a problem-based learning team is still open to debate. Barrows (1988) recommended five to six. In many courses, tutor and accommodation constraints have pushed up this number considerably, while Price (2000a) suggested that problem-based learning in a distance (paper) format could be undertaken by individuals working on their own. Use of PBLonline also needs to address the optimal size of the online group. There is the freedom for potentially large numbers of students to contribute, however, particularly where postings are asynchronous, there are facilitation constraints as tutors will require time to read and respond to comments. Thus group size still needs to match staff, if not room, resources.

Dupuis (2003) writes of the need to open up space for students to extend goals through exploration. The welcome addition of new material from students places demands on tutors to respond. This is especially so when PBLonline is utilised as a form of work-based learning where students contribute experiential learning to the discussion and the problem-based learning scenario not only smells real but *is* real. In Chapter 5, Hmelo-Silver *et al.* write that tutors developed new ways of responding to online postings that enhanced students' ability to follow online discussion. Pelletier (2005) reports that notions of freedom and almost unlimited potential to explore being limited by control are not unique to PBLonline but are also found in face-to-face problem-based learning. Although the freedom to explore beyond the scenario has always been an aspect of problem-based learning, some facilitators close down discussion, keeping the group on set lines (Wilkie, 2002). Pilkington (2001) reports that the amount and type of tutor comments can be seen by students as constraining. The influence of the facilitator is not removed by being distant or invisible.

Clarke (2004) and Dix *et al.* (2004) state that there are benefits related to freedom from the rigid timetable of attendance. PBLonline offers the potential for asynchronous dialogue, allowing students to participate in a time and place that suits them. The authors in this part explore the potential constraints that this places on facilitators as there may be a need to spend more time online than would have been spent in a face-to-face session. Student non-attendance at face-to-face problem-based learning sessions is a challenge for many institutions. Asynchronous design combined with the surveillance potential of online systems may be utilised as a means of overcoming this. However Dix *et al.* (2004) point out that when computer users are tired and pressurised there is an increase in user carelessness and this may be a feature where students use the freedom from a rigid timetable to undertake part-time work. Both tutor and student groups must be actively involved to build up skills.

Collison *et al.* (2000) point out that there is also a need to open up online spaces and provide freedom for students to 'hang out', in spaces that are not facilitated or 'policed' by teaching staff. The issues of space and types of space discussed in Part 1 of this book echo in facilitators' attempts both to open spaces for students and to find ways to respond to the increased freedom, without creating constraints for themselves and their learners.

Technological and pedagogical issues

One theme that occurs repeatedly in respect to PBLonline, unsurprisingly, is the need for training for a range of people in a variety of skills. The need for both tutor and student groups to be comfortable and confident in using the technology is self-evident. However, there are a number of authors who refer to this (see, for example Donnelly, this volume; McLuckie and Topping, 2004; Wood, 2001) and suggest the unfounded assumption that tutors at least will possess the necessary expertise or possess the motivation (and the time) to acquire it. A further assumption is that today's students are competent in all aspects of online technology. In further and higher education in the UK, the drive to widen access has pushed up the student age, particularly in disciplines such as nursing. Students may not be as skilled as is generally believed and thus require some training.

Having acquired skills in the hands-on aspects, tutors further need to gain insight into the nature of online delivery. Tutors may lack skills in developing materials for use online. It is not sufficient to put an existing problem-based scenario into a virtual learning environment and hope for the best. Materials for PBLonline may be created by other staff or adapted for online use by technicians; in either case there is a risk that what was intended is lost. Technologists also require different skills to ensure that material placed online matches the aims and content of the course.

Many facilitators, accustomed to being expert in face-to-face problem-based learning, may now have to contend with PBLonline, in which they are comparative novices. The need for thinking skills to be developed in students remains. Traditional facilitator actions such as questioning, prompting and challenging may still be used, albeit in a different format and with an awareness that group members will pick up the questions at different points in the discussion. As all the authors in this part point out, there are considerable differences in facilitating PBL online; shifts are required in existing techniques and new ones need to be developed. In PBLonline, the tutor is invisible; there is no one to watch and model. Issues of student consent may make tracking of PBLonline discussion as a 'sleeper' problematic. Acting as a co-facilitator may be useful, but asynchronicity of response may bring its own problems, such as perceived inconsistency in responses and resource issues.

In addition to acquiring technological skills, students have learning needs over and above the outcomes of the programme. Just as students in face-to-face problem-based learning need to acquire skills of collaborative working, so ways of working collaboratively in PBLonline need to be found in order to complete the work. Crooke (1997) states that learning gains will not be maximised unless students are adequately prepared for collaborative working. Dialogue also needs to be developed as a vehicle for learning. Further discussion on ways and benefits of monitoring of dialogue and the development of online interactions will be discussed in Part 4.

Another aspect for consideration is the potential for the computer to be programmed to take on some of the aspects of the role and thus relieve teachers from some of the more time-consuming tasks associated with mediating online discussion. The traditional face-to face problem-based learning structure relies on having a single facilitator for each small group, but this is not possible in many settings.

In Chapter 4, Lycke *et al.* explore differences in behaviours of tutors in PBLonline. The balance of time spent on facilitators' civilities changed, not only in respect to the move to PBLonline, but also in relation to individual differences. As there are different approaches to facilitating face-to-face problem-based learning, so also are there different ones to online facilitation. In Chapter 5, Hmelo-Silver *et al.* report on the tensions that may arise as a result of using technology. The online activity structure helps to offload some facilitation functions onto the computerised environment, allowing less experienced individuals to facilitate. However, tensions arise with respect to learning the content versus learning to use the tools, being student centred versus providing feedback, and also issues related to group negotiation of ideas and construction of a joint problem space and solution.

Adoption of PBLonline thus requires consideration about the needs of those who will set up, implement and participate in the strategy. Donnelly (Chapter 6) reports on the use of PBLonline itself as a sustainable method for educational developers to prepare staff and design and run PBLonline.

Human and computer interactions

PBLonline offers many benefits but also some losses, for which compensation is needed. There are benefits in the form of the potential for asynchronous response and extensions of space and time for learners to respond to the learning requirements of the problem situation; there is a plethora of easily available resources; the online tutor may be available more often for comment; opportunities for feedback are more focused and extensive. Conversely, face-to-face contact and direct personal connection with students is lost. Education for professions such as medicine, nursing, social work, teaching and law requires graduates to possess good interpersonal skills in dealing with clients. The ability to role model and develop such people-centred skills, a key attribute of face-to-face problem-based learning, is difficult to achieve in PBLonline. Development of PBLonline is still at a comparatively early stage of development and, as in any new venture, will require time and practice for tutors to develop new skills related not only to the manipulation of the technological tools, but also with respect to developing appropriate user-friendly content and feedback to students.

Miller and Wallace (2002) and Rourke and Anderson (2002) reported that analysis of online 'discussion' showed a preponderance of social/administrative issues rather than intellectually challenging debate. This showed similarities to findings by Jacobsen (1997, 2004) and Wilkie (2002) that focused on 'frame factors', issues for students that were unrelated to the problem-based learning session, such as experiences in clinical areas and receiving coursework results. These distracted student debate from the issues raised by the problem-based learning scenario. Use of online 'cafés' or 'wine bars' may go some way to resolving this, but, as in face-to-face problem-based learning, facilitators need to find ways of preventing the frame factors from taking over the discussion.

Nonverbal cues such as facial expressions and hand gestures form a vital element in face-to-face facilitation, both for facilitators in assisting judgement of students' understanding and for students in deciding the exact meaning of facilitator comments. The ability for active listening is likewise missing. This may lead to a lack of fit with learning style for students who prefer to listen rather than read. Additionally, work in artificial intelligence indicates that computer users tend to focus mostly on the first one or two sentences in paragraphs, thus creating further challenges for the facilitator and pro-gramme developers (Dix *et al.*, 2004). The use of emoticons is increasing in PBLonline. Whether these detract from seriousness of discussion or add to understanding by attempting to present a 'visual tone' requires further research.

Conclusion

The development of facilitation and mediation in PBLonline for both students and facilitators follows a progression that is interrupted as skills/materials for use online evolve, not in a smooth pathway but, like problem-based learning itself, in fits and starts as new understandings are gained and skills adapted or conceived. The authors in Part 2 of this book seek to explore issues of facilitation and mediation, share from their experiences and offer suggestions for those who want to develop PBLonline in their own programmes.

4

Tracing the tutor role in problem-based learning and PBLonline

Kirsten Hofgaard Lycke, Helge I. Strømsø and Per Grøttum

Introduction

Tutors in problem-based learning are more facilitators or coaches than conventional teachers. Their tasks include supporting productive social interactions, promoting suitable progression of group work, facilitating subject discussions and evaluating the processes (Schmidt and Moust, 2000). However, as Dolmans *et al.* (2002: 177) point out: 'Tutor performance is not a stable teacher characteristic, but, rather, is situation specific.' The introduction of computer-supported communication into problem-based learning within a medical faculty at a large Norwegian university definitely changed the learning situation, but there was little knowledge at that time about how the tutor role would be affected by the innovation. This chapter will present a study on how problem-based learning tutors in the field of medical education adapted their role to the new learning context of PBLonline.

Tutor tasks and tutor approaches: issues

Different theoretical perspectives have been brought to bear on problem-based learning and PBLonline (Schmidt and Moust, 2000; Stahl, 2002). While the strongest theoretical arguments for problem-based learning have been derived from cognitive theory (Norman and Schmidt, 1992; Schmidt, 1983), socio-cultural perspectives and knowledge building metaphors are more prominent in computer-supported collaborative learning approaches. Even so, there are noticeable similarities in the learning procedures that are advocated. Engeström's learning cycle with seven stages (Paavola *et al.*, 2002) and the 1999 model of Muukkonen *et al.* of progressive inquiry for computer-supported collaboration, both have much in common with the 'seven jump' procedure described for problem-based learning (Albanese and Mitchell, 1993; Schmidt, 1983). It has also been argued that computer-supported synchronous problem solving does not differ so much from face-to-face problem solving (Orvis *et al.*, 2002). Given the similarities in recommended learning procedures, it would be expected that the tutor role would be much the same in problem-based learning and PBLonline.

The tasks problem-based learning tutors should attend to – what tutors ought to do – have been described in different ways. Schmidt and Moust (2000), for instance, point out that tutors should support productive social interactions, promote suitable progression of group work, facilitate subject discussions and stimulate evaluation of the process. Tutors should pay attention to such areas, but there is little guidance as to how tutors should prioritise their attention. Studies on how such tasks are implemented are fairly rare, but attempts to characterise typical tutor approaches can be illustrative. In a qualitative study of nursing lecturers, Wilkie (2004), for example, demonstrates that the tutors had four approaches to facilitation. The *liberating supporter* used minimal interventions and promoted self-directed learning with focus on content. The *directive conventionalist* retained control over content and processes. The *nurturing socialiser* was student centred, nurturing and supportive, socialising students into good standards. The *pragmatic enabler* adapted their approach to match the self-directed nature of problem-based learning and the demands of the competency-driven programme and thus appears as the most effective approach.

Some of the attempts to classify tasks and approaches may give the impression that there are sets of characteristics for effective tutors. Barrows (1988) however, advised tutors initially to change their role in accordance with the development of the students' roles and his views are supported by recent writings (for example, Hmelo-Silver, 2004). Barrows (1988) pointed to three phases in tutoring: modelling, coaching and fading. For students who were inexperienced with problem-based learning, the tutor should make frequent use of metacognitive strategies and model questioning and reasoning processes. When the students are familiar with problem-based learning, the tutor can limit his interventions to coaching or scaffolding the learning process, for instance if the students miss an important step. Eventually, if group processes develop as intended, the students will be able to work on their own. The tutor at this stage should therefore attempt to withdraw or fade out of the running discussions and become more or less unnecessary to the group (Barrows, 1988).

In spite of a considerable body of literature on the tutor role, conclusions about effective tutor practices are somewhat tentative. When problem-based learning goes online, our knowledge of just how tutors should participate is even more limited (LeJeune, 2005). However, when a problem-based learning programme is adapted to PBLonline it will often be experienced problem-based learning tutors who undertake the facilitating. Knowledge of tutor roles in the two learning contexts and how these roles may differ is therefore important.

Early assumptions related to introduction of information and communication technology into educational practices may have been coloured by a simplistic and instrumental understanding of the relationship between teaching and technologies (Coates *et al.*, 2005; Lund, 2003). For PBLonline the implication is that the early attempts to translate face-to-face problem-based learning to online contexts may at times have been somewhat naïve (Engen, 2005). Today there is a growing understanding that the new learning technologies provide 'dynamic and complex ecologies that require very competent teachers in order to design and orchestrate activities that invite mature participation' (Lund, 2003: 268).

The types of difficulty PBLonline tutors encounter are related in part to the way online communication is organised. Online communication is based on written texts. The advantage is that these messages may be saved and pondered over more thoroughly than oral utterances (Cameron *et al.*, 1999). Contrariwise, the lack of nonverbal expressions (eye contact, gestures) and paraverbal cues (voice inflection, volume) may hamper the communicative flow (Lycke *et al.*, 2002). When the communication is synchronous (real time), the pressure on writing quickly and to the point increases and adds to the complexity of managing the tutorial process (Zumbach and Reimann, 2003). Schmidt and Moust (2000: 47–48) have shown that in order to be effective, tutors need 'social congruence, subject matter expertise' and 'the ability to be cognitively congruent with' the students. Cognitive congruence requires communication skills that may be more difficult to achieve in PBLonline than in face-to-face problem-based learning. It also appears that effective tutoring is related to conditions such as the structure of the learning context and the students' prior disciplinary and technological knowledge. In problem scenarios where the structure is insufficient or unfamiliar, tutoring becomes more important. Tutors familiar with advanced students who need little guidance in the problem-based learning process might well expect these same students to need little guidance in PBLonline processes also. However, even if the students are to use almost the same procedures in PBLonline as they did in problem-based learning, they will need support if they are unfamiliar with, for example, the structure of learning management systems (Lycke *et al.*, 2002).

Attempts to trace a tutor role for problem-based learning and PBLonline should also take account of the conceptions of the tutors. Several studies have shown that different goals or rationales may influence the way in which tutors carry out their functions (Björck, 2004; Lycke, 2002; Wilkersen and Hundert, 1997). 'Different teaching philosophies of facilitators shape the actions of the group accordingly, although there are of course general differences in how the discourse and actions of different groups develop. Nevertheless, the facilitator's role in this process seems to be of great importance' (Björck, 2004: 282).

The relationship between tutors' espoused theories and actions is invariably not given. Hockings (2004) discusses contradictions between the pedagogy tutors express and what actually happens and finds that some of the discrepancy between the two can be traced back to a lack of facilitating skills. It has also been found that tutors modify their expressed beliefs in order to fit their actions (Savin-Baden and Wilkie, 2004) and that tutors shift their approaches dependent on experience, time and context (Wilkie, 2004).

In many cases, tutoring approaches have been studied separately for PBLonline and problem-based learning. It is not obvious, therefore, whether the difference in tutoring approaches that are reported are distinct for each learning context, or whether they rather may be regarded as extensions or variations between tutors, or of approaches tutors use in different settings. The literature suggests several issues related to the tutor role in PBLonline and problem-based learning. We will focus here on two of them:

• How do tutors approach tutoring in problem-based learning and PBLonline?
• How do tutors conceive their role in relation to the two learning contexts?

The research process

Background: problem-based learning and PBLonline in medical education

The setting for our study is a Norwegian university where a 6-year medical education programme had integrated problem-based learning at all study levels. As moves to more flexible teaching and learning gained momentum in 1999/2000, ways to enhance problem-based learning through computer-mediated communication were keenly discussed at the Faculty of Medicine. One reason was the general interest in examining how the rapid advancements of the web, personal computers and new learning management systems could be used to support or even improve medical education. A further more pragmatic reason was linked to the decision to extend the period for clinical placements from 4 to 12 weeks. The tutors considered online communication to be a means to maintain contact with students during their clinical period and to integrate clinical experiences with on-campus learning. Finally, it was argued that the students as future doctors needed skills and competence in using information technology as an instrument for lifelong learning (Roald, 2000).

PBLonline was introduced to students in the fifth year when they were on clinical practice placements in hospitals and family practices in the south-eastern part of Norway. During their clinical placement the students were to meet online twice a week to address a problem scenario. This organisation was similar to the one they were used to from their previous problem-based learning experience. Communication was to be synchronous (real time) with each session lasting for 30 to 45 minutes. After the students returned to campus, problem-based learning was continued face to face. The groups and their tutors were the same for the PBLonline and for the problem-based learning activities.

Participants and setting

Three of the eight tutors in the programme were asked to participate in the study. *Andy* had previous experience as a general practitioner, but was now an associate professor working full time as researcher and tutor. *Ben* had never practised medicine but early on had supplemented his medical studies with courses in social services and group dynamics. *Carl* had a high research profile combined with a dedication to the applied aspects of his particular field. The tutors were academic staff (full or associate professors) who were experienced problem-based learning tutors and who used the internet as part of their daily work. It was, however, the first time they had participated in PBLonline and they were unfamiliar with the use of learning management systems. All tutors therefore were offered, and participated in, a 1-day training course in the learning management system (ClassFronter, Inc., Oslo, Norway).

The students were organised in three problem-based learning groups, two with eight and one with seven members. The groups and their tutors were the same for the PBLonline and the problem-based learning activities. The tutors and students each gave individual written consent to participate in the study. At the beginning of the term the students were given a 4-hour introduction to the learning management system. They also had a trial run in a computer laboratory where the groups used computers to work through a case online with their tutor. The intention was to establish the groups and to familiarise them with the technicalities of computer-supported communication.

During a 12-week period of clinical placements the students were given two problem scenarios. The participants downloaded the problem scenarios and made preliminary notes before meeting online. Each case was dealt with in two synchronous meetings with individual work between meetings. Since students in the same group were distributed and never in the same location during the PBLonline period, all the group communication took place online. Each message was marked with the time the system received the message and the name of the sender.

Design

The study was conducted as a multiple-case design (Yin, 1989) with data from registration of net-based activities (PBLonline), video and tape recordings of face-to-face activities and interviews with three tutors. Research question one on tutor approaches was related to the activity level and content of tutor interventions. They were mainly studied through quantitative analysis of the recordings. Research question two on tutor conceptions was related to conceptions of the same location throughout the PBLonline period. The system provided a chat system with a small space for typing messages at the bottom of the screen, while the rest of the screen displayed messages that had already been posted regarding the two learning contexts and tutoring in these contexts. The research questions were mainly studied through qualitative analysis of the interviews. In discussing the two research questions, however, we will draw on the findings from the quantitative as well as the qualitative data.

The researchers did not participate in the planning of the new online programme, but observed the planning process. Likewise, the researchers were not involved in the implementation of PBLonline, except for questions on technical matters. Access, both to data from the interactions in the two learning contexts and to interview the tutors, was granted by the institution and by individual consent from each of the participating tutors and students.

Data on interventions

The electronic 'chat' discussions were automatically logged as text files with time stamps and names per message for all three groups. Four meetings (two on each case) were logged and analysed for all three groups. The face-to-face discussions were recorded using video- and audiotape. The tape recordings were transcribed and analysed. The videos were used to facilitate the identification of the speakers when the tapes were transcribed.

Activity was estimated in this study through a registration of the number of words in tutor interventions. Tutors' utterances were selected as the unit of content analysis (Rourke *et al.*, 2001). Every time the tutor's identification appeared in the transcript, the utterance following was identified as a message unit. This means that a unit could consist of either a single word or several sentences. After reading the transcripts, the following categories emerged for content analysis of tutor interventions:

1 *Social interactions*
   Statements that were related to the clinical placement and other types of 'small talk'.
   Example:
   Tutor: What's it like out there?
   Paul (student): We're overrun by Chlamydia pneumonia! Must be an epidemic!
   Kari (student): Here too!
2 *Work organisation*
   Statements that were related to technology or to different aspects of the assignment, without touching on the substantial questions in the problem scenario.
   Example:
   Tutor: Hi Anne! Ready to be chair with capital letters?
   Anne (student): YES, THAT'S OK!
   Tina (student): Do we start now or wait for the rest?
   Anne (student): WE START. WHAT DO WE DISCUSS FIRST?

3 *Problem scenarios or subject matter*
Statements related to the assigned problem scenario or to the subject matter associated with the scenario.
Example:
Eva (student): Common problem – experts disagree about treatment!
Tutor: What do we know about treatments? Are there many with such a serious diagnosis?

4 *Task and process evaluation*
Statements that in some way implied evaluation of the task, the group processes, or the tutors' contributions.
Example:
Tutor: Did you all get the learning goals for next time?
Jill (student): Think so!
Tutor: Thanks John – good job on leading the discussion!

5 *Statements not possible to categorise*
(This category is omitted from the following discussion.)

These categories coincided with the 'tasks for tutors' suggested by Hård af Segerstad (2002), Lycke (2002) and Schmidt and Moust (2000); to support productive social interactions, to promote suitable progression of group work, to facilitate subject discussions and to evaluate the processes.

Data from interviews

The three tutors were interviewed separately at the end of the fifth year when the PBLonline and problem-based learning activities were complete. The focus was on the tutors' conceptions of problem-based learning and PBLonline and their role as tutor in these two learning contexts. The interviews were tape recorded, transcribed and content analysed qualitatively by one of the authors. The two other authors checked interpretations. In particular, the analyses were aimed at identifying elements in tutor conceptions that could contribute to understanding the observed tutor activity in the two learning contexts.

Findings

Tutor approaches: levels of activity and content of interventions

First, a comparison was undertaken of *levels of tutor activity* in problem-based learning and PBLonline. The similarity in activity patterns for the three tutors was quite striking. All three had much higher activity levels in problem-based learning than in PBLonline. (These and other findings are more fully reported in Lycke *et al.*, 2002.)

A second observation was that the relationship between tutor and student activity differed for the three tutors. Andy and Carl, for instance, were both approximately twice as active as their students in problem-based learning. In PBLonline, however, Andy was slightly above the student average activity, whereas Carl was well below the student average. Ben showed yet another activity pattern; he had the same level of activity as the student average in both learning contexts. Therefore, in moving from problem-based learning to PBLonline, the activity level for two of the tutors changed from high to low while the level for the third tutor stayed at the student average.

Next, the *content of the tutors' interventions* in the three groups was studied. The categories presented earlier were used to compare the content of the statements in problem-based learning and PBLonline. Considering *social interventions* by tutors in problem-based learning, the registrations showed that Andy used approximately 13% of his time for social statements, but such statements were missing for Ben and Carl. In PBLonline, however, all three tutors spent 5% of their time on social comments.

The attention to *work organisation* was also different in the two learning contexts. In problem-based learning approximately 10% of Andy's time, 24% of Ben's and 6% of Carl's time was devoted to interventions directed at organising the work in the group. In PBLonline the focus on work organisation was much stronger with notable differences between the tutors. Andy spent 28% of his time on work organisation. Ben and Carl used almost twice as much time as Andy on such comments (55% and 52% respectively).

When interventions relating to the *problem scenarios or subject matter* were considered, it was found that tutors gave far more attention to this area in problem-based learning than they did in PBLonline. This tendency was most pronounced for Carl, who used approximately 93% of his time for content-related interventions in problem-based learning and less than 33% for such comments in PBLonline. Andy spent approximately 75% of his time in problem-based learning and 57% in PBLonline on the problem scenarios. For Ben, the percentages were 74% and 40%.

Task and process evaluation was not very prominent in this sample. In problem-based learning the three tutors spent from 1% to 3% of their time on evaluation. In PBLonline this category was somewhat more in focus, with Andy and Carl spending approximately 10% of their time on such statements. Ben used no time for evaluation in this learning context.

One clear difference is thus seen in tutor focus in the two different learning *contexts*; problem-based learning and PBLonline. In problem-based learning the main focus is on the problem scenarios, covering from 74% to 93% of the tutors' time. In PBLonline the main focus for Ben and Carl was on organisation of the work. For Andy, however, the main emphasis in both contexts is discussing the problem scenarios. In addition, there were rather marked individual differences in content focus between the three tutors. Andy divided his time between the four areas in much the same way in problem-based learning and in PBLonline. For Ben and Carl discussions of the problem scenarios dominated the problem-based learning situations, whereas their focus in PBLonline was on organising the work effectively, the difference being more pronounced for Carl.

On combining the data on level of activity and content of interactions in the two learning environments, the individual approaches became clearer. Andy was very active in his group in both learning contexts. His main focus was on discussing the problem scenarios, but he also attended to the other content areas. Ben's activity seemed adjusted to the average activity in his group in both contexts. His focus in problem-based learning was on the problem scenarios and in PBLonline on organising the work. Carl was very active in problem-based learning, but rather passive in PBLonline. The content in Carl's interventions was also rather different. In problem-based learning, scenario discussions were at the centre of Carl's attention. In PBLonline he covered the full range of areas, but his main emphasis was on organisation.

In conclusion, there were both notable differences in tutor approaches (level of activity and content of interventions) in face-to-face and online problem-based learning and marked individual differences between the three tutors.

Conceptions about learning contexts

In order to gain a better understanding of the observed differences in tutor activity the tutors were interviewed about their conceptions of and practices in problem-based learning and PBLonline. Analyses of the interviews were aimed at tracing how the tutors' conceptions matched their approaches (activity levels and content of interventions). In general terms, the tutors conceived face-to-face and online learning to be two rather different learning contexts with problem-based learning as the 'richer' of the two. As Ben commented:

It would be stretching it to call PBLonline for problem-based learning! You lose so much of the usual process such as the element of discussion and direct dialogue. You only have the written comments to relate to. The discussion becomes more restricted – and the learning that comes from rich discussions may be lost.

The tutors also agreed on the difficulties related to the text-based communication in PBLonline. One of these difficulties was losing nonverbal communication. Andy noted:

I missed the direct contact. Group dynamics disappear when we only communicate on the screen. I have used to rely on direct and non-verbal communication, in this setting I never managed to get a proper overview.

The speed of text-based work in the synchronous interactions of the chat format created particular difficulties for the tutors. Carl stated:

While you are writing the discussion has quickly moved on. PBLonline limits communication, much of the spontaneity and dynamics of face-to-face interactions are lost.

In the interviews the tutors said that when they started PBLonline they had hoped to carry on problem-based learning much as before. They were not prepared for the restrictions technology set for PBLonline or for how difficult it would be to communicate with people without nonverbal cues to supplement the written statements. A lack of necessary technical skills and routines in using the learning management system hindered the tutors in managing the group processes and in participating in the case discussions. The tutors also felt restrained by the speed of the communication taking place. With eight or nine participants all interacting in real time, the number of messages presented in a short space of time could be overwhelming. At times the online conversation moved too quickly for the tutors to be able to contribute substantially to the discussions, which made the tutors uncertain how they should participate effectively. The registrations (see earlier) indicate that when faced with such hindrances, the tutors not only reduced their activity but also shifted their focus of attention.

Even so, the tutors noted learning gains for the students through PBL-online, especially where the problem scenarios encouraged the students to draw on experiences from their clinical placements. 'Sometimes the group discussion really gets going,' Andy said, and added, 'They were forced to think through the situations in the districts and how it affected treatment of patients who were seriously ill.' Ben quoted a student who had said: 'I would never have learnt about this part of the subject if we had not worked on this scenario in this way.'

Conceptions about tutoring

The initial experiences with PBLonline as expressed in the interviews were fairly similar for the three tutors, but their tutoring approaches were fairly different. The interviews were analysed for possible relationships between the tutors' conceptions about their role and their registered activity patterns.

The interview with *Andy* indicated that he felt comfortable as a tutor and that he was very conscious of the different challenges posed by problem-based learning and PBLonline:

I enjoy being a tutor. I want discussions on different themes and to promote a critical attitude. The main thing is to encourage the students to learn to ask the right questions, pose hypotheses and gather information – in fact the same as what you do as a doctor! I participate in the discussions about the subject matter. In problem-based learning I can leave a lot of the structuring to the students, in PBLonline I have to be more active!

Andy was keenly aware of his own modelling function as a medical doctor, researcher and tutor and felt that active participation in problem-based learning gave the students an opportunity to encounter him as a suitable role model. In the face-to-face problem-based learning sessions Andy felt little need to focus on the organisation of the work and felt free to do what he really enjoyed, which was to participate actively in the case discussion. When it came to the PBLonline sessions, Andy started out with an idea of how he believed the students should organise their work. He stated his expectations in the first session and was quick to intervene if these structuring 'rules' were not followed. For instance, Andy identified the student who was to chair the session and reminded her to identify her statements by using capital letters. Andy's conceptions were mirrored by his approaches. He had relatively high activity levels in both learning contexts with particular engagement in the discussions of the problem scenarios.

Ben for his part emphasised that facilitating the students' learning processes was his main function, irrespective of whether the learning situation were problem-based learning or PBLonline. Ben was highly student oriented in his approach:

> My starting point is respect for students and their time. I find that tutoring is easier if I get to know them and let them get to know me. I think there should be emphasis on the collaborative aspect – that everybody has responsibility for learning in the group and for contributing to the group. I don't want to be too passive, but usually find a role with some steering – especially when the discussion deviates from focus.

Ben was unprepared for what he experienced as a lack of motivation in the students and how they lost their familiar 'seven-step' (Schmidt, 1983) approach to problem scenarios when they were faced with the learning management system. Ben identified the students' behaviour in PBLonline as that of a malfunctioning group and set up a strategy to overcome their lack of collaboration. Ben decided, for example, to withdraw his group for a part of the first trial case. He judged it more important to motivate the students and to establish 'ground rules' for PBLonline participation than to have the students work on the problem scenario. Ben's focus on group dynamics and processes was reflected in his activity level which, in both learning contexts, coincided with the student average. It was also noticeable that Ben's attention to work organisation in both learning contexts was higher than that of either Andy or Carl.

Carl particularly enjoyed 'bringing students into a field, especially where you have some knowledge of the frontiers of our knowledge. Telling them how this is an open space where we don't know. Asking them to join us in researching the area further!' However, he found it easier to open up for exchanges on such reflections in problem-based learning than in PBLonline. Furthermore, Carl did not want to 'waste time and energy' on organising group work and did not believe that PBLonline was a suitable instrument for academic discussions. Carl's views on face-to-face problem-based learning were very different:

> I am positive to problem-based learning in the sense that it means working with students in small groups – preferably over time on the same theme or case where they can bring in their own experiences. In general I find it easier and more in keeping with academic standards to stimulate good dialogues when the problem scenarios are fairly closely related to my own discipline.

Carl showed marked differences in activity level and content between the two learning contexts. In problem-based learning, Carl's activity level almost exceeded that of his students, but in PBLonline Carl was almost the most passive member of the group. There was also a change in the content of Carl's comments related to case discussions, with a substantial decrease in interventions occurring in PBLonline compared to problem-based learning. In problem-based learning Carl did not participate in the social 'small talk' and paid little attention to the organisation of the work. The dominating focus was on the substantial aspects of the problem scenarios. In PBLonline, Carl displayed a rather passive role with a high degree of organisational interventions. These differences in activity patterns were mirrored in Carl's conceptions of problem-based learning and PBLonline as he expressed them in his interview.

According to the interviews, in PBLonline all three tutors seemed to have less focus on discussing the subject matter and more focus on the organisational aspects of the group work than they would have preferred. This shift in role appeared to be accepted by Andy and Ben, whereas Carl seemed to feel more or less forced into this role. At this point it was difficult to state whether the emphasis on tutor responsibility for organisation and structure was an inherent aspect of PBLonline or the learning management system in use or whether it was a question of becoming more familiar with the computer-supported learning approaches and the consequences this had for online tutoring. The low focus on organisation in problem-based learning, for example, was probably due to the long experience the students had had with this learning environment.

Discussion

PBLonline and problem-based learning tutoring – adaptation or consistency?

The level of tutor activity varied between the two learning contexts and between the three tutors individually. However, there was little evidence that the amount of tutor interventions had a positive or negative effect on the students' learning processes. According to Barrows (1988), tutoring should be adapted to the students' familiarity with problem-based learning approaches. Students who were experienced in the use of problem-based learning, such as the students in this study, needed limited guidance. In PBLonline, by way of contrast, where the structure and technology were unfamiliar to the students, they may have needed rather more guidance than one would have expected, based on their problem-based learning experience (Strømsø *et al.*, 2004). On this basis there were indications that Andy may have been too active in problem-based learning and Carl too passive in PBLonline. In this instance, the tutors were not in conflict with their own intentions as suggested by the interviews, but with the norms for problem-based learning and PBLonline as set down in the literature.

The increase in tutor activity in problem-based learning seemed to be related to an increase in the subject-related content of tutor interventions. To some extent this went against the basic ideas on problem-based learning, which indicated that the students should play the main role in this part of the learning process (Barrows, 1988). The three tutors became worried or frustrated when they had to give a lot of support to the students on organisational matters in PBLonline. Yet such support was emphasised in the literature (Coates *et al.*, 2005). This study indicated that these three tutors practised problem-based learning and PBLonline somewhat differently than prescribed in the literature.

Another point here was the question of consistency in tutor roles. Intuitively, it may have been considered a strength for tutors to develop a certain tutoring style and to use this across different learning contexts. However, it may have been the case that tutors' performance *was* not only situation specific (Dolmans *et al.*, 2002), but that it *should have been* situation specific. The implication of such a normative stand was that all three tutors might have been more effective as tutors had they adapted their tutoring approaches more to the learning context. In problem-based learning Andy could have tried to reduce his engagement in the subject oriented discussions to avoid becoming more dominating than inspiring. By contrast, in PBLonline, Andy could have been more active in the subject-oriented discussions, because these were too difficult for the students to handle by themselves online.

Based on the interviews, the rather striking differences in tutor activity level and content did not seem altogether contextual, but appeared to be the result of individual conceptions about the tutor role in problem-based learning and PBLonline. For example, Andy's espoused approaches to facilitation matched the quantitative data on his intervention activities. In PBLonline as well as in problem-based learning, Andy was rather active, almost more so than his students, with most focus occurring on the subject matter. However, Andy was well aware that PBLonline might present particular challenges and accordingly spent proportionately more time in PBLonline on organisational matters. The implication was that Andy's interventions coincided with his conceptions of his own role. Andy seemed to fit Wilkie's (2004) description of a pragmatic enabler reasonably well in his general approach in both contexts.

Ben's activity level was similar to the average of his students in problem-based learning as well as in PBLonline learning contexts. He appeared to maintain the same approach in the two learning contexts. Ben's interventions were mostly related to work organisation in PBLonline, but even in problem-based learning this area had a fairly large proportion of his attention. The observations were in keeping with Ben's conception of his main role as facilitator and his clear student orientation. The term nurturing socialiser seemed to cover Ben's approach quite well, an approach that was consistent in both settings.

None of the approaches suggested by Wilkie (2004) seemed to fit very well with Carl's approach. His approach and his views on PBLonline indicated his discomfort at not being able to tutor within his own field of expertise. Carl seemed 'displaced' in Savin-Baden's understanding of the term (Savin-Baden, 2003), disliking the changes in the tutor role that were required for PBLonline.

Little is known about how conceptions of facilitation are formed, but it is proposed here that training activities to support tutoring in face-to-face and online learning groups must take into account the ideas and rationale of the tutors, rather than just the need to develop skills. Based on the three problem scenarios presented here it is advocated that tutors receive needs-based training and individual support, rather than merely general courses on using PBLonline. By registering both what tutors actually do and noting how they conceive their role, it can be identified which tasks they emphasise and how they approach facilitation related to these tasks. In spite of suggestions elsewhere (for example Hockings, 2004), the behaviour of tutors in this study illustrated that their espoused theory and practice were congruent.

Influence of technology on tutor approaches

This study supports the notion that tutor performance is situation specific. In this case the most distinguishing aspect of the two learning situations was the use of technology in PBLonline. The tutors themselves related the difference in approach to PBLonline and the use of a learning management system. They had not expected that the technological adaptation of problem-based learning would be so hard to manage. However, all three tutors were quite optimistic, expecting most of the problems to be resolved next time around.

Learning management systems add new dimensions and expectations to teaching. It has been suggested that such systems through their design influence, guide and perhaps even restrict teaching and learning (Coates *et al.*, 2005). With the advance of flexible learning approaches in higher education, and as such systems become more readily used, it is expected that some of the difficulties encountered by the participants in our study will be greatly reduced. There is, however, no straightforward transfer of face-to-face learning modes to computer-supported contexts (Coates *et al.*, 2005; Lund,

2003). Awareness of challenges and possibilities is necessary to exploit ICT for educational purposes. Such awareness however, must be combined with relevant development of the approaches, strategies and skills necessary for tutors and their students. Tutors would benefit from developing a repertoire of tutoring approaches and increasing their understanding of how and when the different approaches could be applied. Tutors also need to become adept at new forms of communication and online dynamics. In order to bring about such awareness and competency, tutors need a combination of planned and structured educational programmes designed for them, and individual follow-up over time.

Conclusion: suggestions for practice

The comparative data here were rather limited, being restricted to only three tutors. Findings and discussions must therefore be regarded as tentative. More in-depth studies of the tutor role in different contexts are needed before any conclusions can be drawn. By way of contrast, the participation of the students and tutors, not as an experiment but as part of their regular study programme, gave a valid picture of tutor approaches and conceptions in problem-based learning and PBLonline. Thus tutors and others who are in the process of introducing online programmes similar to the one described may find our results interesting and suggestions helpful.

Perhaps the most important outcome of the innovation for the Medical Faculty was the way PBLonline connected experiences in the clinical placement to the campus-based curriculum. It also gave the students and their tutors a means to discuss subject matter and social concerns even if they were distributed all over southern Norway. The way the participants, unfamiliar with online communication, made use of PBLonline was impressive. When PBLonline is situated in a clinical context, however, tutors must be attuned to a situation very different from the 'schooling situation' on campus. A number of other factors will compete with the students' attention and task orientation. It is therefore important that tutor and students clarify, not only when they are to meet online, but also expectations related to preparations and follow-up before and after the sessions, for example.

Tutors should not take it for granted that students – even if they have experience with problem-based learning – can transfer their skills directly to online learning. If online discussions are to develop beyond surface exchanges, they need support from the tutor. Barrows (1988) has suggested that tutoring should be adapted to the students' insight and training in the field of study and in problem-based learning processes. He suggests that different phases in student development will call on modelling, coaching and fading. This appears to be applicable to PBLonline as well. Initially the tutor, for instance, must be prepared to model interventions and comments that contribute to in-depth discussions of case scenarios. Later, the tutor must give the students the necessary coaching in their discussions and perhaps also in the mastery of the technology. In later stages again, the tutor should find that he can fade out of the immediate discussion, only staying at hand for particular needs.

Another aspect of tutoring online is structuring the online interactions. In the introductory phase, the students need clear and consistent instructions: what are they expected to do, when and how? Structuring is even more important in PBLonline than in problem-based learning, because the participants must do without the nonverbal communication which subtly contributes to structuring in problem-based learning. As they learn to cope, the structure can become more flexible. To reduce the confusion that may reign in large groups communicating in a synchronous mode, rounds may be introduced just as they may be in other types of group work. It may also be helpful to signal when a point seems sufficiently debated, to suggest that the students move on to a new phase in the discussion or to encourage students to sum up the discussion in turns.

What seems to inspire and regulate tutor activity in problem-based learning are tutors' conceptions of student learning and how it may be further promoted, rather than their distinct tutoring skills (Dolmans *et al.*, 2002). The interviews indicated that this may apply to tutors in PBLonline as well. The implication is that developing understanding of the ideas and processes involved in collaborative learning may be as important as skills training for online tutoring.

Acknowledgements

The research project 'PBL goes ICT: problem-based learning in face-to-face and distributed groups in medical education at the University of Oslo' was sponsored by Hewlett-Packard, Palo Alto, USA and the University of Oslo, Oslo, Norway.

The authors would like to thank tutors and students at the Medical Faculty, University of Oslo, for their contribution to this study.

5

From face-to-face to online participation: tensions in facilitating problem-based learning

Cindy E. Hmelo-Silver, Anandi Nagarajan and Sharon J. Derry

Introduction

Problem-based learning is an effective way to contextualise learning in professional education, particularly in medical education (see Barrows, 2000; Hmelo-Silver, 2004; Schmidt *et al.*, 1996). Medical education is a privileged setting with one facilitator for each small group and students who share common goals, are highly motivated and have been academically successful. Other settings require additional support as there are many groups per facilitator and motivation and prior achievement are more variable. Such was the case when we began to use problem-based learning in teacher education. We developed a problem-based learning course in the learning sciences for students who were planning to become teachers (that is *pre-service teachers*; Hmelo-Silver, 2000). A goal for this course was to help these future teachers understand how *learning sciences* could be a *tool for thinking* about the classroom. *Learning sciences* refers to the current theoretical and empirical scientific knowledge base about student learning and development in educational settings. Originally, several paper problem scenarios were used with one roving facilitator and six to seven groups of students in the class. This course had three major limitations. First, the problem scenarios did not reflect the perceptual world of the classroom and were often oversimplified to focus on one particular topic. Second, it was difficult for one facilitator to work with several groups. Finally, students had difficulty in identifying fruitful learning issues because of limited prior knowledge of learning sciences and pedagogy. These were all issues that could be addressed in an online environment. Moving the programme online presented new challenges for facilitation. In this chapter, we describe eSTEP, a learning environment used for problem-based learning with pre-service teachers; the way we dealt with some of the challenges and how they were resolved.

Activity theory (AT) was used to understand the role of the facilitator and the tensions in facilitating online problem-based learning because, in general, learning was studied in its socio-cultural context and, in particular, there was an interest in how tools mediated human activity. AT was well suited to understanding learning activity as it tries to explain the changes in human practices over time. Learning environments are complex activity systems that involve multiple agents, as well as material and psychological tools that mediate learning. In Engeström's (1999) conceptualisation, each activity system is composed of a subject, object, mediational means, rules, the community and division of labour. The subject is the person(s) directly involved in the activity. The object is the goal of an activity but is often a dynamic aspect of an activity system that shifts over time. Mediating artefacts include material and psychological tools (such as language) that aid the subjects in achieving their goals. This notion of mediation is a key aspect of AT. Tools shape the subject's goal-directed actions and also reflect prior experiences of others and thus can serve to transmit social and cultural knowledge. The community, its rules and norms, and the division of labour account for the larger social, cultural and historical context of the activity system. Learning thus emerges from activity and cannot be separated from the context in which it occurs. AT provides a multidimensional account of activity systems. Therefore, it is an appropriate lens for studying the dynamic complexity of learning environment. To examine learning from an activity theory perspective means that the researcher needs to consider how components interact with each other. These interactions can lead to tensions within the system, which promote change and development (Engeström, 1999). Studying the tensions among different components and understanding how to resolve them allows researchers to develop new forms of practice in collaboration with their subjects[1] and can be the driving force behind innovation (Barab *et al.*, 2002; Engeström, 1999). It is useful to consider problem-based learning as an activity system in exploring how the role of the facilitator changes in moving from a face-to-face problem-based learning environment to an online one. The facilitator plays a critical role in facilitating online problem-based learning groups (Barrows, 2000; Collison *et al.*, 2000; Hmelo-Silver and Barrows, 2003).

The next section reviews a study of face-to-face facilitation and, to develop a bridge between theory and practice, some of the tensions are described that developed in implementing problem-based learning online.

Problem-based learning as an activity system

In the problem-based learning activity system, shown in Figure 5.1, the subjects were students who were engaging in goal-directed activity towards the object of achieving a transformed understanding, for example, of how the learning sciences applied to teaching. Students were expected to take

[1] We use the term subjects here to refer to the student participants in the activity system in order to be consistent with the terminology used in activity theory.

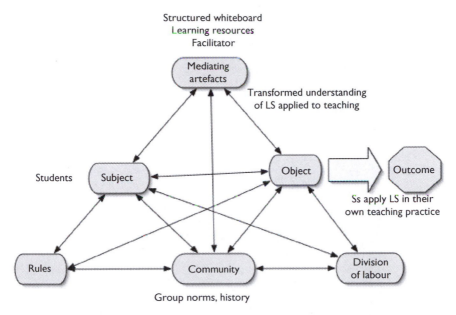

Figure 5.1 Problem-based learning activity system

responsibility for their own learning. Through working together as a community of learners they developed a shared history. The learners could take on different roles within their groups – some official, such as the scribe, or others less official, but no less important, such as helping to facilitate (Hmelo-Silver *et al.*, in press). The structured whiteboard served to mediate learning in the problem-based learning activity system. In the 'standard' model of problem-based learning (see Barrows, 2000), the whiteboard provides a record of the group's deliberation, a focus for negotiation and a means for ensuring common ground.

The eSTEP system

The eSTEP system is an online problem-based learning environment that provides pre-service teachers with an opportunity to engage with learning sciences concepts by using videocases as contexts for collaborative lesson redesign (Derry, in press; Derry and Hmelo-Silver, 2005). The system consisted of three components. One component was the online learning sciences hypertext book, the Knowledge Web (KW). The second was a library of videocases that present examples of classroom practice. These cases presented opportunities both for discussion and the redesign of instruction depicted in the cases. The videocases were indexed to the KW, helping students identify fruitful learning issues (Figure 5.2).

Finally, there was the problem-based learning online module which

Figure 5.2 Videocase with links to case-related concepts in Knowledge Web

included tools that could scaffold students' individual and group problem-based learning activities (Collins *et al.*, 1989). These included a personal notebook where students could record initial observations, a threaded discussion, where students might share research and a whiteboard where students could post and comment on proposals for lesson redesigns (shown later in Figure 5.6). Figure 5.3 shows the roadmap that reminded students of the activity structure.

A typical eSTEP course consisted of three or four problem scenarios each lasting 2–3 weeks. eSTEP courses used a hybrid online and face-to-face course structure to allow students to build trust, create community and make decisions quickly when needed (Arbuagh and Benbunan-Finch, 2005). The asynchronous discussions promoted reflection and allowed one facilitator to work with many groups (Hmelo-Silver *et al.*, 2005; Swan and Shea, 2005). A typical problem scenario would include both a videocase of a student or classroom and a problem statement that sets the students' goal to redesign the lesson (or some aspect of it), based on learning sciences principles. The activity was structured into eight steps plus a poster session as shown in Table 5.1.

During eSTEP activities, students worked collaboratively and engaged with various tools. The tasks ranged from examining student performance and designing assessments to redesigning entire lessons. Despite careful design of the system, with the intent of both offloading some facilitation functions onto the system (such as in the activity structure) and creating the ability to monitor multiple groups, learning to facilitate in an online environment was found to be quite different to facilitating face to face.

Contrasting online and face-to-face problem-based learning

Problem-based learning in the asynchronous environment has many different characteristics from a face-to-face environment. The first difference is the pace. Online discussions are slow compared with the rapid give and take of a face-to-face discussion (Andriessen, in press). This offers facilitator and students the opportunity to be more reflective. Face-to-face discussions occur in real time, with students working synchronously. Online, many hours may pass before there is any response to a posted idea, thus feedback is delayed. In

Figure 5.3 eSTEP roadmap

Table 5.1 eSTEP activities

Activity	Description	Modality
Step 1	Study videocase	Individual, online
Step 2	Record observations and initial proposals in online personal notebook that guides students towards relevant lesson features	Individual, online
Step 3	View other students' proposals	Collaborative, online
Step 4	Identify concepts to explore for redesign	Collaborative, face to face
Step 5	Conduct and share research	Collaborative, online
Step 6	Collaborative lesson design	Collaborative, online
Poster session	Groups present project to class	Collaborative, face to face
Step 7	Explanation and justification of group product	Individual, online
Step 8	Reflection	Individual, online

the face-to-face setting, feedback occurs immediately, requiring on-the-spot decision making about facilitation input. Online, facilitators can take their time and watch how discussions play out. Tools are important in both forms of problem-based learning. Structured whiteboards provide a focus for negotiation during face-to-face problem-based learning, as students decide what facts from a scenario are relevant (and worth recording), which ideas should be considered, which concepts need to be explored and which actions remain to be taken. The tools used in the eSTEP course include some simple tools as students begin and end the problems face to face, using large Post-it Notes™ to record their initial ideas and the concepts to explore and in conclusion preparing a poster to indicate their findings and solutions. They also use a variety of computer-based tools to mediate their communication. The online whiteboard serves as a space that groups use to negotiate their ideas and develop their proposals for solutions. The threaded discussion is the space where students share their research. Students also have individual workspaces where they can develop preliminary ideas before posting to the group.

The role of the facilitator becomes more complex as problem-based learning moves online. In face-to-face courses, the facilitator has several roles. First, the facilitator helps maintain the agenda by guiding the problem-based learning process. This guidance is often subtle and builds on a repertoire of strategies (Hmelo-Silver and Barrows, 2002). Second, the facilitator helps push the students to think deeply by asking questions. Third, the facilitator assists with group dynamics, and in early problem-based learning experiences, with the use of tools. The online environment allows these roles to be accomplished in three asynchronous modes. The facilitator can ask questions on the group whiteboard or threaded discussion board. Without visual cues to address specific group members, the facilitator must develop strategies to keep all group members engaged and help them coordinate among multiple spaces. Email serves as a backchannel to help maintain the agenda, remind students of the timeframe and invite uninvolved students to join the discussion.

The data for this action research were drawn from several semesters of eSTEP courses held at Rutgers University. Qualitative analysis was conducted of online interactions on the whiteboard and in threaded discussions, as well as of student reflections, email correspondence and facilitator journals, to form a composite case study of eSTEP. These data were analysed to look for tensions in the activity systems, characterise them and identify attempted or possible solutions.

Tensions in facilitating online problem-based learning

Examples of the tensions in the system are shown in Figure 5.4. These occurred in all parts of the activity system and some are described in the sections that follow, together with solutions that were used.

Between context and content

Students could become focused on the instructional context of the activities rather than on the learning sciences content as they concentrated on the concrete task of lesson design and did not consider the psychological rationale behind the lesson design activity. In this case, there were competing objects, partly because the students were eager to envision themselves as teachers. One example of this was observed as students were trying to design an assessment for a constructivist classroom as shown in Figure 5.5. In the whiteboard, one student proposed a list of assessments, some of which had good connections to classroom activities. However, the research findings that were supposed to have been their rationales bore little relation to the assessments. This was partly related to the students' understanding of the task. As one student wrote in her reflections:

> I feel that this problem gave us understanding of the multi-facets that teachers must incorporate into a lesson plan. It seems that classes which deviate from the normal class (lecture) style teaching, requires the teacher to be more creative. With being more creative, the teacher must also take into consideration the fact, students must obtain understanding of concepts at the end of the activity.

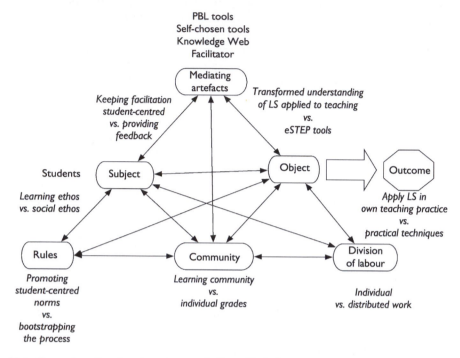

Note: Examples of tensions in systems are indicated in italics.

Figure 5.4   Tensions in eSTEP

This suggested that the student was focused on developing a creative activity rather than theoretically grounding it. To achieve a transformed understanding of how learning sciences applied to teaching, it was important for students to have focused on the connection between content and context. The facilitators used several approaches to deal with this problem.

One way was to remind students of what they were working on. The backward design model of Wiggins and McTighe (1998) required that students thought first about what the enduring understandings for a unit should be ('objectives'); next, what the evidence of that understanding should be and only then about the activity. The facilitators often had to remind the students of the need to connect these aspects of instructional design. In the next example, students focused on the learning sciences, but were not concretely connected to the task of identifying evidence of understanding as they worked on redesigning a foreign language lesson. One student proposed that metacognition was evidence of understanding: 'If students are able to make use of metacognition it will provide an evidence of understanding. While learning a new language students will make serveral [sic] errors. If the children are able to recognize these mistakes and accurately correct them it shows that they are self regulating their learning.' The facilitator asked, 'Can

Proposal
To have the students learn the material to the best of their knowledge, here are different assessments they will receive:
*Lab journal – will assess their ability to explain the process before they do it, observe what worked in the experiment and what didn't and reflect on what they learned. This will be done in a notebook in a certain format, e.g. based on Esther's research.
*Research paper – the individual work/research they came up with in a paper that applies their knowledge to other concepts.
*Objective testing – in class exams with multiple choice, matching, fill-ins, T/F, etc.
*Presentations of their experiment through a car race and explanation of what they did. If they win the race, they obviously know what they did to make this work. However, to prove that they understood the concepts, they have to explain to the class the process they used and why they think it worked. If they lose the race, they still have to explain what they did and figure out what they would do next time to make the car go faster. This will involve peer evaluation.
*Class participation/discussion – this is a combination of all of the above, to clarify concepts, ask questions, and involve themselves in the work they are doing.

Research findings
Scaffolding

Woolfolk:
– Support for learning and problem solving. The support could be clues, reminders, encouragement, breaking the problem down into steps, providing an example, or anything else that allows the student to grow in independence as a learner.
– Gradually allows students to do more on their own.
– Assisted learning.

ERIC digest:
– Scaffolding is described as a means of coaching to the extent that they can perform intellectual tasks on their own. Success with PBL largely depends on whether students have been sufficiently prepared to take on certain new roles, such as those of inquiry seekers and collaborative team players in the classroom. In a PBL classroom, for example, the teacher gauges the difference between what activities students can do on their own and what they need to learn to do to solve the problem. Then the teacher designs activities that offer just enough of a scaffold to overcome this gap of knowledge and skills.
– Effective scaffolding includes activities that help students develop the right mindset, engage students with the problem, divide activities into manageable tasks, and direct students' attention to essential aspects of the learning goals. The effectiveness of PBL depends to a large degree on the scaffolding provided by teachers to students.

Figure 5.5 LBD assessment example

you clarify exactly how students would demonstrate use of metacognition and what objectives that would connect to? I am not sure that I understand what you are getting at (others should feel free to jump in and help).' Thus, the facilitator pushed the group to be more concrete in how this might be enacted. Sometimes, it was helpful for the facilitator to remind students of the problem. This was often evident in a contrasting cases activity in which the facilitator reminded the students about the video: 'Also, remember what the problem is – redesign Blair's instruction using what he learned from Etkina. So you might want to see how the second video might give you some useful ideas in addition to the ones that you are working with.'

Another strategy used to help facilitate was revoicing (O'Connor and Michaels, 1992). Revoicing allows the facilitator to build on ideas that were already 'in the air', to help provide legitimacy for them and perhaps clarify or add a subtle elaboration. In the next example, working on a foreign language lesson redesign, a group member tossed out this idea:

> Since Mme. Beaumont is concerned with teaching . . . the vocabulary that will be used to back up the higher level language classes, Declaritive [sic] knowledge must be worked into her activities.
>
> She is doing a chapter about the culture of France. Since declaritive [sic] knowledge deals with advanced competency in writing, reading, speaking and listening, she will have to frame her unit while concentrating on these objectives. Here is an activity that will help her do just this.
>
> To have students practise reading, she could provide them with a short paragraph about (ex) a French Painter, or War, or King. They would have to read (in groups, in order to work in her emphasis on group work that she would like to create), and translate . . . It will also bring in writing (grammar and vocabulary) two forms of declaritive [sic] knowledge. She will then have them present their product orally, in order to have them practise speaking and listening to the language itself.

The facilitator then revoices what the student has said but adds some interpretation to the students' proposal to help point them towards the mechanism: 'So if I understand what you are all saying correctly, she is using practice and feedback to help the students construct declarative knowledge?' This builds on the theme of declarative knowledge that the student has focused on, but adds to it by noting that it is through feedback and revision that their declarative knowledge could be further refined. The student responds with agreement and takes the idea a bit further:

> Yes, I believe that if she consistently does this project, the practice of writing and speaking, together with group work, will help the students construct a very good range of declaritive [sic] knowledge. THey [sic] will have the necessary background to move onto the next levels of French.
>
> IN ADDITION: Perhaps she can keep a portfolio of the writing, so that at the end of the year, students can see how much wider their range of vocabulary has gotten, and how much more insightful their comments are. This self-assessment can be very useful in helping students understand their own progress.

Here the pre-service teacher got at the importance of both practice and self-assessment in advancing learning for the foreign language students. Thus by beginning the elaboration, in a way that honoured the student's contribution, the facilitator provided a model that the student could continue.

To focus on making connections between learning sciences concepts and the problem, a very simple strategy was to ask students for the psychological rationale for their ideas. For example, one student, working on a science lesson, proposed a class discussion, which she justified using the concept of cognitive apprenticeship and then proposed a detailed set of experiments without a rationale. The facilitator posted a note: 'What is the psychological rationale for having students work on experiments?' The student responded with a concern about whether the students had sufficient prior knowledge to engage in experimentation. Another group member noted: 'It might be useful for the students to explain how they think a scientific phenomenon happens (like objects repelling one another) before they learn it in the classroom. They could write up an explanation about their prior knowledge and then the teacher might have a better grip on where the students are at that point. The direction the lesson plan would take could follow from the student's original ideas, allowing them to prove them right or wrong.' Another student jumped in with a comment about the importance of working with materials. Thus, a simple question led several group members to work at constructing an explanation of why an experiment might (or might not) be useful.

Between learning the content and learning the tools

In the first ever semester of the eSTEP course a mid-course survey showed that 80% of students disliked the online environment the most, of all the activities in the class. It was felt there were too many tools to master. One problem was that rather than viewing the asynchronous discussion as a place where students could be reflective, many students viewed the tools as communication barriers. One student wrote: 'I feel the communication was again a problem. I honestly feel a chat room on this website would bring more strength to this website. Our group didn't communicate as much do [sic] to the distance of the web. I think that perhaps next time, I would ask the group if they wanted to meet together for a half an hour or so to organize our ideas and see what everyone is thinking about the problem. Our group does really well based on our discussions, so this time I think our ideas weren't as creative as our last problems.' This group, like many others, suggested meeting outside class. In subsequent semesters the students were always offered the opportunity to meet face to face as well as online.

One approach to dealing with the issue of dislike of the online tools was orienting students to the activity structure face to face before moving them online later. This has had limited success. In earlier years groups were offered the opportunity to meet with tutors in the computer laboratory to assist them in learning how to use the various tools, but few groups took advantage of this offer. What has subsequently proved to be successful has been to bring wireless laptops into the classroom. This allowed the facilitator to provide contextualised help to the students, as they needed it. In addition, when online activities were occurring, facilitators were able to monitor the groups regularly and be responsive to any technical problems. This assisted students in understanding how the tools could help with their learning related to collaboration and social knowledge construction. It was also important for the students to understand that there was a learning curve in appreciating both problem-based learning and online tools and that the course facilitators and technical support were always readily available to help.

Another tension was between the tools provided (and their limitations) and the tools that students wanted. Students did not necessarily value or realise the role of asynchronous tools in fostering reflection. Another assumption that students had made was that tutors wanted to police them online to 'know what they are doing', rather than understanding that tutors were there to help facilitate their learning. Based on this assumption, one group sent the tutors a transcript from a chatroom they had set up outside the eSTEP system. This excerpt shows that the students focused on dividing tasks but not on discussions of substance:

> *Ced*: has anyone else put anything up on the pbl site?
> *BtWeeN*: for step 3, did we all have to write a proposal or if we agreed would it be fine
> *qtnats*: she said we need to do step 5, but we need to vote and decide which arfe the best
> *qtnats*: yea, thats fine . . .
> *Ced*: which proposals?
> *qtnats*: i revised my proposal to include dynamic assessment and changed elaborative rehearsal to peer assessment
> *BtWeeN*: i think it was step 3
> *Ced*: yeah, I saw that
> *qtnats*: we all have to vote on the proposals, assessment, and activities
> *Ced*: oh i see, but you can only vote two times for each tab . . .
> *qtnats*: and then we submit it for our final, and then we print them and put them on our sticky paper for the gallery walk . . .

This was a striking contrast to the discussion had by the same group on the whiteboard, excerpted in Figure 5.6. All students were involved in this discussion, which involved issues of substance. Pointing out the contrast to the students helped them better understand the affordances of asynchronous tools. The chatroom also provided a lesson for the designers about how a chat tool might be useful when students needed to engage in task management. Such a tool has since been incorporated into STELLAR, the latest version of the eSTEP system that allows flexible authoring of learning activities (Derry *et al.*, 2005).

Related to this was a more general issue of tool design versus user needs. Students (and facilitators) often appropriated tools in ways that were unexpected. The students in the previous example wanted a chat and found a freely available chat tool outside the system to use. In general, the group

Proposal 4 by NatalieV: Last edited: 12/04/2002

Proposal
Assessment should be varied, and formulated around the amount of progress of each student as well as the fulfilment of the National standard's 5 goals. (The goals are: communication, cultures, connections, comparisons, and communities.) Using Vygotsky's idea of the proximal zone of development and dynamic assessment, the teacher can learn how well the students are learning and remembering previous lessons, how well they are applying grammatical rules from both native and foreign language, and how well much more they have learned since the beginning of the year. Also, it would not be necessary for students to have mastered all 5 goals, but the more the better, and the teacher should be aware of the progress of the class as a whole as well as the progress of each individual student and use both as a factor to help the grading process.
Also, participation can be counted as assessment as well as basic formative assessment (quizzes, multiple-choice tests, fill in the blank, etc.) authentic assessment (inquiry, oral participation, interactive exchange tasks).

Portfolios can also be a means for assessment:
• Portfolios may include journals, inquiry, oral presentations, and reports that provide the students with an opportunity to become active in the classroom learning environment. These types of activity promote a deeper understanding of the information being learned and also concentrates on students' ability to communicate to each other and the teacher in their native and foreign languages. They also promote the learning of the foreign cultures, heritage, and history.
• The portfolio can be a compilation of previous activities such as notes, worksheets, quizzes, tests, research for the student's cultural presentation, as well as 'journal entries' for what each student believes he is learning, what he likes, what he is confused about, what he dislikes, and any idea he may have to improve the lesson or learning experience.

Research findings
Diegmeuller, Karen, 'With nod to history, foreign language standards unveiled', *Education Week*, 11/29/95, 15(13), p. 10. Academic Search Premier-11/25/02

Schulz, Renate A, 'Foreign language instruction and curriculum', *Education Digest*, 3/2 99, 64(7), p. 29. Academic Search Premier-11/25/02

Comments by CHmelo:

Please limit your comments to 5 lines. If you need to explain something in more depth, consider using the Group Discussion Board to supplement what you write here on the Group Whiteboard.

What would be indicators that would tell you something about students' zones of proximal development?

Save changes to this Comment   NOTE: Each comment must be saved separately.

Comments by

after giving the students a variety of assessments ranging from multiple choice tests to oral presentations after the first lesson, their zone of proximal development could be registered depending on how well and how quickly they understand lessons to follow before and after the teacher gives an in-depth lesson on the essentials of the lesson. Throughout the course, the students should be able to learn more rapidly and be less prompted due to their prior knowledge from English as well as their previous French lessons.

Comments by ChristopherF:

This ties into attention because one theory of attention is practice meaning that if the activity is practised enough, cognitive resources are used less, thus freeing up those resources for other tasks. it leads to multitasking and in a French classroom, they are without a doubt concentrating on multiple tasks within vocabulary and grammar as they become more advanced.

Comments by ChristineM:

This could also tie in with elaborative encoding because if when the material is taught it's related to the student's prior knowledge then the students will be able to retrieve the information quicker and due to its association it will be transferred into long-term memory.

Figure 5.6   Excerpt of whiteboard discussion assessment proposal of foreign language case

whiteboard has supported student engagement very well but there have been some limitations (Hmelo-Silver *et al.*, 2005). As Figure 5.6 demonstrates, it provided a context that anchored students' discussions (Hmelo *et al.*, 1998), but there was only a single space for comments, so as students or facilitators posted new comments, their old ones were erased. The facilitator adopted the convention of adding to her notes, labelling them old and new. In groups with extended discussion, the students have appropriated and extended this practice as shown in the next example. This was a set of comments made by one student in response to a very elaborate proposal for activities in the foreign language case:

> *New comment*: I agree A. with the acting out vocab words! I remember my Span 101 prof made us do that all the time – the one that sticks in my head the most is when we had to act out the words for shower, dress, comb hair, etc when we were learning about daily activities. I like that idea! I remember my 101 prof saying that even though we are in college, we are like children learning how to write and read for the very first time because we haven't been exposed to this language before, so it's okay to be silly, have flash cards, words hung up around the room (or at home) to label objects for us to learn because that is how little children learn to speak and write . . . in English.
>
> *Old comment*: S. – I agree about the skits! I hated doing them, especially when teachers pushed to do them early in the year/semester rather than after getting used to the class and people because I felt like a moron getting up there and doing a skit in front of a classroom full of people I didn't know. But maybe skits could be done in the middle to end of the year after students have gotten to know each other (personally as well as in the class and language ability). By doing skits after knowing each other, people may not feel as weird getting up in front of the class performing them because they know that everyone has to do them, and they are all in the same boat by doing them, and working in groups in skits are also helpful too . . .
>
> *Old comment*: Yeah I agree M. about being more specific, I just wanted to collect everyone's initial ideas so we have a frame to work with – to add/delete things from. Then we could also divide these things up somehow maybe in order to get the research from online and textbooks from.

By appropriating this practice, students could address each other as well as the group and deal with task management issues as well as design and conceptual issues. This example shows how both the facilitator and students redefined how a tool could be used to meet their needs.

Tensions related to facilitating

Students did not always appreciate the role of the facilitator; sometimes facilitation was ignored. Our log data suggested that this occurred because students did not check the website regularly. This could have been a tension between the ill-structured demands of problem-based learning and the well-defined demands of more traditional courses. Thus, when students did not appear actively engaged, email served as an important backchannel for communication since it was sent to the concerned students. This helped the facilitator maintain the agenda and kept all group members involved, as shown in this email, written to move a group towards problem completion near the end of the semester:

> You have made and are making some good progress towards completing this, the last problem. Now you need to work together (meaning every-one needs to get online and make some comments and refine pro-posals). A few of you have not been real active on this problem. Be sure that you use the instructional planning rubric to check that you have touched all the bases. Also, don't forget the psychology. Email me if you have any questions.

This served to encourage the students, remind them of the timeframe and provide pointers to help them be successful in working on this final problem. The artefact-centred discussion has proved helpful for facilitation when students were online, because it was integrated with student work (Hmelo-Silver *et al.*, 2005).

Another tension was that the students sometimes saw the facilitator as someone who impeded their work or 'interrupts too much and slows us down'. Students sometimes did not understand the role of the facilitator or assumed that she was there to judge what they were doing. In this example, from a group that was struggling with problem-based learning, both these tensions have been addressed by the facilitator explaining her role:

> *Student:* . . . I always get nervous that when you ask questions, our group may be on a totally wrong path to solving this problem or else you would not be questioning it. Therefore, I just try to verify what we're doing is ok.
>
> *Facilitator:* The reason for my asking you questions is to see whether you can clearly explain what you're referring to and can adequately justify it. So take it easy and take my cues as constructive feedback – Whenever you go totally on the wrong path, you'll find me spending more time in your group.
>
> (Chernobilsky *et al.*, 2005)

This group subsequently engaged with each other and was more respon-sive to facilitation. Their subsequent problem-based learning activities were increasingly successful.

New facilitators, in particular, struggled with the tension between being student centred and providing feedback. In an early facilitation experience, one of the eSTEP facilitators was concerned that the group was developing a misconception about the concept 'transfer' and commented:

> Alright first and foremost, transfer is not a strategy or skill that can be 'used' so it wouldn't be appropriate to say 'use transfer'. Transfer is a process of applying your knowledge or understanding to solve new problems so for example . . . formative assessment. When you apply that knowledge in designing assessments for this problem . . . transfer is said to occur, but it won't be correct to say that you used transfer – rather you transferred knowledge or used and applied your knowledge. Do you see the difference?

More experienced facilitators tended to use questions that tossed the responsibility for learning back to the students, as shown in Figure 5.6. The facilitator built on the ideas that the student offered ('zone of proximal development') and how that connected to the problem of assessment.

Related to this was the issue of remaining student centred but bootstrapping the process of engaging with online problem-based learning and using the tools effectively. Students got frustrated when they were working online with the tools and did not understand how they might be used. It was particularly useful during early online experiences for the facilitator to provide some explicit guidance, as shown here:

> One way to use the whiteboard more effectively is to answer the questions I've posed to your proposals. For example, under assessments, you might want to address how each of your assessments will be administered and how your research relates to your design and use of assessments.

Without this guidance, students might have resisted the use of the online tools.

Facilitators had to struggle with students' desire for expediency, on the one hand, and their goal of preparing students to be lifelong learners, on the other. A major goal of education is to prepare students for future learning (Bransford and Schwartz, 1999) and the self-directed learning goals inherent in problem-based learning are consistent with these goals, but facilitation often involved explaining to students why they needed to go beyond cutting and pasting their research. Students were reminded of the importance of processing information, as in this exchange:

> *Facilitator*: It is really important for you to summarize the information and not just cut and paste. By summarizing you are engaging in elaborative processing which helps you learn and providing the source reference allows others to read the original material. It is also helpful if you (and the others in the group) can think about how this connects to the problem – either the original video or the solution that you are working on.

Student: i think the reason we are doing so much cutting and pasting is so that all of our group members can view all the information that we are when we research it. Although we are narrowing down information, i feel that it is important for each of us to draw our own conclusions on the material that we read on the discussion board.

Discussions of issues related to self-directed learning are now orchestrated, so that students can be focused on issues related to constructive processing and critically evaluating information. These occurred in the context of the students' self-directed learning during initial problem-based learning experiences. Whole-class discussions focused on the range and reliability of resources that students identified.

Studying the tensions that developed and how they could be resolved provided important pointers for the ongoing development of PBLonline. It was useful for the designers and facilitators of problem-based learning to consider the differences between the intended and enacted design, to understand the difficulties experienced by both students and facilitators and to be aware of the kinds of resistance offered by students. It was critical to provide new students with immediate help and hands-on opportunities. This could occur in a computer laboratory, with laptops in the classroom, or by using a chat programme in a distance learning environment. Other lessons related to strategies for facilitation. Facilitators needed to honour students' ideas yet at the same time restrain them from wandering too far afield. Strategies such as revoicing, asking for explanations of important ideas, asking about group consensus, and sometimes reminding students of the problem they were working on, could all be helpful. It was also important to help students understand the nature of problem-based learning and the role of the facilitator. Students will have spent most, if not all, of their past education being accustomed to their teachers taking the role of information provider and evaluator. Some students will need to be reminded of the different roles for students and tutors in problem-based learning.

Conclusion

Activity theory, with its emphasis on mediation, provided a useful lens for identifying the tensions in the system and how they might be used to improve a technology-mediated problem-based learning environment. Facilitation was a critical part of the problem-based learning process, even more so when problem-based learning moved online, although the online eSTEP environment made some aspects of facilitation part of the activity structure. Many tensions needed to be resolved in facilitating online problem-based learning. Some of these were the same tensions as in face-to-face problem-based learning, such as being student centred and providing feedback to students. Students might want to get the task done quickly, but the facilitator might need to slow them down to encourage explanation, connections and reflection. Others were unique to the online environment, such as the use of tools. There were tensions between spending time learning to use the various tools (and when to use which) and spending time reaching the content goals. It was also important to realise the importance of the backchannel in helping to maintain the agenda.

We have worked to design eSTEP by providing opportunities for pre-service teachers to engage with perceptually rich and meaningful tasks. The eSTEP system provides effective scaffolding through tools that communicate the problem-solving process, elicit articulation, and provide hints for concepts that might be explored (Hmelo-Silver *et al.*, in press). Despite this additional support, there were many tensions to resolve in order to facilitate problem-based learning effectively in the online environment. Online environments provide real potential for implementing problem-based learning on a large scale and in ways that can be adapted to fit alternative schedules. Our work has demonstrated one way in which the associated challenges can be recognised and addressed.

Acknowledgements

This research was funded by NSF ROLE grant No. 0107032. Any opinions, findings, conclusions or recommendations expressed in this material are those of the authors and do not necessarily reflect the views of the National Science Foundation. We thank Ellina Chernobilsky, David Woods and Matt DelMarcelle for our many absorbing discussions during the periods of system design and course implementation.

6

The academic developer as tutor in PBLonline in higher education

Roisin Donnelly

Introduction

This chapter is written from the perspective of an academic developer engaged in blending e-learning and problem-based learning as a means of delivery of professional development for academic staff in higher education. There is undoubtedly a wide range of e-learning technologies available for use with the more traditional teaching and learning/instructional strategies. The challenge faced by today's academic developers is the development of e-learning technologies to support constructivism and social constructivism in learning approaches among the academic staff with whom they work, so that this is, in turn, carried forward into their own classrooms and subject disciplines. The learning approach supported by e-learning technologies explored in this case study research is problem-based learning. The chapter presents a review of the relevant literature that informed the design of a module for academic development of teaching staff in higher education, together with subsequent case study research exploring the role of the academic developer as tutor in this form of continuing professional development.

Research question and objectives

A hugely important area in any form of instructional delivery is the role of the tutor: in an online environment, it is even more crucial. This chapter aims to address the question of what the academic developer's role as tutor in sustaining/propagating the best features of e-learning and problem-based learning is. The tutor's cognitive, social and managerial role in a blended problem-based learning module will be explored in this chapter, as will how this form of facilitation of the learners can build a sustainable model of academic development. In particular, matters such as the locus of control within blended problem-based learning sessions will be considered, alongside the issue of whether combining two innovative pedagogies such as problem-based learning and e-learning can empower learners. The premise for the original research study was that a tutor who values a cohesive, supportive and productive blended problem-based learning class will accentuate exchanges of positive affect in learners; they will encourage collective and achievement orientations towards learning in students; they will show appreciation for the uniqueness of each particular learner; and they will facilitate open and diffuse discussions about the problem in both virtual and face-to-face learning environments.

The objectives of the research study were to:

• explore the principal tutor skills required in facilitating blended problem-based learning
• identify tutoring strategies that academic developers adopt in tutoring learning through blended problem-based learning in higher education to appraise the effects of the tutor's cognitive, social and managerial presence (if any) when facilitating blended PBL tutorial sessions
• to inform the personal and professional development needs of individuals who facilitate blended PBL for academic staff in higher education.

What was the motivation for the innovation?

The current and emerging higher education environment in Ireland, as elsewhere, is placing high demands on staff and learners to deal with changes in education influenced by both the rapid development and implementation of information technologies and their use for teaching and learning. The use of these technologies impacts not only on the ways in which staff teach but also on the ways in which learners learn. There are, however, a significant number of staff and learners who are not adequately prepared or equipped to operate effectively in emerging alternative learning environments, particularly those environments that are technologically mediated. The need for staff development programmes is apparent, but it is doubtful that any one strategy or approach would have much effective long-term impact on developing the skills and experiences necessary to create effective teaching and learning activities in the emerging teaching and learning environments. Therefore, the motivation behind delivering a model of academic development using a blended problem-based learning approach is seen as a way in which innovative approaches to teaching, learning and assessment in a virtual and face-to-face setting can aid the development of a fully professionalised teaching force in Irish higher education.

Context of blended PBL

The focus of this chapter is a 10-week module entitled 'Designing e-learning' which is delivered using a blend of face-to-face and online problem-based learning. Module participants are drawn from very diverse fields and have spent varying lengths of time as lecturers. There is also a wide range in knowledge and experience about both e-learning and problem-based learning. All participants are self-selecting and choose to come on the course. A specific approach was taken to the design and delivery of this module by using problem-based learning as the dominant pedagogical model. The online delivery component and support of the module is in the online learning environment, WebCT.

The aim of the module 'Designing e-learning' is to enable the participants (lecturers, librarians and educational technologists), through a blended learning approach to problem-based learning, to become aware of the practicalities of designing, delivering, supporting and evaluating an online module in their own subject disciplines.

In the context of this module, the term 'blended learning' refers to a merging of classroom and online activities that must be integrated by tutors in ways that allow them to deliver learning (both content and tasks) as a coherent and effective whole. Blended problem-based learning has evolved as both a delivery and facilitation approach in the module, in which an online environment has been created to complement a series of face-to-face problem-based learning tutorials with a puzzlement that engages the group of learners in inquiry activities consistent with the learning outcomes of the module.

Review of the tutor role

The study recognises the abundance of research and literature on the role of the tutor within problem-based learning and also the wealth of work in recent years on the classification of tutor roles in an e-learning environment (see Berge 1995; Collins and Berge 1997; Hootstein 2002; Salmon 2000). A variety of terms for such a role has emerged. In this chapter, e-tutor, e-moderator, e-facilitator will all be used interchangeably when referring to literature. Carlson in Winograd (2001) provides a straightforward definition of a moderator online as one who:

> helps people get started, gives them feedback, summarizes, weaves the contributions of different folks together, gets it unstuck when necessary, deals with individuals who are disruptive, or get off the track, brings in new material to freshen it up periodically, and gets feedback from the group on how things are going and what might happen from the group on how things are going and what might happen next ... [Further the moderator needs to] communicate with the group as a whole, sub-groups, and individuals to encourage participation.

McConnell (2000) identifies and classifies a variety of differences in teaching and learning between online and face-to-face group work. Areas pertinent to this proposed work will centre on the differences in the level of tutor control and impact over learners' behaviour; the permanence of online discussions and impermanence of face-to-face ones; that online discussions may have several simultaneous foci, whereas face-to-face ones usually work on one issue at a time; the differences in group dynamics, with difficulties for interpretation of behaviours online due to lack of nonverbal cues; the differences in levels of anxiety; the psychological stress of rejoining a group is much higher online than face to face; that feedback on others' work is much more detailed online than face to face; that people cannot hide online; that the total effort of the group is likely to be greater online than face to face.

Multiple methods for online instruction are utilised throughout academe. One method, described as the online learning community, has become pre-eminent in online instruction. Boettcher and Conrad (1999: 88) define an online learning community as one that 'consists of learners who support and assist each other, make decisions synergistically, and communicate with peers on a variety of topics beyond those assigned'. It is this building of the learning community by the academic developer/tutor in face-to-face problem-based learning tutorials and sustaining it online that led to the evolvement of this module in its present form.

Outline of the blended module

The research builds on a previous action research study (Donnelly, 2004). There are three main areas that were initiated by the tutor in the face-to-face problem-based learning tutorials and continued in the online environment: self-directed learning, learning by practice and learning through modelling. Figure 6.1 illustrates these.

The concept of self-directed learning emerged in the 1970s through the efforts of educational researchers such as Malcolm Knowles (1984) who proposed that 'most of us have never learned how to learn'. His early identification that the world was *beginning* to become a place of rapid change certainly has resonance in today's fast-paced society. He believed that the knowledge that we 'transmit' to students will have a short life span and may indeed become obsolete: this is more applicable today than ever. Knowles subscribed to the idea that the main purpose of education should be to develop skills of inquiry to enable students to learn how to learn what they needed to know. Currently self-directed learning can be designed in a number of ways including:

- self-directed learning tutorials where learners 'master' predetermined material, at their own pace without the aid of a tutor (Piskurich, 1993)
- self-directed inquiry-based learning where learners are guided to develop independent and self-directed learning skills critical to the discipline or profession.

This second realm influenced some of the module learning outcomes.

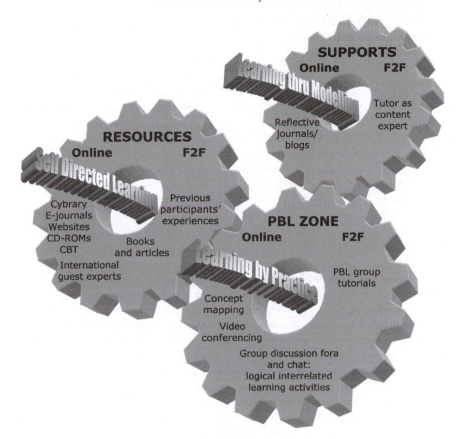

Figure 6.1   Blended problem-based learning module

Learning through modelling by the tutor

On taking up the post of lecturer, most new lecturers have no idea of how to teach or, in many instances, how people learn, other than what they themselves have experienced. Some may try to model themselves on someone whom they thought was a good teacher, someone from whom they themselves felt they learned well. In online education, the teacher is unable to stand up in front of a class; hence the link that once existed between teacher and students is broken. This means that we have to think more about *how* people learn.

It is vital for the tutor to promote blended problem-based learning through how they model it themselves. This involves developing learners' skills in subject and topic specific skills alongside generic learning skills such as critical evaluation, writing, finding and accessing resources, note taking, summarising, problem solving and prioritising.

It is argued that the tutor in a blended problem-based learning environment must be able to:

- model these skills explicitly
- break complex skills down into smaller units (tasks) to scaffold skills development
- take different approaches depending on subject area (e.g. text based, fact based, practice based)
- encourage peer and self-evaluation of students' skills
- know when to separate/distinguish and when to integrate ideas
- use techniques such as games, simulations, debates and role play
- model (or be explicit about) quality and etiquette of online and face-to-face contributions in the problem-based learning tutorials.

Learning by practice

Most e-learning programmes present information with little or no opportunities to practise the tasks or skills that the information is supposed to help learners perform. There is no opportunity to practise a sequence of decisions and actions in a realistic situation or to practise complex skills and decision making in multiple cases where variables are systematically manipulated to reflect common variations that occur on the job. There is no attempt to diagnose and correct misconceptions or flaws in reasoning that will lead to inaccurate application of the 'information' covered.

Authentic practice in varied contexts, with appropriate feedback, is what leads to learning and transfer of skills on this module (Donnelly, 2004). The most effective learning activities induce the same cognitive processes that expert performers use in real situations. Information and feedback are organised by the tutor so that each learner automatically receives the scaffolding he or she needs to complete an activity.

Role of online activities with the problem-based learning problem

In the module, problem-based learning provides an authentic context and activities that the participants may well come across in their practice. Specific online learning activities in the module include researching information regarding the authentic context outlined; discussion of ideas within the online discussion forum and submitting a document outlining potential solutions to the problem. These activities allow participants to attempt to solve the problem by researching and discussing among themselves – thus the task is driven by the problem, not the content/theory. Learning supports include the module and problem information. The 'Introduction to the module' section gives a clear outline of the objectives, problem-based learning, study schedule and assessment. The 'How to study this module' activity provides support for the participants and clearly outlines how they should approach the problem and what they can do to help themselves along the way. The support for the problem itself also provides guidance including a clear outline what activities to do, what readings to look at and so forth.

The tutor can provide formative feedback via the discussion boards. Participants submit both the problem work-in-progress and extracts from their online journal for feedback before final submission allowing them to reflect on their work and make additions/changes to their final submission. Learning resources include reference to textbook readings, online articles, discussion forum, CD-ROMs, images, and so forth, all of which create a useful starting point for participants. Access to the discussion forum also gives participants the knowledge that they can ask for expert help (from fellow participants or the academic tutor) if need be. As the resources provided are quite varied, participants can look at the problem from different perspectives before making a decision on how to tackle it. The online activities are planned to provide participants with information on what the problem is; information they can use to 'solve' it and supports for gaining extra information if necessary.

Case study research

The principal area of concern within this section involves the case study approach. Yin (1994), considered to be one of the leading exponents of case study research, believes that case study is the preferred methodology to use when questions such as 'how' or 'why' are posed, considering the essence of this method is its enquiry into real-life context. He also suggests that case study is ideally suited to educational research. Bassey (1999) believes that an essential feature of case study is that it is conducted in its natural context, which is the situation pertaining in this study.

The methods, methodology and theoretical perspective indicate that a subjectivist position has been adopted within this study. The epistemological stance is significant because the subjects of the research are individuals (academic developers in higher education) who each view the world differently. The research involves four academic developers, each with a range of prior experience in using learning technology or new pedagogical approaches in their practice; therefore the methods used are 'soft' and predominantly qualitative. Both Crotty (1998) and Cohen *et al.* (2000) agree that where qualitative methods are predominant, the subjective epistemology may be the best approach. Crotty (1998) does, however, caution that qualitative methods combined with subjective epistemologies can lack scientific rigour. The research question that forms the basis of this submission, combined with the participants (academic developers), was ideally suited to the case study methodology.

Qualitative online evaluation

A qualitative questionnaire was distributed online to a number of colleagues internationally, who work as academic developers and offer programmes to academic staff using some form of e-learning and/or problem-based learning. These academic developers were chosen for this study, as they each had a guest tutoring role on the 'Designing e-learning' module, outlined earlier.

This qualitative questionnaire was designed to explore two angles to the tutor role. One was aimed specifically at the guest tutoring role in the module, exploring why the guest tutors acted or thought the way they did. The second angle was wider, to delve into their academic development role in their own institutions, engaged in e-learning or problem-based learning or a combination/blend of the two. The questionnaire was designed as 'open ended' as the research is concerned with obtaining opinions and feelings. The data are used to explore the total picture of utilising these pedagogies to deliver continuing academic development, rather than the separate components.

Delineation of the findings

The participants' online questionnaires contained a series of open questions relating to tutor perceptions of the module, and to e-learning and problem-based learning as a means to deliver academic development in higher education. A content analysis of questionnaire data was used to identify themes, concepts and meanings using code categories recommended by Burns (2000). To set the scene for the research, the participants were asked to share their past experience, as academic developers, in tutoring e-learning and problem-based learning.

There are a number of key findings emerging from this study. They are labelled as follows and are detailed separately.

- Core components involved in the act of tutoring.
- Key differences between online and face-to-face learning in academic development.
- Tutors' requisite communication skills in a blended environment.
- Empowerment of learners by blended problem-based learning.
- Principles of blended problem-based learning.
- Rounded tutor skills in blended problem-based learning.
- Professional development opportunities and concerns about blended problem-based learning.

Tutoring in academic development
The maxims for good practice in online and face-to-face tutoring are derived from Brookfield's (2001) analysis that good learning relationships are based on reciprocity, authenticity and credibility. In addition, it is believed that in

order to develop deep understanding, high-quality learning and teaching, a tutor has to set ground rules, provide alternative modes of participation, exemplify models of engagement and give access to their experience as tutor.

Participant 1
I will emphasise the two key aspects for me in tutoring or teaching in other roles too, as well as for an online or face-to-face context. First, a focus on revealing the key questions that illuminate the subject matter to be learnt. These questions might be raised specifically by the teacher/tutor or by the students or a combination of both. It will depend on the teacher's approach. Second, creating 'space' in which the teacher/tutor and the student can engage about the subject matter. Space is my metaphor for this, but it is all about leaving the opportunities for students to create their own knowledge, and not having the teacher fill up all the space with their own knowledge, views, etc.

Participant 2
From the learner's perspective, it is important to identify their learning needs, set their learning outcomes, engage with the learning activities; as a tutor, one needs to facilitate learning by motivating the learner, provide scaffolding and guide the learner to achieve their learning needs; if a tutor is involved with curriculum design, and not just hired to tutor an already designed and produced course, s/he needs to be aware of and use sound educational and pedagogic principles to underpin the course design, planning, implementation, assessment, evaluation and review. This is to ensure that the course is fit for purpose in meeting the stakeholders' needs and enhances the students' learning experience.

Key differences between online and face-to-face learning in academic development
Teaching online does share similarities with teaching in the classroom; however, even the best traditional tutors may still find that teaching in an online environment can lead to feelings of inadequacy and being ill prepared. Providing training and tools for e-pedagogy is one way to build confidence and create successful outcomes in the online classroom. Even experienced online tutors can glean helpful and time-saving ideas from knowledge shared by others.

For the practice of blended learning in the context presented by this chapter, it is argued that it is not necessarily the case that a good face-to-face tutor will be a good online tutor, even if the necessary technical abilities are added. Many online tutors are already face-to-face tutors and will have developed their own style and pedagogical assumptions. Becoming an online tutor, or a tutor operating in a blended learning environment, may involve a shift in some of these, especially for tutors who rely very much on their face-to-face skills of reading body language, establishing rapport and working with groups. The face-to-face tutor needs to make these core skills work equally well in an online environment. Distinguishing a good online tutor from an excellent one may rely on an ability to deploy technologies effectively and imaginatively: a pedagogic skill rather than a technical skill.

Participant 3
. . . I always try to create a 'conversational' environment and place key questions up front as a focus and often as the starting point for engagement. Application often occurs away from the online environment, in the classroom, etc. but the participants' responses and experiences are always brought back to whatever type of forum is available for sharing across the group.

Participant 4
This is very variable and depends on both individuals' differences and likes as well as the nature of the topic being discussed. For content-based topics, engagement is about the same in face to face and online. Again, this depends on the facilitator's ability and effectiveness in engaging the participants. For practical-based elements of a topic and or involving human contact, most participants engage better in face-to-face settings than online.

Tutors' communication skills
Collaboration and dialogue are pivotal to any discussions about the role of a tutor in the blended environment of e-learning with problem-based learning. Laurillard (1993) has famously presented a conversational model of student learning: a way of thinking about the role of dialogue in the learning process and the practical implications for student and tutor roles. A telementoring taxonomy developed by Levin (1995) and a variation more recently by Brescia *et al.* (2004) highlight a number of key areas for this research: coaching through participation, providing structure, supporting individual students, community building and institutional structure.

Participant 2
From my own experience – this is relatively easy. I communicate using a diverse range of media to suit the content, context and situation.

In relation to the academic developer role, what does 'empowerment' by e-learning and/or problem-based learning mean for participants?
Eklund *et al.* (2003: 9) suggest that at its worst, e-learning 'can disempower and demotivate learners by leaving them lost and unsupported in an immensely confusing electronic realm'. Salmon (2000) advises that 'educators wishing to get the best from e-learning opportunities need to concentrate on engaging their learners (and not just on providing reading materials)'.

Participant 4
For me, I would answer most strongly that it would result in the learner being confronted by alternate perspectives, views (solutions – perhaps, but might be a bit too strong a notion for what I am trying to do, which is to impact on how a teacher approaches their own role as an educator). Quick fixes don't work; it is about changing a mindset and how the teacher understands their role.

A PBL approach probably describes reasonably what I try to do and have done for some time in my practice. Frankly, I try to place learners in situations that are realistic and which require them to expose their own thinking, often the foundation of their practice but not often revealed. Then, I try to expose them to alternatives . . .

Participant 3
They will turn out to be self-directed, self-regulated and autonomous learners who are well equipped with the required skills to learn and manage their own learning, but above all else, can solve problems and reflect on their learning and use the outcomes from their reflection to improve practice and performance.

Important principles of e-learning and problem-based learning and how they can be related to academic development
A number of key well-recognised principles were named and detailed: the importance of feedback, active, social, affective, collaborative context for learning.

Participant 1
Feedback should happen very soon after the commencement of the learning experience/course/programme, etc.

Active learning is vital, but active can mean the extent to which the learner is positively engaged in the learning process (i.e. the extent to which they approach the material, rather than passively receive it) and does not mean making lots of activity.

Learning is essentially a social experience and therefore must involve considerable collaboration.

Much learning takes the learner into uncomfortable territory . . .

Learning is definitely an affective experience too.

Participant 2
PBL and e-learning can contribute in helping people learn and develop the relevant knowledge and skills through appropriate contextualisation of their learning needs, rather than basing the teaching on a 'content-driven' approach.

The principles of . . . pedagogy, facilitation of learning and supporting learners in different contexts and situations, assessment and the effective use of technology in teaching and learning . . . specifically . . .

Role of feedback: very critical in enabling the learner to know what it is they know and do not know, how well they are doing and how they can make progress.

Active learning: good understanding of the pedagogy ensures that the curriculum is based on constructivism and not instructivism. That way learning is active and not passive.

Collaborative learning: If a socio-constructivist approach is used, then learning is set in a social domain involving a learning community or community of practice.

Learning as a painful yet rewarding process: The teacher through their training and experience needs to appreciate that learning is painful and rewarding and should be equipped in providing the following: appropriate induction for learners at the start of the course; and the necessary support, encouragement and guidance at the various stages for the learner.

Learning as an emotional as well as an intellectual process: This involves cognitive (intellectual) and social presence. The teacher's presence can deal with content and both the teacher and learner through social presence and socialisation, can deal with the emotion involved in learning.

E-learning and problem-based learning offering an opportunity for
lifelong learning
E-learning also offers the opportunity for lifelong learning; an important consideration for the academic staff enrolling on this module. In an Australian study for lifelong learning through higher education, P.C. Candy (2000) identified four categories that graduates participated in to continue their educational development. These were workplace-based learning; continuing professional education; further formal study; and self-directed learning. The study found that 'this category of learning has been significantly strengthened by the spread of the Internet; an aspect of lifelong learning that deserves a study in its own right' (Candy, P.C., 2000: 110).

Participant 3
E-learning has potential if used well to be a positive influence in any of these categories: workplace-based learning; continuing professional education; further formal study; self-directed learning. However, the potential does not lie just in the format/technology. It is about the approach adopted and it is in this area that the greatest challenge and potential lie.

Important rounded tutor skills in e-learning and problem-based learning
The tutor's role has been key in this module in these four areas: managing how the participants engaged with the resources; a consideration of how the tutor promoted social interaction individually and collaboratively; and a cognitive responsibility as to how the tutor facilitated the participants building knowledge together (Figure 6.2).

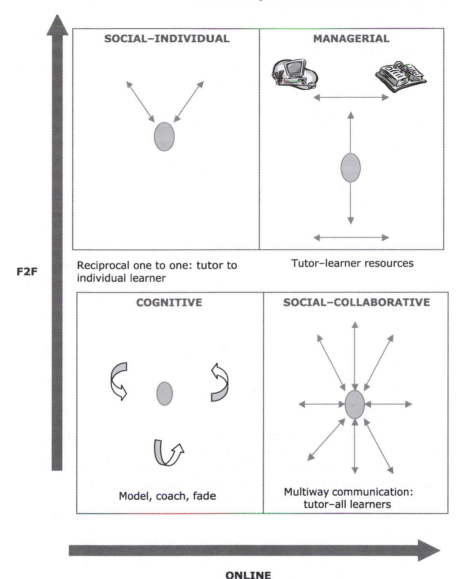

Figure 6.2   Tutor roles in a blended PBL module

Participant 4
Developing a sense of 'self' by the teacher in order to help the students engage with this out-of-body teacher on their computer.

Participant 2
The need to develop competency in the use of technology to support learning for individual learners in different context and situations.

The social context of tutoring is very critical for the success of any such course. Both students and tutors must have a social presence to enable them to effectively communicate, engage and to achieve the intended learning outcomes. The social context will involve socialisation, ground rules, language of engagement, content, etc.:

- have a sound knowledge of pedagogy: both online and for PBL
- good facilitation and moderating skills
- have good assessment and feedback giving skills
- ability to motivate, engage, guide and support learners
- ability to engage in analytical reflection
- ability to evaluate the outcome of a learning activity or course/ curriculum
- can time manage.

Tutor's role on this module

The tutor's role in this module is not at the content level, but at the meta-cognitive level, where they model, scaffold and support learner thinking both face to face and online (Figure 6.3).

Participant 1

My approach was to draw on my considerable experience and to try to make this available for the students to provoke ideas, comments, etc.

Participant 2

Construction of participant knowledge: providing prompts and scaffolding.

Promotion of lifelong learning skills in participants: highlighting the pedagogical imperatives of helping people to learn by doing and support-ing them through appropriate activities to engage in self-directed learning.

Participant completion of interrelated learning activities: facilitating and consolidating connection learning.

Learning by practice: enhancement of knowledge, skills, practice and performance.

Use of self-directed learning: promoting the skills required to develop the autonomous learner.

Learning in authentic contexts: makes learning relevant for the learner and provides them with the language of discourse to enable them engage effectively with the learning process.

Engaging in critical reflective thinking: helping to develop metacogni-tive skills in the learners, i.e. equipping them with the skills to stand back and critically evaluate their work and use the insight gained to improve practice and performance.

Using well-supported reasoning: to develop ability to engage in relevant critical discourse and debate; develop the ability to critically think, analyse, make links and deduce facts from information or data.

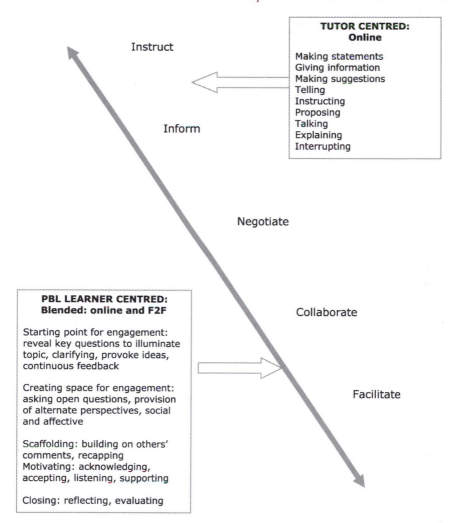

Figure 6.3 Continuum of blended communication strategies: e-moderating and PBL

Implementing time management skills: it is important that learning is appropriately paced and the student is progressing well in relation to her ability and in line with set targets (individual and/or institutional, etc.).

Scaffolding learning: providing and deploying scaffolds at appropriate times based on individual needs.

In relation to the academic developer acting as a tutor on this module, the guest tutors provided a synopsis of their experience in three areas: enjoyment of role, resources they brought and any challenges they encountered in the role.

Enjoyment of tutoring role on this module
    Participant 3
    I enjoy the excitement of engaging with new people and the expectation
    of what might occur . . .

    Participant 4
    Sharing knowledge and experience and learning with others.

Resources one brings as a tutor
    Participant 2
    Experience of being both an online learner and tutor.
        Reading and reference text; acting as a resource person/sounding
    board for learners, e.g. through responding to their questions via CMC and
    videoconferencing.

Challenges of tutoring on this module
    Participant 4
    Learning something about the context in which the students were studying
    and knowing a little about them.
        Focusing on the assessment process – how to do it, how to make it
    meaningful for the students.

    Participant 3
    Reliability of the technology; limited number of sessions which impacts
    on not getting to know the students well with regard to their progress and
    development on the module.

Professional development opportunities and concerns about blended
problem-based learning
Online instruction is new to many tutors in higher education, and for good
reason. In just a few years, it has grown from an academic experiment to a
recognised alternative to traditional classroom learning. Even traditional
classes have embraced many of the teaching methods popularised by online
education.

    Participant 2
    Technology is good to use as a medium for teaching and for supporting
    learning . . . for a number of reasons: it provides versatility and flexibility;
    it provides convenience; individuals can access learning any time, at any
    place and in the format they wish it; it can be used to support individual-
    ised and group learning; it is good for developing collaborative, cooperative
    and reflective learning.
        Concerns: technology must not drive learning – it should act as a sup-
    port medium; most of the technology are technologically driven and are
    not pedagogically sound; educators do not match available technology to
    appropriate use – we all seem to use them because they are available or

because others use them; some learners and teachers do not have the skills and know how to use the technologies effectively and this can cause both frustration and/or give the use of technology a 'bad name'.

Tutor pitfalls in blended communication

There is also potential for problems to occur in tutoring blended PBL. It is important to be aware of these, so appropriate strategies can be designed in advance or to deal with them as they arise (Figure 6.4):

- Asking too many questions – balancing between those asked face to face and online.
- Transferring tutor anxiety onto the student.
- Finding a quick solution – only dealing with the presenting problem.
- Feeling inadequate with the student.
- Wanting to do everything for the student.
- Blocking the student's emotions.
- Wanting to be liked by the student.
- Being too busy to listen.
- Dictating and imposing your own values on the student.
- Not being clear about what you can and cannot offer in the way of help (fuzzy boundaries).

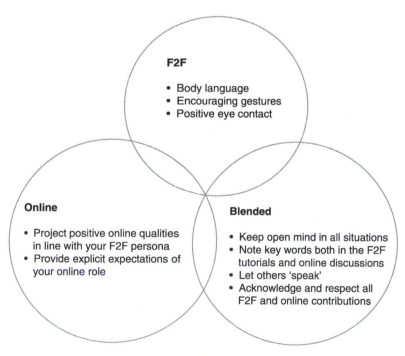

Figure 6.4 Avoiding pitfalls in tutoring blended PBL

How does the innovation relate to macro issues in online learning and problem-based learning?

This section of the chapter will offer practical implications and suggestions for other educational developers and academic staff interested in blending online and face-to-face problem-based learning. Emphasis needs to be placed on developing generic and scalable processes and providing feedback to enable learners to influence their education provision. The findings from the questionnaire indicate the following as important when planning to blend problem-based learning and e-learning.

Planning and management

- Plan how e-tutoring will be employed with face-to-face tutoring.
- Establish the technical facilities necessary to support e-tutoring.
- Provide administrative support online.
- Provide learners with technical and subject matter expertise.
- Initiate activities that will facilitate learning.

Communicating with learners

- Establish relationships with new learners.
- Communicate appropriately with learners.
- Provide learners with support and encouragement.

Integrating technology tools

- Use email for individual communication with learners.
- Use bulletin boards and discussion forums for group communication with and between learners.
- Use text, audio and videoconferencing for communication with and between learners; choosing between communication technologies such as email, conferencing, chat or videoconferencing by the tutor will depend on what is appropriate to a given learning situation, rather than a knowledge of the technologies per se. Information retrieval skills will determine whether the tutor makes good use of the easy access to web resources as well as an ability to evaluate the quality of materials held on remote websites.

Reflecting on participant and tutor experiences

- Assess learners' performance formatively.
- Evaluate and continuously improve e-tutoring and face-to-face tutoring support.

Conclusion

While it is not feasible to extrapolate the findings of the investigation beyond the present context, the analysis of this blend of face-to-face and e-tutoring in academic development raised a number of issues worthy of comment. One particular issue concerns the leadership and facilitation of the learning community by the responsible subject tutors. In essence, there was a sense that the tutors were working to release participants from traditional control structures of time, space, content, discourse, assessment and teacher direction. The style of their response was public, shared, engaging and not judgemental. This can only be achieved by a tutor who knows when to change hats from being peremptory to moderate in their facilitation.

Part 3

Technopedagogy

Part 2 of this book focused on facilitation and the influence of the facilitator in the management of PBLonline. In Part 3, the focus shifts towards the experiences and activities of tutors and learners using PBLonline. It explores issues related to the combining of pedagogy and technology in PBLonline, including the design of curricula for PBLonline; the skills required to engage with the approach and those acquired through the engagement; and the position of the technology within or outside the pedagogy: is the technology (the virtual learning environment (VLE), Flash Player™ and so forth) an integral part of the pedagogy (online, flexible, blended learning) or is it simply a means to a pedagogical end?

Part 3 addresses some of the issues raised in Chapter 1 with respect to the evolutionary relationship between technology and pedagogy. Cousin (2005) raises the debate as to whether pedagogy makes use of the available technology or if the technology influences the pedagogy; making the point that teaching and learning strategies have always been linked to the technology available at the time, be it chiselling in stone or palmheld wireless computers. She contends that the technology contributes to or, in some cases (brainstorming and flipcharts, for example), drives the teaching strategy. L. Candy (2000) likewise argued that the internet deserves to be pedagogy in its own right. Dupuis (2003) cautions that learning will only be improved by the use of technology if the chosen technology is matched to a planned educational strategy. Without this considered planning, there is a risk that the intended learning will not take place. With a planned education strategy the shift is made from computer-based instruction where the computer is merely an adjunct, to a pedagogy of e-learning where the programme is integrated into the teaching methodology. Cousin develops this further, arguing that neither the pedagogical approach nor the media by which it is delivered drives the other, but that both elements are inextricably intertwined integral parts of the whole. PBLonline has evolved as the pedagogy has utilised developing technology, often for reasons associated with the learning environment (student:facilitator ratios; geographical distances;

accommodation constraints) and, conversely, as online technology adopted problem-based learning as a method of promoting discussion and learning from online material, rather than providing material which is simply viewed, read or played with.

Pedagogical considerations

Three different versions of PBLonline linked to professional education with learners at different points in their careers are presented in Part 3. Starting from differing perspectives on combining problem-based learning with technology, the authors of each study linked problem-based learning with online learning. Jennings used facilitated synchronous PBL sessions and unfacilitated asynchronous chatrooms; the learners in the Savin-Baden and Gibbon study had face-to-face problem-based sessions with supporting resources being provided online; while the online learners in Lee's study used the problem-based learning scenario as a focus for chatroom discussions, to which the facilitator contributed.

In Chapter 7, Jennings presents a case study that examines the ways in which PBLonline promoted collaborative working for a group of university lecturers. Jennings' group members were experienced both in utilising VLEs and in problem-based learning, allowing the study to run without concerns of skill development or unfamiliarity with the principles of problem-based learning. Savin-Baden and Gibbon (Chapter 8) report on work with a learner group that also had some experience of problem-based learning and VLEs. Their chapter reports on a project that designed online resources to support problem-based learning scenarios for the second year of undergraduate nursing programmes. Although their student group had had some exposure to face-to-face problem-based learning and in accessing web-based materials, it is unlikely that they possessed the same level of skill in either element as the learners in Jennings' study. Registered nurses were the participants in Lee's research (Chapter 9), into the value of PBLonline in creating communities of practice for infection control practitioners. Unlike the groups in the other two studies, this group had had little prior exposure to learning online and none to problem-based learning. Comparison of the studies points up the dichotomy of pedagogical and technical issues in PBLonline.

Cook and Dupras (2004) in a study of PBLonline in medical education found that placing material on the internet was insufficient to generate learning. Students required frequent prompts and reminders to engage with the material and complete the set learning tasks. As highlighted by Dupuis there is a need for the pedagogy to be considered when planning a shift to learning online. Alur *et al.* (2002) examined medical teaching websites for attributes of modern teaching philosophies. Only 17% of the online courses examined met all the criteria (critical thinking, independent learning, evidence-based learning and feedback), while 50% showed little evidence of promoting learning. Even when consideration has been given to the pedagogy, learners may need further support through a planned pedagogical strategy, such as PBLonline.

Recent work on learning styles (CLaSS 2005) suggests that some students may be disadvantaged by being presented with a teaching/learning strategy that relies heavily on visual material. The SONIC project reported by Savin-Baden and Gibbon did introduce a spoken element, however, this was fixed and not available for discursive aspects of the programme. Rosenberg and Sillince (2000) found that nonverbal communication supported social activities that could impact positively on problem solving and task completion. Thus the loss of nonverbal cues may also disadvantage some students. Wood (2001) reports on the development of computer programs to facilitate learning which included a non-human voice structure in response to student postings. The programmed responses were drawn from observation of human facilitative responses. The potentially unstructured format of PBLonline makes it unlikely that this type of package in its current format would be suitable for use with PBLonline.

Learner issues

A study by Bayne (2005a) reports on the concepts that learners hold of their online selves. Students in the study reported the opportunity to develop a persona which differs from the 'real' self, known to friends and family. However, the students told of anxieties related to this created self, of loss of control and of making postings that they later regretted. Conversely comments in course evaluations (University of Dundee, 2005) showed that learners report feelings of 'shyness' and being unwilling to expose themselves in the 'permanent' setting of discussion boards. The threads are there for peers to see, scrutinise and respond to over time. Spoken words were regarded as being impermanent, related to the idiosyncrasies of human memory, perhaps now not as well trained as in the days before the technology of print, and were thus somehow perceived to be less threatening. Yet those same learners who claimed to be unwilling or unable to post online and share their thoughts and findings with others appeared to have little problem in online café settings, where they freely shared opinions about the running of the course or organised nights out. Concepts such as Ritzer's (1996) 'infotainment', or Land and Bayne's (Chapter 1) 'playful experiment' suggest that boundaries between work and play are becoming more blurred. This may make it more difficult for students to remember (or indeed recognise) what is work and what is play. One result of this may be the sort of situation reported by Bayne's student, where an online persona is created for online learning in a way similar to computer games such as *Tomb Raider* where the player assumes the character of Lara Croft. Another result may be an inability to distinguish between what should be posted in virtual cafés and what should be contributed to online discussion threads.

Technological issues

The degree of interactivity with the resource as well as the amount of discussion generated depends not only on students' cognitive abilities and willingness to contribute but also on their ability to navigate sites and find their way around the VLE. Given the literature on 'infotainment' (Ritzer, 1996) and the development of the net generation, there is, perhaps, an expectation that today's students will arrive on (virtual) campus fully equipped with all the technological skills required for online learning. This is a questionable assumption, particularly given the diverse nature of the student body. Students who opt for online courses may do so from a convenience and access perspective, rather than online learning matching their preferred learning style.

Atack (2003) in a study of Canadian qualified nurses undertaking web-based learning reported that much of the learners' time, particularly early on in the module, was devoted to acquiring technical skills, such as posting to discussion boards, sending email, and conducting web searches, rather than engaging with course content. The learning of these skills took time, up to half the time dedicated to the module in some cases, which learners had intended devoting to content.

Atack's online learners cited having 'one's own room' to work in as a benefit of online learning. Savin-Baden and Gibbon's learners however, provide different insights of learning, indicating that study space became more flexible, amalgamating with family and working life rather than being separate from it; working online at home or during breaks or quiet periods on work placements. Jennings' chapter does not indicate where the online learning took place, but for university lecturers computer use is much more likely to be part of the fabric of their work than it would be for either group of nurses in the other studies. However, coursework could have been undertaken by the lecturers between teaching sessions or between other computer-based work.

As Deepwell and Syson report in Chapter 3, the rapid growth of technology and the increasing number of packages available often mean that students are required to download programs in order to access materials. Although the plugins are freely available, the additional navigating required may be sufficient to discourage students, particularly those who do not have, or may be unable to afford, fast broadband access in the home setting. Problems with technology itself, such as systems crashing or websites being unavailable during updating, also create difficulties that may deter the less computer-literate student. Many institutions devote considerable resources to providing training in the technological skills, despite the aforementioned statements about the new generation of technology users. Dennis (2003), reporting a study which compared PBLonline with face-to-face problem-based learning, stressed the need for training sessions to manage the software. Donnelly (2004) found that lecturers lacked the necessary preparation to work with technological settings. Atack's (2003) learners, like those of Hmelo-Silver *et al.* (Chapter 5) preferred to learn about computer use under human instruction rather than working solely from guidance by the machine.

Conclusion

Online learning requires a different type of cognitive process or at least a different cognitive use of the material. Matching of the technology with the pedagogy seems to be necessary for the process to be truly online learning, rather than online information searching or use of the internet as an e-book. Savin-Baden and Gibbon's experience, working from the perspective of problem-based learning experts, indicates that forward planning of the pedagogy would have enhanced the use of the technology with problem-based learning. Jennings and Lee, both working from a technology-focused perspective, rather than a problem-based learning position, found that applying a problem-based pedagogy to the online learning situation enhanced the students' experience and contributed to the use of the technology as an active learning experience rather than as an information source. The benefits of problem-based learning applied online appeared to be present regardless of the degree of technological skill possessed by the learners.

As pointed out by Deepwell and Syson, technology has grown and developed rapidly in the past decade. Further applications of technology to problem-based learning with respect to student interactions are discussed in Part 4. From an educational perspective the use of technology is still regarded as being 'new', with many experienced teachers lacking the skills to capitalise fully on the benefits of VLEs. The current situation may be another example of a 'theory–practice gap' where the learning theories required to explain how students learn online and ways in which that process may best be supported, have yet to develop with the opportunities offered by the technology.

7

PBLonline: a framework for collaborative e-learning

David Jennings

Introduction

This chapter presents the results of an exploratory case study to explore the mechanics of collaboration within PBLonline and to examine how individual learners share the cognitive load of groupwork and its effects on individual educational development. The case study is based on a cohort of ≤10 adult learners, all members of university staff, who used the virtual learning environment Blackboard™ (v6.3). A number of educational theories are examined in relation to collaboration and how these apply to e-learning, leading to an exploration of the effects of social learning, student-centred approaches, socio-cognitive conflict and co-construction of shared knowledge. A quasi-experimental approach was used to test cause and effect by observing the subjects' reaction to phenomena (the phenomena being the collaboration).

The online collaboration was set in a problem-based scenario, offering the opportunity for maximum interaction among participants. The use of a structured online problem-based learning situation can be seen as a key trigger in provoking communication and collaboration. It is offered as a potential framework within which to increase collaborative learning. Participants were seen to engage in the task and develop cooperative learning skills, sharing experiences and visibly constructing new knowledge.

Purpose of research

This study examines the impact and level of collaboration within a specific online task, to determine if there is a measurable difference in one's way of learning within a group dynamic (the concept of shared cognition), and how this dynamic may affect an individual's own particular learning preferences: 'In a world of ambient technologies, pervasive knowledge, networking, and multitasking learners, the dynamics of the learning experiences must change to provide value to new generations of learners' (Norris *et al.*, 2003: 22). This study presents such a change to invigorate online interactions and offers a means by which learners may enhance their approach to deeper learning and develop critical thinking skills.

This study places the methodology of problem-based learning at the heart of the research as a means to leverage the maximum amount of cooperative participation by engaging the cohort in a problem-solving task. Many papers have discussed the psychological and practical implications of collaborative learning (for example Dillenbourg, 1999; Johnson *et al.*, 2002; Salomon, 1993; Strijbos, 2004) and many more offer guidelines for appropriate online mentoring and facilitation that may engender such situations (for example Laurillard, 2002; Mason, 1998; Salmon, 2003). This chapter offers an exploration of the phenomenon of collaborative learning and its perceived linkage to shared cognitive load and metacognition (Schoenfeld, 1987) within the framework of problem-based learning and asks whether this can act as a suitable framework to allow for the genuine occurrence of group interactions that lead to deeper learning and shared understanding.

With the almost ubiquitous presence of virtual learning environments (VLEs) throughout further and higher education (BECTA ICT Research, 2003), both for distance learning and as a supplemental element to campus-based learning, it is crucial to achieve a genuinely blended approach to the implementation of education technology and traditional teaching practices. It is taken for granted that the use of VLEs offers opportunities for advancing collaborative learning and provides a means to extend the reach of resources to today's students, who are often in professional roles as well as studying. The need to offer a dynamic and holistic experience to learners heightens the responsibility of the tutor to provide the opportunity within which to find these.

Many institutional portals or local VLEs attempt to offer such opportunities in the format of online resources, chatrooms, message boards, formative multiple-choice questions (MCQs), interactive tutorials and so forth. There are many more resources and learning opportunities that are found by the learners themselves and run outside the usual curriculum, for example, wikis, blogs, SMS (short message service) and VOIP (voice over internet protocol). There is an apparent lack of integration that is almost impossible to remedy. By the time it would take an 'institutional portal' to implement the 'latest' technology and complete the appropriate testing within its own environment, that technology may be superseded. There is a need to offer, and more importantly facilitate, a flexible means of providing an engaging environment in which to learn collaboratively. This environment needs to be monitored to enable the provision of feedback and advice to participants; it must be able to meet the needs of individual learners (student centred) and at the same time provide ample opportunity to work collaboratively and finally it must provide a means by which learners may be assessed in a clear and transparent manner so that learning outcomes, once identified, are achieved. This study presents a scenario within which these needs may be met as well as providing a means of helping individual facilitators to enhance their distance learning offerings or indeed to add further structure to supplemental usage of VLEs within campus-based courses.

Research aims and objectives

The research aimed to monitor how individuals work together collaboratively within an online problem-based scenario. A number of the key objectives were to:

- Identify how and where collaboration occurs.
- Determine how one may facilitate and engender collaboration.
- Measure/note the occurrence of shared cognition.
- Identify if this is task specific or reliant on group dynamics.

Other identified objectives were to:

- Analyse whether facilitation is key to successful collaboration.
- Analyse if shared cognition is predetermined by teaching and learning methodologies.
- Determine if a framework may be used to achieve shared cognition where it may not otherwise occur.

Context and background

The definition of collaboration is seen by many as problematic (Dillenbourg, 1999). It may refer to the opportunity to learn within a given situation where more than one learner participates, it may refer to the actual interactions of learners or it may apply to particular mechanisms (such as internalisation, self-explanation, conflict). What is clear is that it provides an environment in which two or more individuals may learn together.

The element of interaction is increasingly seen as one of the fundamental components of successful online learning (Paulus, 2005). Collaboration is not seen as a division of tasks among learners (Dolmans *et al.*, 2005) though this may occur, with students often inadvertently dividing up a task into its constituent parts to complete them individually, only to reassemble them as a collective. It is this collective action, this mutual interaction and shared understanding that is crucial to the process of collaboration.

Constructivist theory overarches many current instructional design choices as it provides the view that learning is an active process in which learners construct new ideas or concepts from current and/or past knowledge (Kearsley 1994). There are three major theories that pervade the arena of learning in collaboration: socio-constructivism, socio-culturalism and shared cognition. Each of these is now discussed briefly in an online/e-learning context.

Socio-constructivism

Socio-constructivism advocates the mastery of new approaches to learning by interaction with others (Doise and Mugny, 1984). An individual's interaction within a given social environment enables the production (development) of a new personal state. This new state makes it possible to return to or move into another social environment and allows for more sophisticated interactions to take place (Dillenbourg *et al.*, 1994). In essence, collaborating may unlock and produce a series of criteria (culminating in a new state) within the individual. It focuses on the personal development of the individual as a result of social interactions. Crucial to any successful online experience is the establishment of a community and sense of personal ownership. This is often achieved through peer inductions/icebreakers and social forums (Billet, 1996).

Socio-culturalism

The concept of socio-culturalism ideals springs out of Vygotsky's (1978) concept of proximal development, whereby individual development is a casual result of social interaction. In effect the individual internalises any processes while party to social interactions and brings them to light at a later date independently. Notably Vygotsky goes further to state that instruction is most efficient when students engage in activities within a supportive environment and when in receipt of appropriate guidance. This is never more apparent than in an online environment, where it is essential to provide an identified framework, in the form of peer support/mentoring, clear instructional design and learning outcomes, to enable a learner to engage in a learning process whereby they may attain their own personal learning objectives.

Shared cognition

Shared cognition is seen as being situation dependent; it specifically enables social interactions (and knowledge sharing) within a given context that is immediately applicable to the task at hand. By linking context and knowledge the learner is made aware of the conditions under which the knowledge should be applied. In the wider realm the learner may thus see how such knowledge can best be applied in outside situations – thus fostering critical and creative thinking, Within an online environment, as with traditional face-to-face teaching, the relevancy of case-based scenarios or contextualised data is essential to focusing the learners' attentions on the immediate needs of a problem or example and on the identified module learning outcomes in assuring strategic approaches to online experiences (Evans *et al.*, 2003).

Socio-cognitive conflict

Inevitably, the role of interaction and collaboration involves an element of confrontation among participants, akin to debate, discussion and argument. The idea of conflict as a precursor for cognitive change has been explored in many papers, most notably by Doise and Mugny (1979, 1984) and Doise *et al.* (1976), whose experiments with groups holding different perceptions demonstrated the role of 'socio-cognitive' conflict when individuals were observed to formulate arguments in favour of a 'new position' that had not been demonstrated in previous social interactions. This interaction offers an insight into the group dynamics on display within online situations – in most cases groups are allowed to grow together, performing induction programmes, social tasks and the inevitable course work (collaboratively or individually). There is a strong indication that groups (and individuals) need space and time to breakout, reformulate ideas and plans, only to reconvene and 'strike' off one another once more.

Co-construction of shared knowledge

The idea of co-construction of shared knowledge supports the premise that shared cognition is not just reliant on the factual knowledge and the common social grounding around that knowledge, but on the processes and practices in which one may attain knowledge (Resnick *et al.*, 1991). This implies that collaboration is most effective when there are common objectives and individual participants are working towards the same goal or set of goals. However, work by van Boxtel *et al.* (2000) noted no discernable differences while testing collaborative and individual learning outcomes.

Communities of practice

In discussing the concept of shared cognition one inevitably has to consider the social element; how individuals interact within an environment and with one another. Etienne Wenger (1998) developed the concept of communities of practice, in which there are three key elements: the domain, the community and the practice. The key to each of these elements (and indeed the community itself) is the interactions between individuals, their joint purpose and their actual endeavours. Wenger (2004) views a community of practice as a living curriculum; it is this entity that may form the foundation for collaboration and, in turn, the structure within which shared cognition occurs on an ongoing basis, promoting both lifelong learning and continuing professional development.

Experiential learning and facilitation

Fenwick (2000) reviewed five contemporary perspectives on cognition based around the premise of experiential learning as reflected by the current literature. The five perspectives (reflective, interference, participation, resistance and co-emergence) offer a means of reconsidering how we may develop and place in practice methodologies that may take heed of how individuals interact and provide the basis for further dialogue and understanding of experiential learning. Thus it is the interactions that are central to this study, providing the impetus for sharing knowledge among the cohort.

Thomas (2002) puts forward the proposal that the use of discussion boards may aid the level of thinking undertaken by students, in particular the attainment of critical thinking and deep cognitive processing. She explores the idea of measuring the environmental impact of the use of facilitators and collaborative tasks. Cooke and Sheeran (2004) also cite the use of moderators to determine behavioural changes in cognitive relations.

Collaboration, the individual and the group dynamic

An individual's construction of knowledge can be suggested as being a 'collaboration with oneself', drawing on experience, practice and implementation to achieve a desired objective. This is brought into a group dynamic where such implicit experiences are often made explicit via cognitive conflict (that is challenging and exploring concepts cooperatively). Each group member may demonstrate a 'personal' interaction with the curriculum elements that is interpreted internally yet shared externally. This interaction offers an increased range of experience demonstrated, explored and shared via the entire group (see Figure 7.1).

Figure 7.1 attempts to draw together the current elements in constructivism and collaboration and show how each perceptual development may add to the development of an over arching view that is encompassed by the concept of communities of practice. This, in turn, is adapted to fit within this research study by adding a structured domain (the curriculum), providing external guidance (the tutor/facilitator) and identifying key tasks (T) or events that require achievement in order to arrive at collaboration. This collaboration will ideally lead to a shared understanding that may be mutually transferred between participants within the community and beyond (see Figure 7.2).

Engaging in online learning may often prove disorienting (Palloff and Pratt, 1999) and, in an attempt to provide a framework within which to hang this research, the concept of problem-based learning has been utilised. Problem-based pedagogy is widely used throughout higher education particularly in the field of medicine. It offers the potential to not only deal with its actual discipline specific arena, but to offer a holistic approach to

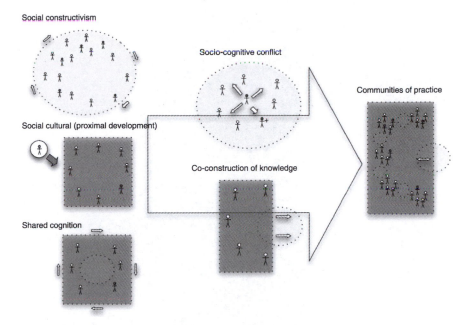

Figure 7.1   Move towards inclusive, collaborative and constructive domains of sharing knowledge within an online environment

learning, to instil in students a sense of 'how to learn' and to reinforce the premise of lifelong learning.

Methodology

Overview

Participants were drawn from two sectors of the university: those who had experience of problem-based learning and those who were users of the local VLE (Blackboard). A cross-section of academic disciplines was represented from veterinary medicine to the arts; computer services to medicine. The roles of individuals varied from administrative and academic to support and technical. Of those partaking only one had no prior experience of online learning; the majority considering themselves 'advanced users' of the VLE. Furthermore, most had at some time partaken in a form of collaborative online work, whether within a VLE, via online discussion boards or through the use of email.

The cohort was invited to partake in a problem-based scenario within the online environment of Blackboard. This problem-based session occurred over a 2-week period and required in the region of 4–8 hours work. Two identified sessions were synchronous (two 60-minute online tutorials) and

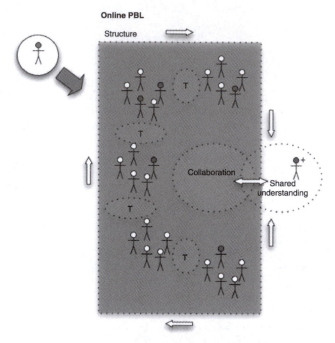

Figure 7.2   A model for collaborative interactions in an online PBL environment

therefore compulsory. The first of these was to discuss and identify the problem. The second tutorial was to report back on stated learning outcomes. The remainder of the time was to be self-directed and required posting to discussion threads asynchronously, accessing phase-released data and acquiring external resources.

The research model in practice was that of the 'time series design', whereby a number of observations (pretests) were used to establish an existing pattern among the participants (LoBiondo-Wood and Haber, 1994). The participants were then exposed to the curriculum (the online problem-based scenario), which was designed to encourage and promote the use of collaboration. Finally, further observations and interviews were conducted after the online task was completed. Empirical studies (Harvey, 1998) have validated this experimental approach and results prove indicative of the differences between individual and collaborative learning.

Problem-based learning

Educational technology is often seen as the solution to many curriculum issues, the area of communication and collaboration being a particular case in point. However, just because technology provides us with a means to collaborate does not necessarily imply that it will actually occur (Roschelle and Pea, 1999). Problem-based learning is a relatively new phenomenon within this writer's university. From participation in a number of workshops and facilitating part of a problem-based module in the 'theories of teaching and learning' it was evident that the majority of participants found it not only a worthwhile and stimulating experience, but the level of communication and interaction achieved was outstanding. It was therefore deemed that problem-based learning would provide an ideal methodology and framework within which to set the online study for collaborative learning.

The method of problem-based learning was chosen for this study to further add to the potential for interaction and increase the need for conflict resolution, debate and discussion (Avouris *et al.*, 2003). A variation of the Maastricht model was chosen, whereby a seven-point task list is presented to aid in the problem resolution. The group were asked to familiarise themselves with this process (see Appendix 7.1) so that they might be better able to structure their ensuing discussions. Following this preparation they were invited to review the 'problem' prior to a live tutorial.

The online structure: a framework for collaboration

The university has chosen Blackboard (see www.blacboard.com) as its virtual learning environment (VLE). Blackboard is extremely functional in terms of a course management system, however, it lacks certain intuitive and flexible approaches that may be more apparent in a socially derived learning management systems such as Moodle (see www.moodle.org) or one designed specifically around collaboration and research such as Sakai (see www.sakaiproject.org). The online session was designed in such a way that participants were able to explore the key structures and components from the outset. After each synchronous tutorial (all of which were immediately archived for reference and reflection), discussion threads were established to act as guides to learning outcome completion and further enquiry. Simultaneously relevant literature and resources were released to accompany the identified learning outcomes.

In line with good practice related to online facilitation and mediated support (Palloff and Pratt, 1999; Salmon, 2003), a number of constructs were provided for the participants. One of these was an introductory and localisation task to familiarise learners with one another and the imminent course work. Although the actual structure of the session was mapped hierarchically (as predetermined by the design features of Blackboard), participants were invited (and encouraged to explore) all available elements as time and needs dictated (see Appendix 7.2).

Blackboard has a series of 'collaborative tools' built into its academic system. Two in particular were chosen to facilitate the live tutorials and discussions. The synchronous (live) tutorials were run using the 'virtual classroom' and 'chat' tools. The virtual classroom allowed participants to post queries and questions while viewing a generic whiteboard and/or slide show. This enabled an agenda for each session to be posted in the whiteboard area and act as a guide to the following discussions. The chat tool, as implied, was a more informal device to facilitate discussion; this was used for the final feedback session.

The 'discussion board' was used to house the numerous asynchronous threads that were established throughout the session, from the initial ice-breaker (identify your favourite piece of chocolate and explain what it says about you) to the series of identified problem-based learning outcomes decided on in the first synchronous tutorial. Participants were thus enabled to post reflections on questions/problems at a time suitable to themselves. Other collaborative tools in use were the 'digital drop box' (a file sharing process), the 'electric blackboard' (for taking 'live' notes) and email.

Having completed the preliminary questionnaires related to the research study (see later) a time was arranged to hold the first synchronous tutorial to discuss the problem. The participants were presented with a recognisable problem that was applicable across the multitude of disciplines represented among the cohort, namely, 'How to engage students in online activities'. Background was provided to set the scene: the participants were invited to reflect on their current work in their chosen VLE and how it was being used in conjunction with their face-to-face teaching. Context was provided by introducing a new member of staff with experience in distance learning. This recent arrival has offered to share their expertise and participants must now consider how they may integrate such methodologies into their current practices. Concepts such as networked learning and virtual field-trips were given as possible scenarios to explore. A number of concerns and issues were presented that would need to be addressed, for example, student computer access, assessing online contributions and using online collaborative tools. This was presented in textual form from the point of view of a module evaluation, and a graphical representation was also used to highlight the nature of possible collaborative situations within the given environment. Further to the actual problem an 'information teaser' was offered to give further insight prior to the online session, acting as a guide to the imminent discussion. This posed a number of questions relating to the problem and offered a suggested guide to identifying possible learning outcomes.

The first tutorial was held in the 'virtual classroom'. An agenda was posted to facilitate the discussion, which included: discussion of problem, identifying valid concerns and issues and establishing a plan of action (defining the learning outcomes). Individual discussion threads were then created for each learning outcome and participants invited to post reflections and findings prior to the next synchronous tutorial. Specific resources relating to the learning outcomes were released in the resources section to further aid discussion and cogitation. The second tutorial provided a forum to discuss the learning outcomes and possible solutions to the key issues identified within the problem. One final live 'chat' session was convened to garner feedback on the process and to organise a face-to-face session as a group forum.

Results

Conceptions of online learning

Part of the initial survey asked participants to reflect on their conceptions of online and collaborative learning in an effort to gauge how they might interact with one another in the forthcoming session and to determine any predefined notions. The majority of participants were 'comfortable using online communications as a means to working collaboratively'. However, in the same breath almost all admitted to liking to discuss matters on a face-to-face basis. While most 'enjoy the rapport of peer interaction' many are reticent to become involved in 'arguments' and possible flames.[1] Likewise, many use the web on a regular basis both for collecting resources and for research purposes but prefer reading 'books'. Finally, many agreed to being 'aware of limitations in online interactions' citing that face to face is both 'preferred' and required to establish an initial rapport or to provide context.

Although these answers are not unexpected, it does show that people have adjacent opinions to the nature and expectations of online learning. The question posed is do these notions interfere with one's preconceptions of online learning and interaction – thereby hindering engagement or participation? Or do they merely reflect what most academics/facilitators would like to be achieving – in that a blended approach to e-learning is a fundamental necessity to its success – and it is what everyone (every learner) naturally expects?

Evaluation tools

There were two particular questionnaires key to the pre-test methodology: the Index of Learning Styles (ILS) (www.engr.ncsu.edu/learningstyles/ilsweb.html) and the Approaches and Study Skills Inventory for Students (ASSIST) questionnaire (www.ed.ac.uk/etl/project.html). Participants were requested to fill out the ILS questionnaire online and post their results on the discussion board. Additionally, they were invited to provide any remarks about the test itself, its format and design and their own results. Participants were also requested to fill out the ASSIST form and deposit this in the digital drop box or email it to the facilitator.

---

[1] **Flaming** is the performance 'art' of posting messages that are deliberately hostile and insulting, usually in the social context of a discussion board; www.Wikipedia.com.

Index of learning styles

The index of learning styles devised by Soloman and Felder (1991) provides a gauge of an individual's or group's particular preferences to learning. Devised on a sliding scale within four dimensions (active to reflective, sensing to intuitive, visual to verbal and sequential to global), it offers a means to see where possible strengths or tendencies lie. However, it must be noted that this was only seen as an indication and participants were invited to comment on their personal results. Most acknowledged that the preferences highlighted were what they expected, but perhaps not to the degree shown. It was also interesting to note the diversity of learning preferences within the group; representation was present from each particular learning preference. Although every dimension was present, some were more dominant than others; these included a strong showing from active, visual, intuitive and global learning preferences.

Of those participants who undertook to revisit the Index of Learning Styles Questionnaire, one in particular showed a number of changes that resulted from having engaged in the online problem-based session. There was a marked move from a reflective preference to that of an active learner, perhaps evidenced by the amount of collaboration and group work required while online. Furthermore, there was a perceptual change to preferring a global and intuitive way of learning (over that of sequential and sensing). This can be related to the methodology of problem-based learning, which at its very ethos promotes the exploration of facts/data and the personalised contextualisation of events. Further research needs to be done in this area to validate the potential of learning experiences and their effect on learners within an online context.

Approaches and study skills inventory for students

The ASSIST questionnaire is designed to allow the participant to describe systematically how they undertake to study and learn. This provides an indication of learning orientations and approaches to study (Entwistle, 1998; Entwistle *et al.*, 2002). The questionnaire used was divided into four areas: the first deals with conceptions of learning, the second and largest deals with the approaches one might take, the third explicitly deals with the environment and one's preferences for teaching methodologies and the fourth area is a reflection on one's own progress to date in the particular course.

Participants showed a high level of acknowledging learning as a transformative and challenging process, allowing for individual engagement and a deep approach. There were some elements pertaining to a surface approach to learning, in particular, referring to the ability (or lack of) in coping with large amounts of content. Strategic approaches were also represented, specifically in the realm of 'monitoring effectiveness', this may indicate participants' desire to control and review their contributions and offer an insight into how they may interact online – perhaps reflected in a possible reticence to post during synchronous discussions.

Finally, the participants primarily chose to align their own learning strategies with that of the deep approach. This relates clearly to the idea of constructive alignment (Biggs, 1999), with which the majority of participants would be familiar, whereby all components of a specific course/module, including its environment, are integrated to enable learners to engage critically, be self-directed and receive encouragement to take a deep approach to their learning.

Synchronous tutorials: collaboration in action

A number of initial queries with regard to the online content and structure were made. However, it was interesting to note that few, if any, enquiries were related to the chosen methodology (problem-based learning), and although some of the cohort were familiar with it, none had partaken in an online session prior to this. The Maastricht process identified was not followed to any great extent, but merely acted to inform the participants of the 'suggested' procedure. The very nature of a problem-based discussion can be intimidating in its seeming lack of structure and rationale. The participants were allowed to explore the scenario by placing it within their own contextual knowledge and often appeared to veer off the topic and draw on a diverse range of experiences and knowledge.

Tutorial two allowed the informed discussion of the learning outcomes to take place. Participants had had time to review the materials released online relating to these outcomes and to seek out and share further relevant resources. Once again the discussion was diverse in its coverage; participants appeared happy to engage in the discussion quite freely, drawing on personal experiences and possible areas for concern within their own disciplines.

A feedback session completed the trio of synchronous discussions (not usual in problem-based learning, but the facilitator felt it necessary to offer closure on the previous sessions where a wide range of experiences and material had been covered). The asynchronous threads dealing with the learning outcomes had been revised to reflect how a possible 'action plan' or solutions might be presented for each particular area (learning outcome) of the problem. These were gathered and presented at the feedback session to assess their potential workability and possible realisation and also to allow for the opportunity to reflect on the final outcomes. It was felt that although much material had been covered and indeed dealt with, the nature of the problems meant that individuals found it difficult to imagine implementing any definitive solution/action plan, preferring rather to take what had been presented as a series of guidelines on which they might inform their own practice.

Usability, navigation and layout

The very nature of Blackboard means that one is required to lay down data in a sequential manner and that the folder hierarchy predetermines how content is accessed. In this regard all data concerning the online problem, resources, questionnaires and the actual research details, were on constant display. Although clearly demarked by their respective folder structures, it did give the impression of 'information overload'. The alternatives, to bury information deep within folders, thereby moving beyond the 'three-click golden rule' (Nielsen, 2002); or to 'turn off', make invisible content after a set duration, were not seen as viable solutions. Some participants remarked on the suitability of the chosen VLE to carry out its functions, noting that it was sometimes difficult to navigate through the content structure. In a face-to-face course-based situation any extraneous materials to the actual problem-based scenario itself would not be housed in the same environment but provided at a separate induction session and its accompanying online presence.

The synchronous ('live') tutorials proved, for some, difficult to follow and engage with 'need for quick responses make reflection difficult'. The multitude of ideas, comments and debate that occurred proved overwhelming and yet at the same time provided the stimuli for the most productive discussions. This anomaly can only be overcome with exposure to this process, and the most fruitful situations are those that are set in a given 'session or module' context, thus no number of induction sessions will provide the right setting. It is thus envisioned that a sliding scale of interactions needs to be designed throughout the lifespan of a course, enabling learners to engage with one another and with the process in a meaningful and deep manner.

Discussion

The prospect of committing to a 2–3-week online session was a daunting prospect for some participants, whether because of work or personal needs, or by the very nature of working online and not seeing one's co-learners. In this manner, the cohort provided a genuine reflection of normal anxieties and concerns that confront every potential online learner. One respondent remarked it was 'disconcerting to engage views with strangers in the ether'. Though all participants were members of university staff, there was a wide range of experiences with technology and in particular online learning, some feeling that they did not have the requisite skills to engage in online chat. In fact one experienced user remarked that the chat in particular was 'wholly disconcerting'. However, as time progressed a number of the participants found that their confidence rose with their use of the technology and consequently their ability to communicate online.

Although noted as being problematic for some, the synchronous collaborative discussions were highlighted as being one of the activities that most influenced participants in collaborating and sharing information.

The other was the asynchronous discussion board. The participants views of e-learning ranged from 'being learning via the web, accessing resources as a supplement to traditional face to face teaching' to 'self-paced user-defined direction' and 'access to multimedia content'. One participant identified it as an opportunity to interact and collaborate with peers. Although engaging fully with the task presented one participant acknowledged the need and preference to work face to face.

Facilitation

An integral part of running this online problem-based scenario was the presence of the facilitator and the role that they adopted. Donnelly (2004) noted that in online learning the tutor/facilitator is often required to become more of an authoritarian figure, going against the norm of the 'traditional' role acknowledged within problem-based learning. Apart from the creation and design of the session, serious consideration and time resources were allocated to the content and process management. Central to this process were the dual issues of learner support and discussion facilitation. Every attempt was made to provide a seamless operation, with the provision of an induction, guidelines, task roles and resources. Few technical difficulties were encountered. Those that did occur were resolved almost immediately. Acting as the discussion facilitator was eased by adhering to the problem-based structure along with the provision of continuous 'announcements' (a separate area within Blackboard) and clear agendas. Nevertheless, the onslaught of multiple suggestions and queries in a live session can prove to be daunting; the temptation to attempt to answer everything is even more troublesome. The structure of problem-based learning allows for a free flowing expression of ideas and suggestions, so by its very nature it can appear unmanageable at the start. What is required is a soft approach to guide discussions to their desired learning outcomes. As these are dictated by the group's own directions, decisions and learning needs, it is essential that this process is allowed to occur in full. Thus, it is at times better that the facilitator remains quiet but whether this is possible often depends on the established communication dynamics of the group.

In terms of comparing this process to alternative means of teaching the same content, most participants were engaged by the concept, finding it novel, and even 'quicker' by having elementary resources on hand to read and reject as required. However, one issue that concerned most participants was the generic nature of the problem posed. Many felt that, although recognisable, it still lacked an immediacy or sense of impact within their own disciplines to be considered authentic. This caused a sense of misplacement, causing one participant to comment that they 'lost track slightly'. Although all agreed that collaborative problem solving was encouraged, one remarked that they were not sure it had actually happened.

Conclusion

System vs perception

Invariably the major question asked of the researcher was 'why should we do this online?' Or perhaps more accurately 'what benefit is there to doing it in this manner?' Many academic institutions use VLEs to manage and support their curriculum. For many institutions campus-based e-learning provision has proved problematic – is it there to enhance current face-to-face learning or is it a means by which to deliver courses to a global market and publicise the institution's potential? Systems often over-emphasise the management elements and not enough attention is paid to the learning experience. By utilising the methodology of problem-based learning online, an array of communication and collaborative tools naturally comes into play. Educational technology is often perceived as a 'bolt-on' to traditional teaching methods and this seeming lack of integration has been used as a reason for poor uptake. Like all good instructional design, a well-aligned module will enable the tutor to use those tools that suit the teaching and learning needs best.

Although the participative cohort were experienced practitioners in education, many were wary of fully engaging online, citing lack of technical knowledge, reluctance to show perceived ignorance and want of face-to-face or indeed face-to-'book' interaction. Yet most agreed that this would be of benefit to their own student cohorts in a variety of situations. Follow-up studies aim to refine the problem-based model for online usage and implement it across a variety of disciplinary contexts.

PBLonline – hit or miss?

The first question one may ask is 'Was this a genuine problem-based scenario?' Due to the online nature and the emphasis on achieving and visibly promoting collaboration, changes were made to the traditional structure. It is perhaps more accurate to state that the process was influenced by 'problem-based learning' and multiple layers of constructivism. Figure 7.2 laid down an 'instructional design model' on which the ensuing research model was based. It hoped to provide a structure within which the collaborative, social and constructive elements could be both prompted and captured.

Dealing with the 'problem'

Although solutions were offered to the 'problem' and much debate ensued, no firm resolution was fully agreed. At best, 'guidelines' to inform practice were established. This may be due in part to the facilitator not ensuring a plan of action was firmly in place. Furthermore, it may have been a factor that 'too much' was expected of the participants; this will need to be reviewed for future projects. More often than not the topics provoked vibrant discussion that did not appear to directly capture the identified learning outcomes, but nonetheless were highly engaging and offered insightful commentaries from all involved. Participants felt that they were working together collaboratively and sharing knowledge, but were unsure at the end if the designated learning outcomes had been achieved. Many comments reflected on this opportunity to interact and engage with peers, with one participant remarking how possibilities have emerged to attempt in their own practice. One other issue of note was the size of the cohort. For this research study it was kept purposefully small, but one would now need to upscale this and apply it over a longer duration for a more in-depth analysis to be undertaken of group dynamics (social elements) and the cognitive development therein (shared cognition).

Group dynamics and shared cognitive development

The process of cognitive freedom is never more apparent than in the arena of e-learning. The ability to reconstruct experience (as evidenced by the synchronous discussions) and create meaning (the culmination of the problem-based process) allows for the combination of collaborative (public) and reflective (private) approaches to learning to be fully explored (Garrison and Anderson, 2003). The group believed they were learning from one another and the context. Certainly the structure present allowed for this dynamic to occur, although to evaluate the actual measure or level to which it did so is more problematic. Mapping the intangible degrees of differences in learning may only be possible over a more sustained course. Certainly changes were noted in individuals' learning preferences, but to what degree this can be attributed to the collaborative interactions that preceded this along with other external circumstances is perhaps unclear. Participants commented on the 'energy' and wealth of experiences shared online, further adding that they 'would attempt to integrate these new experiences into their practice'. Perhaps this is where the key lies to determining the benefits of shared cognition in such future developments.

Problem-based learning: a framework/scaffold for collaboration

The overarching success factor of the project was the usage of a problem-based framework to provide a scaffold on which to offer an engaging and genuinely collaborative experience. The question arises as to whether this could have been achieved in a didactic or resource-driven online course. The nature of problem-based learning offered the clear opportunity for discussion, indeed, *vigorous* discussion. While other courses may falter with online discussion threads being supplemental to the proceedings, within this context the discussion (collaboration) element was centre stage, inviting the participants to 'wade in'. Although some participants expressed doubts to the worthiness of their contributions, these were quickly dispelled, as more and more personal experiences were shared, thus validating each individual contribution.

Questions arise around the notion that online learning is often seen as an asynchronous and an asynoptic enterprise, offering little time for genuine collaborative endeavours. A problem-based pedagogy requires a synchronous spark to engage learners and must be developed to allow for the opportunity to provide that social and collaborative interaction. The von Glasserfeld (1988) concept of social construction of shared perspectives suggests that concepts are developed through a process of 'fine-tuning' by interaction with others; learners are thus exposed to multiple perspectives that aid understanding. The problem-based pedagogy has offered this as a tangible achievement within an online environment, but much research is still required to overcome the array of challenges faced by the academic community in offering engaging and learned experiences online.

Acknowledgements

Many thanks to those participants of the research study who gave over their valuable time and made the experience thoroughly enjoyable and extremely worthwhile.

Special thanks, once again, to my colleague Brendan Dixon, whose energy and generosity goes to keeping our VLE afloat!

Appendix 7.1

PBLonline guidelines

1 *Clarify terms* (collected resources and a glossary were provided online as a mutual starting point).
   Participants were invited to ask for or be given explanations as required.
2 *Define the problem* (presentation of the problem and its context were provided online).
   Participants are required to define the major issues captured by the problem.
3 *Analyse the problem* (facilitated by the online group tutorial).
   Participants expected to brainstorm associative connections to the problem, activating any previous knowledge within the group. Participants then invited to list any relevant aspects, questions/queries etc.
4 *Systematic clarification* (facilitated during online group discussion and asynchronous discussion threads).
   Participants begin by classifying themes that emerged at the brainstorming session into higher order groupings. Further refinement may present itself in discussion threads.
5 *Formulating learning objectives* (facilitated by online group discussion).
   On the basis of knowledge that is lacking, participants formulate learning goals in unambiguous, well-defined and concrete terms.
6 *Self and group study* (facilitated by discussion threads, shared resources and group presentation/paper).
   Participants having established keywords and terms, seek out appropriate resources, systematically checking sources and working towards synthesising all relevant material to achieve the identified learning outcomes.
7 *Reporting via a joint presentation/discussion* (facilitated by second online group tutorial).
   Participants share collectively with other group members the results of one's inquiries, and decide on an appropriate action plan to resolve the initial problem.
   (Based on the work of Tseëlon, E. (2002) www.ucd.ie/sociolog/PBL/index.html.)

Appendix 7.2

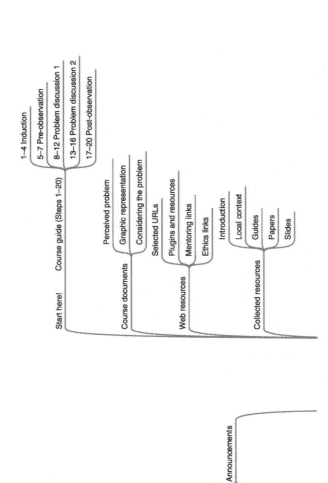

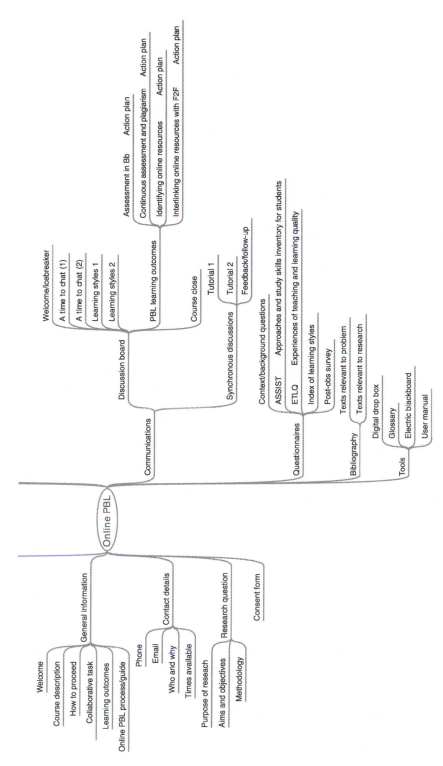

Figure 7.3 Schematic of PBLonline scenario within the VLE Blackboard

8

Online learning and problem-based learning: complementary or colliding approaches?

Maggi Savin-Baden and Carolyn Gibbon

Introduction

This chapter presents an evaluation of a project concerned with the interrelationship of problem-based learning and interactive media in schools of nursing at four UK universities. It is argued that there is an increasing interest in using interactive media with problem-based learning but, as yet, there are few illustrations of this combination and even fewer pedagogical evaluations of such examples. This evaluation sought to analyse and to understand the pedagogical tensions of bringing together interactive media and problem-based learning. The findings suggest that a focus on the underlying pedagogy at the outset of the project would have enabled those developing the materials to take a more constructivist stance. However, it is a project that appears to have produced a successful amalgamation of problem-based learning and interactive media in a way that reflects some of the pedagogical priorities of problem-based learning.

Background

The combined use of interactive media and problem-based learning is complicated, since, on their own, problem-based learning and interactive media each demand that staff and students possess a complex array of different teaching and learning capabilities. Together they could be seen as a formidable combination, however, it is not yet clear if they are approaches to learning that collide or are complementary. An evaluation of the interrelationship of problem-based learning and interactive media within a project titled 'Students online in nursing integrated curricula' (SONIC), which took place across schools of nursing at four UK universities is presented in this chapter. The findings suggest that appraisals of combined problem-based learning and interactive media to date have not extrapolated the complexities of amalgamating these two approaches. Further, there is a lack of clarity about the use of the term 'problem-based learning' by both virtual and face-to-face communities.

The nature and process of interactive media has changed considerably over the last few years. Britain and Liber (2004: 8) have noted that considerable effort has been expended on the development of managed learning environments rather than the pedagogy of such development. There is also continuing debate at both local and global levels about what counts as problem-based learning and what does not. Problem-based learning has expanded worldwide since the 1960s, and, as it has spread, the concepts associated with it have changed and become more flexible and fluid; however problem-based learning is an approach to learning that is affected by the structural and pedagogical environment into which it is placed in terms of the discipline or subject, the tutors and the organisation concerned.

There has been much discussion about the implementation of problem-based learning and the possibilities for its execution (for example Boud and Feletti, 1997; Duch *et al.*, 2001; Glen and Wilkie, 2000). There are those who claim that problem-based learning is an approach that works best when implemented wholesale across the curriculum, while others believe that the issues relating to problem-based learning and curriculum design relate less to the positioning and adoption of it across a whole curriculum and more to the quality of curriculum design, however large or small the problem-based component happens to be. This debate is now further complicated by the addition of online applications.

The objective of combining problem-based learning and interactive media is in itself complex. Terms such as 'computer mediated problem-based learning' and 'online problem-based learning' have been used to define forms of problem-based learning that utilise computers in some way. These offer little indication about the ways in which computers are used, the areas of interaction of the students, the quality of the learning materials or the extent to which any of these fit with problem-based learning (see, for example, Barrow's (2002) discussion of distributed problem-based learning). Furthermore, there are other issues that need to be addressed, such as developing tutors' online facilitation capabilities; providing some synchronous events to support students; encouraging collaborative interactive participation and finding ways of engaging those students who seldom participate in the online problem-based learning team. In the SONIC study the term 'interactive media' (following Laurillard, 2002), was chosen because it represents the idea that students learn through the web-based materials that include text, simulations, videos, demonstrations and resources. Additionally, the use of the site is student guided, but the materials support the learning students undertake in face-to-face problem-based learning groups.

Another concern is that of the positioning of the 'problem' in the learning. What is on offer in the SONIC project is a form of problem-based learning that has many of the hallmarks of the original models developed in the 1960s. However, in the online community, problem based learning (without the hyphen) is seen as being where the problem is defined as a discrete learning object. Essentially, this would seem to be an acknowledgement that online education needs to be more creatively situated and thus 'problems' are a means of providing students with more creative ways of learning, while also being a means of preventing virtual learning environments (VLE) from becoming merely information repositories. This distinction is important:

- Problem-based learning (*with* the hyphen) is an approach to learning in which students engage with complex, real-world situations that have no one 'right' answer and are the organising focus for learning. Students work in teams to confront the problem, to identify learning gaps, and to develop viable solutions and gain new information through self-directed learning.
- Problem based learning (*without* the hyphen) is where problems are used as prompts for learning in online environments. The problems often have a single correct answer and may demand little more of the students than linear problem-solving skills.

At first sight the SONIC project may be seen as problem based learning, however, problem-based learning (with the hyphen intact) is actually taking place through the onscreen prompts and the face-to-face facilitation of the groups of students by a tutor. Although the SONIC project has embraced problem-based learning, an examination of the position of problems (i.e. problem based learning as a learning object in other areas of the curriculum) would bear further exploration in order to understand the interrelationship between these two forms of learning.

The SONIC project was developed to provide students with interactive problem-based learning scenarios that encouraged independent learning and student inquiry. Web-based resources supported each of the scenarios for second-year students in a problem-based learning module. The SONIC website uses standard web technology and Flash Player™ components that are available on the project website, as well as in each university's virtual learning environment (VLE). The VLEs include assessment information, which is not required by the wider community; hence the two locations for the materials. This, in turn, gives students a choice of route for accessing materials.

This evaluation was undertaken using rhetorical criticism (Foss, 1989) to examine artefacts used within the project, such as the website and student/ facilitator guides, and documentation that emerged as a result of the project, such as reports and qualitative data.

Overview and context of the project

The project was commenced in autumn 2002 by four UK schools of nursing that each utilise problem-based learning in their undergraduate programmes. The impetus for the project came from a desire to support nursing students in their learning. Previous quality reviews of nursing education had indicated that students' knowledge of anatomy and physiology was generally regarded as poor (QAA, 2001). The project aimed to provide Flash Player™-based physiology resources as a different approach to learning and thus improve students' expertise in this area of concern.

The website materials comprise five scenarios, two adult, one child, one mental health and one for learning disabilities, matching the corresponding undergraduate nursing programmes. Each scenario is studied within the first module of the second year (termed 'branch programme') and, following pilot studies with groups of approximately 15 students per scenario, the resources are now embedded within each curriculum. The students meet face to face in problem-based learning teams, study the scenario on the website and then use the website resources to support their learning. The problem scenarios remain on an open website at all times and, depending on the programme, students meet two or three times per week over 3–4 weeks to engage with the scenarios and to decide how they will manage the problem situation with which they have been presented.

Evaluation

The evaluation was conducted by an educational researcher external to both the project and evaluations that had already been undertaken. This chapter presents a meta-evaluation of the project as a whole. Rhetorical criticism was used to examine both project artefacts and data that emerged from various research methods. Rhetorical criticism is the process of investigating and exploring acts and artefacts through systematic analysis and understanding the use and meaning of symbols, whether symbols of speech, web-based symbols or symbolic representations of curricula. The method is thus concerned with the analysis and interpretations of meanings expressed in rhetorical artefacts (Foss, 1989). Rhetorical criticism was adopted because it helps to understand the way in which information and narratives are projected and helps to distinguish the characters, plots and storylines that are at play within the project. Explaining the SONIC project from the stance of rhetorical criticism offers an opportunity to explore both the medium and the message of the approach.

Symbolic convergence theory, developed by Bormann (1972) from Bales' studies (1970) of small group dynamics, was used to examine symbols or symbolic terminology. Through the consistent use of symbols, forms of communication are created that are particular to the problem-based learning community. Symbolic convergence theory is based on the belief that communication creates reality. For example, in group interaction people try to make sense of what is occurring and they do this by using symbols to frame their understanding. The theory is appropriate for examining problem-based learning as it focuses on learning with and through small groups. In this evaluation, symbols might be the use of models of problem-based learning (for example Savin-Baden, 2000) or particular symbolic terminology that helps learners to describe what is taking place.

Method

This pedagogical evaluation analysed 16 artefacts from the project including: the original document submitted for project funding, annual reports, evaluation reports, data from student focus groups, the SONIC website, pedagogical evaluation questionnaires from both tutors and students, and a videoed focus group with the project team leader from each university.

Process of interpretation

Data were interpreted through analysing the artefacts and through discussing, exploring and negotiating meaning with those involved in the project. Although artefacts can appear 'fixed', it was acknowledged that there was a fragility and an instability in terms of changes in materials and personal and pedagogical shifts within people and their contexts and thus both the data and the management of data were constantly on the move. However, data were interpreted through the exploration of subtext and oppositional talk. The exploration of subtext focused on 'sense making' by staff involved in the project when they answered questions and shared views. The analysis also involved an exploration of the subtext of materials presented to students in order to understand what was being said and to identify any conflict between what was being espoused and what was happening in practice. Further, participants in research often speak oppositionally and share their perspectives in ways that are mechanisms for explaining and justifying their conduct and values. By exploring such perspectives it was possible to see how participants saw and defined themselves.

Findings

The findings illustrate that by combining problem-based learning and interactive media different types of learning contexts were created that were not previously evident in any of these curricula. The pedagogical positioning of interactive media and the nature of support and dialogue were important factors in the way students perceived and managed knowledge. Further, the types of problems on offer to students illustrated the ways staff expected students to manage knowledge and knowing.

Learning context

In the SONIC project the context was different at each site due to both curricular differences and the way in which the materials were used. Themes that emerged were connected with notions and understandings of space. Lefebvre (1991) differentiates between representational space (lived space), perceived space (spatial practice) and conceived space (representations of space). Lefebvre's conceptions of space were drawn on in the data analysis when it became apparent that understandings of space had shifted in terms of staff's and students' perceptions of it. However, it is important to note that the themes used have emerged from data rather than imposing Lefebvre's conceptions of space on the data. What is particularly important about Lefebvre's work in this context is that virtual space, real space and lived space, as classified here, are defined by spatial practice.

Virtual space

Boundaries around conceptions of time and space were spoken of by students as 'being different' for example, 'work' occurred in different ways from other components of the course and learning tended to transcend home/university boundaries because of the accessibility of the SONIC site. Students spoke of learning to use the site together at university in their problem-based learning group and then undertaking further exploration at home. As one student pointed out: 'I mean at home, we spent quite a bit more time on it at home, sort of finding your feet, you're investigating in all the different areas, you know, seeing what it's got to offer, and then using that at a later date for when its relevant for your study.' Learning, knowledge, relationships, communication, home and workplaces were no longer seen by students as static, bounded and uniform but instead became ongoing, variable and emergent.

Real space

Real space is defined by the physical world, such as the design of the buildings and the space that exists between and within structures shaped by the organisation's function and activity – past and present. With the rise of telework there is now a shift towards a notion of 'flexible spaces' in homes, and this is particularly important in relation to students involved in a project such as this. Thus the notion of real space no longer represents an integrated idea of the use of space in the home or the workplace. This notion of changing real space was evident in the ways the students worked and spoke of work in relation to the SONIC scenarios, which for some impacted on lived space.

Lived space

The notion of lived space is one symbolised by activities that necessarily occur within it. Therefore it is no longer an integrated concept. Lived space changes according to weather, for example, when workers move indoors from the outside office (shed), it changes with time when the children go to bed and the laptop is put on the kitchen table so that one partner can work while the other cooks. The SONIC project merely reflects what is happening in many universities across the world: that is, students' local cafés become communication centres. At the same time complaints are made both about learning groups in campus bars and the noise in the library – the latter is no longer either a symbolic or an actual silent work space.

Accessibility 1 and 2

The nature of accessibility in e-learning normally relates to two concerns: first, accessibility to the site, second, accessibility for people with disabilities.

Accessibility 1
This form of accessibility is concerned with access to the site. Across the universities many of the initial problems for students were connected with speed of connection, up-to-date equipment and software. To some extent the problems raised by staff and students related to the design of the material but more often they related to the policy decision of the institutions and the type of VLE that had been implemented institution wide as well as the particular version of the given VLE. One of the advantages raised by a number of students was that SONIC was an open system. This meant access to it was easy, unlike other areas of the university where there was a lack of managed learning environment (MLE) integration, leading to separate signing on for each different service, e.g. library, students services, WebCT or Blackboard.

Accessibility 2
This form of accessibility related to the mechanisms used to ensure accessibility for students with disabilities, such as Alt Text and LongDesc. All potential pre-registration nursing students are invited to declare a known disability, so that arrangements can be made to accommodate their needs. During the pilot study there were no known disabilities reported by students, but in the current round of evaluations, one student has come forward. There is evidence on the site that the needs of this student can be accommodated. The site uses Flash Player™ for the animations and it was felt that there was little point in providing large amounts of texts to describe them. Audio is being implemented, allowing students the opportunity to either read the text or listen to the text: it is not possible to carry out both activities at the same time. Clark and Mayer (2003) point out that words placed alongside images are more effective than words alone and that words presented as audio instead of text are even better. Caution needs to be exercised, as, while this reduces the cognitive load for the student, it increases the processor load for the computer and may have implications for access off campus.

Pedagogical positioning of SONIC

The SONIC project aimed to promote resource enriched scenarios but there remain difficulties about the relation between the form and content of online education. This has been captured by Mason (1998: 4) who has argued that: 'Many computer-based teaching programs whether stand alone, or on an Intranet or the Web, fall into one of two categories: all glitz and no substance, or content that reflects a rote-learning, right/wrong approach to learning.' In many curricula it could be argued that this is still very much the case. However, the more recent focus on students as customers, and approaches such as problem-based learning have forced a reappraisal and a redesigning of online education, so that it can facilitate the development of knowledge management, problem solving, critique and learning how to learn.

Nature of support and dialogue

The nature of dialogue in problem-based learning is affected by the way in which problem-based learning groups are set up, the pedagogical stance of the facilitator and the pedagogical content knowledge within the discipline. The SONIC project uses face-to-face problem-based learning with interactive media as a support mechanism. Britain and Liber (2004: 25–26) have argued that: 'If e-mail is used as the tool for communication between tutor and student in a given VLE we need to know how the use of e-mail is embedded within the context of the dialogue about a specific topic or set of learning goals.'

In SONIC, dialogue is largely face to face and electronic communication is undertaken between students by email. There is currently no plan to use conference facilities for students or to shift the problem-based learning facilitator role into that of an e-moderator. This is because SONIC is designed to 'support' students' learning. Although the notion of support differed between the staff interviewed in the video focus group there were some commonalities. There was a sense from all participants that the SONIC materials had helped students to synthesise knowledge across different subjects within the nursing specialty they were studying (for example, learning disabilities, paediatrics, mental health). Staff at one school particularly felt that SONIC had helped their students to understand anatomy and physiology better than more traditional ways of learning these subjects. Tutors at two other institutions felt that the relevant and up-to-date links to other websites had provided students with support that fitted with many of their preferred approaches to learning. For example one tutor said: 'It links with the way students want to learn – it's the fast click that they seem to want.'

The 'fast click' was seen by many of the tutors to have advantages in terms of saving students time in looking for resources and enabling them to access credible resources. Yet there were concerns that the fast click also meant that at times the SONIC site was seen and used by students as infotainment: a liberal mix of information and entertainment (Ritzer, 1996). However, it was also argued that it was important to ensure that the problem-based learning groups commenced as face-to-face learning groups away from the computers, so that students would first work together before doing the 'fast click' in a computer lab.

One student stated in their evaluation that they started off in small groups, which worked well, but then they worked at home, before coming back to groups which they liked because 'they could bounce ideas off each other'. Another student liked working in pairs, but also enjoyed working individually 'because I had control of the mouse!' From the staff perspective, SONIC provided more learning support to the students than they had envisaged and they found that the SONIC site and particularly its animations fitted with students' approaches and motivation to learn.

Problem typology

The complexity of problem design presents a challenge for many tutors in implementing problem-based learning. To date much of the discussion in the field of problem-based learning about the nature of problems has centred on cognitive psychology. There have been discussions about the role of problem solving in problem-based learning and whether problem solving is a generalisable skill or not (see, for example, Eva *et al.*, 1998; Norman and Schmidt, 1992). In many curricula little attention is paid to the different types of problem available or how they might be used. The SONIC project utilises 'fact-finding problems' throughout (see Table 8.1).

In practice this means that the scenarios always guide the students towards descriptive knowledge. For example, if the students were asked, 'what would you do if you were this man's nurse?' then the emphasis becomes one of action rather than explanation. The assumption is that the student always understands the explanatory knowledge and can take action, thereby using procedural knowledge. Such a distinction is important because it helps students to begin to understand how they recognise and use different types of knowledge.

Discussion: complementary or colliding pedagogies?

The initial aims of the SONIC project have been realised since a resource-enriched interactive media environment has been created to support problem-based learning. The findings of this evaluation suggest that a number of issues affected the extent to which interactive media and problem-

Table 8.1 Types of knowledge and types of problem

Types of knowledge	*Explanatory knowledge*	*Descriptive knowledge*	*Procedural knowledge*	*Personal knowledge*
Types of problem	Explanation problem	Fact-finding problem	Strategy problem	Moral dilemma problem
Examples	People in the 15th century used to believe it was possible to fall off the edge of the earth	Following recent political changes relating to land use in Zimbabwe many internal borders have changed	A 43-year-old woman cannot lift her right arm more than 45° and she complains of pins and needles in her hand	A mother breaks into a chemist's shop at night to obtain life-saving drugs for her baby. She contacts her local physician the next day to explain what she has done
Example of question	Explain why	What would a legal map look like?	If you were this client's physiotherapist, what would you do?	What should the doctor do?

Source: Adapted from Schmidt and Moust, 2000: 68.

based learning were complementary or colliding pedagogies; these are now discussed.

Interrelationship of problem-based learning and interactive media

One of the primary criticisms of a project such as this would appear to be the lack of initial pedagogical underpinning in terms of the type of problem-based learning on offer and the design of the interactive media environment. Cultural and institutional constraints affect the design of problem-based curricula, as do issues that tend to differ across disciplines, such as the way an essay is constructed or the way that knowledge is seen. When adopting problem-based learning, the extent to which the curriculum is designed as a whole entity is an important concern. Curriculum design thus impinges on tutors' and students' roles and responsibilities and the ways in which learning and knowledge are perceived. However, through analysis of the project artefacts it has been possible to map the way that problem-based learning is in operation within a programme, in terms of the *mode of curriculum practice*. These modes were developed by Savin-Baden and Major (2004). They are not meant to be an exhaustive list of types of problem-based learning curriculum but rather are a means of considering what occurs in some programmes, as well as the impact of opting for a particular design. Several modes are in evidence in this project because of the different approaches to the curriculum at each university. Each curriculum has been guided by the same principles (DoH, 1999) but has been implemented in individual ways in line with various local regulations.

Problem-based learning on a shoestring (Mode 2)

In this mode, problem-based learning occurs with minimal cost and interruption to other areas of the curriculum. The McMaster model serves as a blueprint and modules appear almost in isolation from the rest of the curriculum. Problems used are usually subject based and rarely transcend disciplinary boundaries. The modules tend to be scattered throughout the curriculum with students not understanding the rationale for the use of problem-based learning and tutors frustrated by the lack of departmental or institutional support.

The foundational approach (Mode 4)

In this mode, the decision has been made to design the curriculum in a way that enables students to commence with lecture-based learning in the first year, then move on to problem-based learning in their second and third year. This is built on the assumption that basic concepts have been taught in the first years. The second year will comprise problems that are set within, and bounded by, a discrete subject or disciplinary area, but students start to determine the interdisciplinary links. In the third year problems are designed that build on each other, using a cohesive framework. Thus the focus of problem-based learning is on the students being able to build on foundational knowledge in order to undertake problem-based learning.

E-resources directing or guiding student learning?

There has been much criticism in the last five years or so about interactive media environments that fail to create effective settings for learning (Noble, 2001; Oliver and Herrington, 2003; Reeves, 2002). One of the reasons for this has been that the focus in interactive media environments has been on technological rather than pedagogical design and there have been suggestions that there is a need for a reengineering of the concept of learning design rather than just a simplistic repackaging of the course content into interactive media formats (see for example Collis, 1997). Despite the criticism here that SONIC lacked a clear initial pedagogical underpinning, data on the student experience indicate that they have valued and enjoyed utilising SONIC. Students have argued that engaging with SONIC has helped them to become familiar with learning online and using the internet. They have particularly valued being able to revisit the interactive media materials at home and have begun to see learning as less time and context bound through using the SONIC site at home, university, cyber cafés, alone and in groups. Further, what is important about the SONIC project is that the interactive media has been designed as an integral part of the learning process, as Oliver and Herrington (2003) argue:

> In learning environments that support knowledge construction learners need to be exposed to a variety of resources and to have choices in the resources that they use and how they use them. An important aspect of resource development is to provide content that provides them with perspectives from a multitude of sources . . . The materials need not all be on-line.
>
> (Oliver and Herrington, 2003: 15)

In the context of problem-based learning there needs to be clarity about how scenarios are created so that they produce robust educational discussion. Perhaps different types of scenario need to be used in online learning than in face-to-face problem-based learning. At one level the interlinking of problem-based learning with virtual learning environments has brought creativity to problem-based learning and the development of innovative multimedia materials. It is clear from much of the literature that this is not always the case and that focusing on the achievement of outcomes and tasks is instead causing a narrowing of the definition of problem-based learning and a certain boundedness about the types of problem scenario being adopted, and the way that problem-based learning is being used.

Recommendations

Although much of what has been undertaken in the SONIC project would suggest that interactive media and problem-based learning are complementary approaches, there are a number of recommendations that would enhance this relationship. For example, using the model proposed by Oliver and Herrington (2003) it would be possible to make student learning more constructivist in nature than it is currently. They argue that this three-stage design process is an effective organising strategy for promoting knowledge construction, which involves:

- The design and specification of *tasks to engage and direct the learner* in the process of knowledge acquisition and development of understanding.
- The design and specification of *supports for the online learner* to scaffold the learning and to provide meaningful forms of feedback.

- The design and specification of *the learning resources* needed by the learner to successfully complete the set tasks and to facilitate the scaffolding and guidance.

(Oliver and Herrington, 2003: 3)

A further possibility would be to further develop the interactive media so that the online formative assessment strategies, videoclips and problem scenarios are extended to prompt the use of procedural and personal knowledge.

However, the strongest recommendation would be to develop the use of the SONIC materials towards computer-mediated collaborative problem-based learning (CMCPBL). While many of the current models of online education focus on tutor-centred learning, CMCPBL needs to be focused on a team-orientated knowledge building discourse. Scardemalia and Bereiter (1994) have defined three characteristics of this discourse:

- A focus on problem scenarios and depth of understanding.
- Open knowledge building that focuses on collective knowledge so that inquiry is driven by a quest for understanding.
- An inclusion of all participants in the broader knowledge community. Thus learning involves students, teachers, administrators, researchers, curriculum designers and assessors. This brings a wide range of perspectives and an acknowledgement that anything done by one person means that others must adapt.

The impact of the inclusion of these three characteristics means that learners and facilitators may take on different roles in the course of a collaborative learning situation, which again brings online education of this sort in to line with the dialogic nature of problem-based learning. Facilitation occurs through the tutor having access to the ongoing discussions without necessarily participating in them. Tutors also plan real-time sessions with the CMCPBL team in order to engage with the discussion and facilitate the learning.

Conclusion

This study has examined artefacts in the form of speech, interaction and text, in order to examine the existent and emerging pedagogy of an innovative interactive media project that was based in a problem-based learning module. This project typifies some of the trends of designing materials first and locating them pedagogically later (if at all). However, the evaluation highlighted that a focus on the underlying pedagogy at the outset of the project would have enabled those developing the materials to take a more constructivist stance. This would have enabled them to develop a constructivist learning setting by avoiding the use of text written only in the teacher's voice and content that was largely aimed at familiarising students with propositional knowledge. Early pedagogical underpinning might also have enabled the development of CMCPBL at the outset of the project. However, it is an innovative project and possibly one of the first worldwide that has produced a successful marriage between problem-based learning and interactive media.

Acknowledgement

The SONIC project was one of the phase 4 projects supported by the Fund for the Development of Teaching and Learning (FDTL), a UK fund that promotes the development of best practice in teaching and learning.

9

Developing expertise in professional practice, online, at a distance

Karen Lee

Introduction

This chapter examines the effectiveness of using problem-based learning as an online learning activity within a paper-based undergraduate distance learning module for practising specialist nurses, in a Scottish university. The module was supported by the use of a virtual learning environment (VLE). The evaluation of this support found online problem-based learning to be valuable in achieving the learning outcomes of the module by promoting development of expertise within an online community of practice. The role of problem-based learning in facilitating development of a community of practice is examined and a framework to guide its use proposed.

Context of problem-based learning use

The students on the programme were qualified nurses with a remit for infection control in a wide variety of settings, who wanted to complete a degree in conjunction with a specialist practitioner qualification in infection control. Initially the module was designed to be run face to face but a decision was made to offer it exclusively in distance learning format, with the aim of targeting nurses across the UK and abroad. There were approximately 20 learners in each cohort. The module was rated at 20 Scotcat credit points at Scottish undergraduate level nine and was required to meet the competencies set by the regulatory body (UKCC, 1998). At this time the university department had expertise in paper-based distance delivery, but no experience of providing e-learning tuition.

Learning considerations

According to the professional regulatory body, the hallmark of a specialist practitioner is the ability to demonstrate higher levels of judgement, discretion and decision making in clinical practice (UKCC, 1998). The role of the specialist practitioner includes the following components; clinical expert, consultant, researcher, educator, change agent, advocate, clinical auditor, leader, manager and accountable practitioner (McGhee, 1998). The aim of the module was thus more than the acquisition of knowledge; it required learners to acquire the ability to apply and use the knowledge in many different scenarios where the answers are often not clear cut and are rarely to be found in a textbook.

Members of the module team were familiar with the use of problem-based learning in the pre-registration taught undergraduate nursing programme and recognised the value of problem-based learning in developing critical thinking skills in a face-to-face context. The module team believed that problem-based learning could offer similar benefits in an online programme. It was proposed, therefore, to write three problem-based learning scenarios into the distance learning workbook across the 12-week module, and to explore the potential use of a VLE (Blackboard v5.0) for communicating with and supporting students.

Motivation for the innovation – potential benefits of an online component

A key issue identified was that of learner isolation. It was unlikely that students would have face-to-face contact with fellow students or tutors. In addition, it was recognised that the students, as mature adults, had experience that could be used as a learning resource and were likely to be internally motivated, wanting to learn in response to a perceived need to know (Fry *et al.*, 2000). However, as mature adults, the students might also be unfamiliar with computer technology. Furthermore, until nurse education moved into higher education in 1992 with the 'Project 2000' initiative, training was by apprenticeship on the wards (Casey, 1996). Returning students might therefore have an expectation that knowledge will be delivered to them, might lack study skills such as self-direction and time management and might not have been exposed to groupwork.

Nonetheless, clear benefits of utilising the VLE were the ability to provide further resources and to enable communication with peers and the teaching team. These abilities could be used for teaching or support. Use of the VLE moved the module from second-generation to third-generation distance learning, allowing a greater degree of interactivity (Calder and McCollum, 1998). Research on second-generation distance education identifies that the opportunity for discussion with a tutor is crucial and that lack of contact with peers is a disadvantage. In addition, the sense of isolation frequently experienced can lead to high attrition rates. Students also lack socialisation into the academic system (Marland, 1997), miss out on help from other students' questions/answers and are unable to compare their performance with others (Race, 1994). In addition, Simpson (2002) suggests that it is feasible to use computer-mediated conferencing (CMC) to support students in learning skills such as self-direction and cognitive skills. Online tutorials were therefore proposed in order to reduce isolation, scaffold learning skills, allow students to benefit from their colleagues' questions, compare their understanding with their peers as they would do face to face and enable vicarious learning from observing the learning of and interactions among other learners.

In addition, there were strong pedagogical drivers to utilise the computer-mediated discussion (CMC) capabilities of the VLE to enable collaborative learning, such as the problem-based learning scenarios in the workbook and to provide a social dimension of learning. Particular drivers were the current shift from an acquisition metaphor to a constructivist view of learning and from a focus on the individual to an emphasis on the social context of learning (Mayes, 2001). Alexander and Boud (2002) argue that learning does not occur in isolation, but requires emotional and personal support from others, context, feedback and reflection. In addition, Ryan (2001: 73) identifies a motivational layer of student support in the form of the class group, which also 'provides a socializing, civilizing experience where individuals learn how to behave in groups and to negotiate community'. Furthermore, Thorpe (2001) highlights research illustrating the importance of conversation, community, enjoyment and relationships both in learning and in facilitating personal transformation.

Rationale for implementing use of problem-based learning via CMC

It was felt important to use the full potential of CMC. CMC does not provide a set environment with intrinsic educational outcomes, but offers a customisable environment that can be tailored to a range of different purposes (Salmon, 2000). One of these is a return to 'real' (collaborative, group-based) education based on the best features of group interaction and independent study (Kaye, 1989). However, Harasim (1989) warns that, although CMC was developed with the purpose of facilitating interactive group communication, many-to-many communication is not the same as collaboration. Collaborative learning theory sees the student as an active participant in the learning process, who constructs knowledge through interaction and discussion with peers and experts (Harasim, 1989). Collaborative learning activities therefore are those based on cooperative tasks requiring active participation and interaction with peers in achieving a common goal, of which problem-based learning is an example. Thorpe (2002) observes that facilitating collaborative learning as part of a community and with access to experts is a challenge for open and distance learning (ODL) that was not always met in the past.

The use of CMC to enable students to collaborate in problem-based learning therefore seemed a valuable addition to the paper workbook. The benefits to learning of CMC are thus in understanding and commenting on other people's understanding/perspectives; in being able to accept criticism on one's own position, and to reflect on and reformulate one's point of view accordingly (Klemm, 1995). In addition, Kaye (1989: 3) observes that CMC 'has the potential to provide a means for the weaving together of ideas and information from many people's minds regardless of when and from where they contribute'. Evidence from communication research (Harasim, 1989: 3) demonstrates that the text-based discourse of CMC allows critical, thoughtful and intellectual analysis, with asynchronous messaging enabling reflection and the ability to read through an archive as many times as required. Collaboration allows debate, negotiation, mentoring, peer review, reflection and helps learners validate their learning experience. Furthermore, the articulation required promotes deeper understanding (Vonderwell, 2003).

Advocates of good e-learning practice promote a social constructivist approach (see Chapter 7). This approach appeared well suited to the module, as learning takes place in an authentic environment, content and skills are relevant to the learner and understood within the framework of their prior knowledge and experience and all this occurs in a socio-cultural context. Within this model, the tutor's role is to facilitate and guide learning, encouraging multiple perspectives. Oliver (2001) summarises a constructivist approach to e-learning as follows: active construction of knowledge supported by various perspectives within meaningful contexts rather than the memorisation of facts, learning embedded in realistic and relevant contexts and learners bringing their own needs and experiences to the learning situation, thereby providing experience of and appreciation for multiple perspectives, all within a context for learning that supports both autonomy and relatedness. These are, of course, also the tenets of effective use of problem-based learning. The use of CMC to facilitate online, asynchronous problem-based learning scenarios was therefore congruent with the principles of good e-learning and the collaborative affordances of CMC (Koschmann *et al.*, 1996). It was also consistent with the basic elements of problem-based learning with authentic problems in a professional context and communication between peers (Ronteltap and Eurelings, 2002).

Experiences from elsewhere in academe (Rogerson and Harden, 1999) and the RCN Institute (Price, 2000b) suggest that problem-based learning can be integrated successfully into paper-based distance learning design for post-registration nurses. In addition, Oliver and Omari (1999) found online problem-based learning to be a 'sound alternative to conventional delivery' for on-campus students across a variety of departments. Ocker and Yaverbaum (1999) found it as effective as face-to-face delivery with regard to learning and the quality of the solution, while Benbunan-Fich and Hiltz (1999) found it more effective as a result of asynchronous discussion promoting deeper reflection.

Delivery

Students were sent a paper-based workbook and a core textbook. In addition, all students were enrolled on the VLE where additional resources, support and learning activities were provided. Activities took place on the discussion board and consisted of an introductory socialisation 'welcome' activity, followed by three problem-based learning scenarios within a 9-week period. In addition there was a 'café', a forum to ask questions of the teaching team and an assignment surgery. Participation online was optional, the alternative being to complete the problem-based learning scenarios in the workbook independently and post the work to the tutors. It was anticipated that the opportunity for online contact would encourage students to participate, as proved to be the case.

Evaluation of the use of online problem-based learning within the module

The desired outcome of online problem-based learning was to facilitate collaboration, with individual and social construction of knowledge. Evidence for this was examined by retrospective review of the discussion boards. Following a review of the literature, two complementary methodologies of transcript analysis were chosen: interaction-based coding, which puts emphasis on the message as part of a larger discussion (Spatariu *et al.*, 2004) and sociocultural discourse analysis, which examines language as a tool for developing shared understanding over time (Mercer *et al.*, 2004).

Within interaction-based coding, the 'holistic' method of Jarvela and Hakkinen (cited by Spatariu *et al.*, 2004), which categorised the online discussions into 'levels', appeared to correlate most closely with collaborative learning. 'Low-level discussions' were those where there were mainly separate comments and opinions. 'Progressive discussions' included generalisations and some joint knowledge building; there were some cross-references. 'High-level discussions' were shared, theory-based discussions involving new points or questions, with rich cross-referencing. To assess social construction of knowledge in CMC by discourse analysis, the constructivist model of content analysis of Gunawardena *et al.* (1997) was chosen. This examines whether knowledge is constructed within the group, and whether individual participants change their understanding as a result of interactions within the group. The five stages are:

1 Sharing/comparing of information.
2 Discovery and exploration of dissonance/inconsistency.
3 Negotiation of meaning/co-construction of knowledge.
4 Testing and modification of proposed synthesis/co-construction.
5 Agreement statement/application of newly constructed meaning.

In addition, the standard module evaluation questionnaires were examined for the student's perspective of the VLE. These are Likert scale questionnaires on all aspects of the module from the library to tutorial support. Those relating to Blackboard were examined to allow evaluation of the quality of the students' learning experience (Lockwood, 2003). Transcripts from the discussion board of the first and last runs of the module were analysed. Only the second and third problem-based learning scenarios were examined, so that students had some familiarisation with the method and each other. The triggers and instructions are given in Appendix 9.1.

Results

Discussion board transcripts

High-level discussion was present in both transcripts demonstrating collaboration. All five stages of individual and social construction of knowledge were achieved. Examples can be seen in the (abbreviated) dialogue given here, among four students addressing one part of a scenario surrounding meningococcal meningitis (Appendix 9.1).

KL: Having read the scenario, what is one question that sprung to mind?

Pam: If meningitis was suspected and as benzyl penicillin was given, confirming that this was suspected, why was the patient admitted to an open ward? All hospital staff should be aware that the patient must be isolated due to the risk of airborne transmission. Therefore I would feel that the patient being nursed in an open bay prior to 48 hrs of treatment could pose a potential risk to others. Immunosuppressed patients, visitors and staff could all be affected.

Janette: The patient should be isolated for 24 hours worth of antibiotics but perhaps there were no cubicles available and so strict observations of standard precautions would be needed.

Mel: Meningitis is spread by respiratory droplets, nasal or oral secretions. I believe from my conversations with HPA [health protection agency] that it is not as easy as is commonly thought to pass on to others. One method is by kissing which would not be taking place (I hope!) between the patient and healthcare staff, or patient to other patients. Meningitis does not survive for a long period outside the body. Therefore with the above in mind, . . . perhaps this is not necessary.

Janette: I was reading in Chin this morning that meningococci are no longer a threat nasally or in nasopharyngeal secretions after 24 hours of antibiotics, and that is why he recommends isolation for 24 hours.

Pam: The HPA site has an article describing an outbreak of meningococcal disease among university students which I have found interesting and is useful comparison to this scenario; *Communicable Disease and Public Health*, Vol 2 No 3 September 1999. However going back to my original questions regarding isolation. The trust I work in follows a 48 hour rule of isolation including antibiotic treatment during this period. The contacts to follow up include household, kissing contacts and anyone who has stayed overnight in the same residence during the last seven days. Therefore I would feel that the patient being nursed in an open bay prior to 48 hrs of treatment could pose a potential risk to others. Immunosuppressed patients, visitors and staff could all be affected.

Gemma: . . . I agree with the other points made by Pam re – resus. but i dont think the open ward is a huge risk, it depends on what kind of patients are there and their immune status, it is however best practice to isolate.

Mel: I feel that there is perhaps an increased risk of others being susceptible within a hospital as patients are immunocompromized, and perhaps this is the reason we isolate, but I have a feeling that it is because it has a feel good factor to isolate. It is certainly something I will think about and look into, but also one of the symptoms of meningitis can be photophobia and therefore the patient may prefer a side room.

Gemma: I suppose a risk assessment should be made with regard to isolation, there is evidence to show that patients isolated for the purposes of infection control are less likely to receive care from staff (all grades) so the morbidity may increase. If this patient is very sick it may be unsafe to isolate

Pam: OK, I'll defend my position! I have found a reference which states that on admission to hospital all patients with known or suspected meningitis should be isolated in a single room, for at least 24 hours following the start of antibiotic therapy. Damani N (2003) I will continue to look for further evidence to support my previous statement of 48 hours. The HPA states that the meningococcal bacteria is not highly infectious and rarely develops into meningococcal disease.

However, if infection does occur it can spread rapidly and is fatal in about 10% of cases. Statistics demonstrate that 1 in 8 people who do recover can experience long term effects, including headaches, joint stiffness, epileptic fits, deafness and learning difficulties. As contact in residential accommodation, such as student halls of residence and schools can be places that allow the bacteria to spread, (HPA website) surely this indicates that there is also the potential for spread in an open ward. After all nurses have a duty of care to all patients under their care. (Ethics module kicking in. 'Do no harm!') As one of the symptoms is vomiting and the bacteria is found in the naso pharynx this must also be a potential risk. I suggest that the risk of mortality and the evidence of morbidity following this infection would be factors indicating that isolation is advisable! References Damani N (2003) *Manual of Infection Control Procedures*, Greenwich Medical Media London, HPA website Meningococcal disease. I'm not on my high horse just putting my thoughts down!

Mel: I would agree . . . that it seems sensible to isolate especially as although it may be relatively difficult to transmit, the consequences of having it transmitted to you can be enormous.

Module evaluation forms

That the students found the VLE of benefit was apparent from the module evaluation questionnaires. The following comments have been taken from the first module. Eleven students (66%) returned the questionnaire. Those comments selected are those that relate to benefits of group working. There were no adverse comments:

> I like to have contact and reassurance that what I am doing/thinking is along the right lines or completely off the wall. Blackboard has given me that communication.

> It was all so new to me, I mean looking at everything from an ICN's point of view. I felt I couldn't contribute much to the discussion but I did enjoy reading what everyone had to say. I feel more confident about using Blackboard now and I'm sure I will give my opinion more in the next module.

> Blackboard has been a great support throughout the last few modules. Being able to see other people's comments has helped me learn and sometimes look at things differently.

> Although I didn't often have much to say I've enjoyed reading the messages and have picked up on things that I hadn't thought of, or was just about to ask myself.

The results from the questionnaire are given in Table 9.1: 90% of students

Table 9.1 Results of questionnaire on use of Blackboard

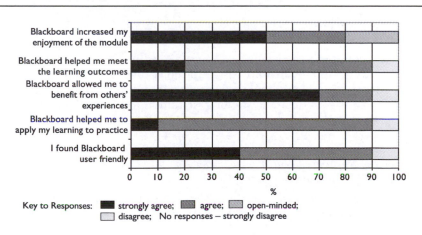

Key to Responses: ■ strongly agree; ▨ agree; ▥ open-minded; □ disagree; No responses – strongly disagree

agreed or strongly agreed that Blackboard had helped them to meet the learning outcomes, and to apply their learning to practice; 90% agreed/ strongly agreed that it allowed them to benefit from others' experiences.

From evaluation of the transcripts and the students' experience it was apparent that problem-based learning had been very successful in facilitating collaboration and social construction of knowledge. Indeed, it appeared that it had facilitated the development of a community of practice that is a 'group of people who share a concern, a set of problems, or a passion about a topic, and who deepen their knowledge and expertise by interacting on an ongoing basis' (Wenger, 2004: 1). Wenger (2004) proposes that in the real world we learn most in becoming part of and contributing to what a community is doing.

To determine whether an online community had developed, the discussion boards were examined using criteria developed by Palloff and Pratt (1999: 32) on the premise that the ability to collaborate and create knowledge and meaning communally is 'the hallmark of a constructivist classroom in which an active learning process is taking place'. The indications that an online community had been forming were:

- Active interaction involving both course content and personal communication.
- Collaborative learning evidenced by comments directed primarily student to student rather than student to tutor.
- Socially constructed meaning evidenced by agreement or questioning, with the intent to achieve agreement on issues of meaning.
- Sharing of resources among students.
- Expressions of support and encouragement exchanged between students, as well as a willingness to critically evaluate the work of others (Palloff and Pratt, 1999: 32).

All the criteria for community and a healthy, online, collaborative classroom were met in the problem-based learning scenarios, as illustrated in the following with messages from the scenario two discussion fora on scabies.

Active interaction involving both course content and personal communication

> *David*: I could share personal experience on this. As one of the many healthcare professionals who has acquired scabies I can tell you that I was among those who was misdiagnosed by my GP. I was prescribed prednisolone to reduce the swelling/irritation for more than a month until I gave scabies to someone else in my family who was then diagnosed by the very same GP!

Collaborative learning evidenced by comments directed primarily student to student rather than student to tutor

> *Sue*: I totally agree with you, the hydrocortisone cream would actually mask the problem while it established itself in the index patient and

once it had been stopped as a treatment, the resulting flare and itch would have been twice as bad for the patient ... I feel skin conditions of any sort are commonly misdiagnosed and inappropriate treatments prescribed especially by GPs unless they have a particular interest in skin!

Socially constructed meaning evidenced by agreement or questioning, with the intent to achieve agreement on issues of meaning

Sue: ... I believe the chance of transmission happening is so small, minute even it [isolation] is not worth mentioning and in fact only serves to augment the fear and stigma around having scabies and supports unenlightened healthcare workers rituals of using non-evidenced-based infection control practices like isolating patients with scabies. I base this comment on the fact that my understanding is the immature mite is so fragile when it reaches the surface of the skin if not being transmitted directly to another host it desiccates and dies within a couple of minutes.

I would agree that there is a slightly higher risk (but still small) in cases of crusted scabies due the larger number of mites and their being shed within a protective layer of skin cells.

Patsy: Wilson (2001) and Ayliffe *et al.* (2000) also agree that it is not easily transmitted from person to person and suggest isolation is only necessary for Norwegian scabies. When first diagnosed, will we always know which one it is? As isolation is recommended for only 24hrs after treatment, isn't it better to be safe than sorry?

Chin (2000) in the *Control of Communicable Diseases Manual* doesn't make any distinction and again suggests isolation.

Janet: If you mention even a suspicion of a scabies infestation, the 'victim' is almost invariably subjected to a period of involuntary isolation by carers and even relatives, due to a widespread belief that scabies is 'highly infectious'. This is often a knee-jerk reaction based on fear and misunderstanding. Surely it is the role of the CICN [community infection control nurse] to look at the evidence surrounding infectivity and transmission, and formulate reasoned and reasonable plans for treating and caring for sufferers, as well as educating about the parasite.

Sharing of resources among students

Linda: There is an interesting article in the nursing times supplement about scabies. There is a good picture of a female scabies burrowing in the skin! You might be able to access it at www.nursingtimes.net.

Expressions of support and encouragement exchanged between students, as well as a willingness to critically evaluate the work of others

Carrie: Thank you Alison for writing this up – it was a great help ... I also felt there was an educational issue for the staff involved who were contacts of the initial patient. Were they washing their hands after assisting her? . . . this i feel is a big educational issue for community staff as well as hospital staff.

Alison: Carrie, an important point that I certainly hadn't thought about thanks.

Discussion

That CMC has the potential to support virtual communities of inquiry and significantly enhance learning environments and outcomes as a result has been proposed (Garrison, 2002). Indeed it has been observed that 'community' and 'communicate' have the same root *communicare* which means 'to share' (Palloff and Pratt, 1999). What are the theoretical means by which this occurs, and what role might problem-based learning play in this process?

In a community of practice, learning is situated (Lave and Wenger, 1991), with understanding and knowledge being a product of the learning activity and learning situation, and embedded in that context (Miao, 2004). Lave and Wenger (1991) demonstrate that in many contexts learners initially learn from observing others but gradually gain knowledge and skill, along with the values and thought processes of more experienced practitioners – legitimate peripheral participation for enabling. In a community of practice the learner's identity is shaped by participating within the community, which models the role and language of a practitioner (Wenger, 1998). This is a form of cognitive apprenticeship (Brown *et al.*, 1989). More competent peers or the tutor can also provide scaffolding to enable learners to reach higher cognitive levels (Faggiano *et al.*, 2004) akin to Vygotsky's 'zone of proximal development'; the difference between independent problem-solving ability, and potential ability under guidance (Hung and Chen, 2001). Mentis *et al.* (2001) introduce the concept of a 'collective zone of proximal development' in online communities where there is both participation and mutual guidance between peers, resulting in group as well as individual learning. Community also produces, and is supported by, integration of learning with the workplace, and this is demonstrated by the analysis of CMC transcripts showing that the knowledge gained in discussions is applied and tested back in the workplace, developing the learner's own professional practice. The results of this are then taken back to the group and used in its collaborative activities, thus integrating work, theory and practice (McConnell, 2002a).

These themes have resonance with those recognised in effective problem-based learning. It has been observed that 'problem-based learning in its best moments is a form of cognitive apprenticeship' (Steinkuehler *et al.*, 2002: 32), providing modelling and scaffolding by the facilitator and peers (Savery and Duffy, 2001). After reviewing the literature, Hung (2002: 393) argued that 'problem-based learning is fundamentally congruent to situated cognition'. Macdonald and Isaacs (2001) noted some 'important links' between the theory of situated learning and problem-based learning. Putz and Arnold (2001) recognised presence at a university seminar as legitimate peripheral participation in a scientific community and Harland (2003: 263), from action research, proposed 'Vygotsky's zone of proximal development as a possible theoretical foundation for problem-based learning'. Furthermore, by using authentic tasks in problem-based learning, it is accepted that students are encultured into a community of practice (Chernobilsky *et al.*, 2004; Hung, 2002), developing professional language, knowledge and skills. This allows students to develop their identity as practitioners (Chernobilsky *et al.*, 2004; McConnell, 2002b; Mentis *et al.*, 2001).

Conclusion

The results demonstrated that students in professional practice, 'meeting' each other for the first time, can form a community of practice within a 12-week period, and that this community can enhance learning. High-level discussions were very evident. The indications that an online community was forming were simple to assess from the discussion board, which provided a very good framework for examining what was happening in terms of the social and collaborative aspects of being online. The students' module evaluations indicated that they found Blackboard enjoyable and helpful. Many benefits of bringing students together in a group that were identified in the literature were seen on reading the transcripts. These include the sharing and learning from each other's experiences and perspectives, the integration of learning with workplace issues, social support, reflection, debate and negotiation, knowledge construction and a final product that addressed more issues than any one individual in a single field of practice could have generated. Modelling the role and language of the practitioner was also evident. All these aspects of a community of practice are of benefit in meeting the learning outcomes of preparing nurses for specialist practice and congruent with the learning needs of the students. Problem-based learning provided an effective framework to achieve these outcomes. A suggestion why this might be is provided by Hung and Chen's (2001: 8)) 'communities of practice' model. This identifies four 'principles of situated cognition and Vygotskian thought' which contribute to a 'vibrant and sustaining' online community: situatedness, commonality, interdependency and infrastructure. From these, Hung and Chen provide design principles for good e-learning as shown in Table 9.2.

This experience demonstrated that problem-based learning can be designed and used to enable these principles and thus act as a framework for guided social participation towards a community of practice. It has been proposed that when problem-based learning is used online the approaches of problem-based learning and computer-supported collaborative learning merge (Zumbach *et al.*, 2004). The findings of this study could be viewed as proposing that they are actually synergistic.

In summary, as demonstrated by this module, it has been observed that online learning enables the development of collaborative learning

Table 9.2 Design considerations for e-learning

Situatedness	• Learning is embedded in rich cultural and social contexts, acquiring both implicit and explicit knowledge • Learning is reflective and metacognitive, internalising from social to the individual
Commonality	• Learning is an identity formation or act of membership • Learning is a social act/construction mediated between social beings through language, signs, genres and tools
Interdependency	• Learning is socially distributed between persons and tools • Learning is demand driven – dependent on engagement in practice
Infrastructure	• Learning is facilitated by an activity – driven by appropriate mechanisms and accountability structures

Source: Hung and Chen, 2001.

environments in which students can increase their knowledge and skills, and develop their identities as practitioners within a professional community (Mentis *et al.*, 2001). Online problem-based learning is congruent with the pedagogical underpinnings of situated learning and the effective use of computer-mediated conferencing and provides an effective framework to guide social participation in the development of a community of practice. Its use can therefore be recommended in facilitating the development of professional expertise at a distance.

Appendix 9.1

Problem-based learning – triggers

Unit 3 Etivity; ectoparasites

Purpose
This activity is an alternative to sending your answers to your tutor for feedback.

Preparation
As preparation, it is assumed that you have already completed activity 3.4 – reading the trigger, identifying the issues and your learning questions.

What to do
Your task now is to ask one of your learning questions to the group, to see if anyone else can answer it. If you know the answer to another person's question, then please make a contribution.

Telephone message

Caller: Mrs H Smith (Social worker)

Phone no: 01592 268888

Date/time: *Monday, 3pm*

Message: There are three home carers in her department who are complaining of an itchy rash that started two or three days ago. One of them is the regular carer for a client who has recently started prednisolone for an allergic skin condition. The other carers have attended the same client in the last couple of weeks or so when the regular carer has been on days off. She wonders if there is something spreading. Please contact her as soon as possible.

Unit 4 Etivity; meningitis
Here is the scenario or learning trigger.

David and his girlfriend Julia have returned from university. It has been a busy week – exams, parties and then back home where they are about to become godparents to Julia's sister's first baby. David and Julia are very sociable – David sings in the university choir and Julia plays in the women's rugby team.

David was feeling 'off colour' but assumes it is the result of too much partying. During the day, his condition deteriorates and by late evening he has a severe headache, photophobia and muscle pain. Julia attempts to get him to the car to take him to accident and emergency, but eventually has to call an ambulance. In A&E, David is given a provisional diagnosis of '? Meningitis'. He is given IV benzylpenicillin and is admitted to an open Nightingale-style ward. Unfortunately, his condition deteriorates further and a resuscitation call is put out in the middle of the night. He is successfully resuscitated, intubated and transferred to ICU. By this time a purpuric rash is spreading rapidly on his limbs.

The hospital infection control nurse is called by a porter who claims that during David's original transfer from A&E to the ward he had to assist in restraining him and he now wishes to be treated with prophylactic antibiotics.

Julia, on visiting the next day, says she has been contacted by friends from university to say that one of the girls in her rugby team has also been diagnosed with meningitis.

Part 4

Developing technology

Part 4 focuses on the ways in which technology has been developed to support and enhance the pedagogy and the practice of problem-based learning. What the authors of Part 4 point out, although not always specifically, is that PBLonline largely prevents students from being subject to online instruction and the economic application of decontextualised learning objects. In PBLonline students are expected to engage with constructivist approaches to learning, thus the notion of reuse as an economic possibility that will ensure students all learn the same input at the same time and in the same way is not a possibility; it is merely an impoverished picture of learning – whether online or face to face. Instead what is evident in the chapters here is the development of tools and media that not only support the pedagogy of problem-based learning but have been designed with both this pedagogy and student-centred learning at the forefront of the developments.

In terms of design and creativity it is clear from these studies that sound online discourse requires effective and creative design of online environments. A framework that would appear to be helpful to such design would be a learning framework proposed by Ravenscroft (2005), which, to paraphrase, is:

- based on relevant theory, in particular a blend of pedagogical approaches that will addresses particular learning problems
- holistic and integrated, so that dialogic process and cognitive change are linked as well as being located in an appropriate cultural context and community
- able to reconcile behavioural and motivational approaches with social constructivist approaches, because online dialogue needs to be fostered and stimulated in ways face-to-face dialogue does not. Ravenscroft suggests it is important to adopt behavioural notions of affordances so that we acknowledge the importance of inviting people in and encouraging them to participate.

Although such a framework has not been adopted in this particular way by the authors of Part 4 there is the sense that design and pedagogy have largely gone hand in hand.

In Chapter 10, te Winkel *et al.* describe how an evaluation of problem-based learning curricula indicated that, due to a continuously growing number of students at Erasmus University Rotterdam (EUR), students reported a decreasing number of opportunities to meet and discuss their learning issues, and also an increasing distance between students and tutors. As a result of this the psychology department at EUR began developing a number of tools to address this. In particular, an asynchronous communication tool was developed that could extend discussions with tutors and student peers and provide a shared work environment. After developing and considering other tools they realised that many of these did not build on the cognitive constructivist approach to education that was felt to be central to problem-based learning. The form of problem-based learning adopted at EUR is predominantly a collaborative form of learning designed so that students are able to both acquire and organise subject matter. In short, it is 'cognitive constructivism' or more specifically, 'information-processing constructivism', whereby knowledge construction processes are organised around problem situations that challenge students' reasoning and help them to contextualise and organise the information that needs to be learned. What the authors illustrate here is that there have been, and continue to be, a number of tools that have been developed to support and enhance problem-based learning curricula, yet few of them support a cognitive constructivistic approach to education. In Chapter 10, te Winkel *et al.* demonstrate that PsyWeb, a learning content management system which has been designed to mirror key principles of problem-based learning, such as self-direction and elaboration, aims to extend students' possibilities for individual knowledge construction during self-study.

In Chapter 11, Ronteltap documents how the tool POLARIS, which was originally a forerunner of PsyWeb, was designed as a means of empowering student learning in problem-based learning through the use of network technology. POLARIS was developed as a new tool for group communication which was initially based on the pedagogical principles of self-directed learning and situated learning. The communication tool looks like a threaded discussion board but it supports creative work and continuous improvement of ideas by writing, sharing, discussing, comparing, integrating, reorganising and restructuring of information. An interesting aspect of this study is that the researchers sought to understand the role of the tool in the learning process and adapted it to meet the needs of tutors and students utilising problem-based learning. Of particular interest is the recognition of the complexities involved in group discussion, even when it is asynchronous and thus specific features and functionality were designed to accommodate this. However, in the final version of the tool discussed here, Ronteltap documents the most recent version of POLARIS which contains two components: a group environment *Knowledge Builder* in which information is exchanged and participants then feed information back to one another, and the personal environment *Knowledge Manager*, in which the products of the collaboration can be manipulated and stored for later access.

In the final chapter, Beaumont and Swee Cheng analyse the use of communication tools for collaboration in PBLonline. The motivation for study emerged from an interest in the use of communication tools such as SMS text, webcams, ISDN videoconferencing and the integration of some of these into virtual learning environments (VLE). The authors' motivation for this study was to investigate how such tools could best be used in problem-based learning, and if particular tools had specific advantages for the different purposes needed for problem-based learning. The development of a purpose-built student-centred learning portal for the School of Information Technology (INT-SCL Portal) being launched at Temasek Polytechnic, Singapore, afforded an opportunity to examine the extent to which instruments and materials in the portal could be used in problem-based learning programmes. The development of resources, material and technology along with an interest in the pedagogy of problem-based learning prompted the decision for this exploration. In many ways, this chapter exemplifies the issues raised by Ravenscoft about designing a learning framework that both supports and is supported by problem-based learning. The authors found that the range of tools facilitated students' learning but there were also findings that seem to be common to other studies, namely that students regarded synchronous discussion as essential for decision making and clarifying issues of understanding.

Across this volume it is interesting to note the emerging importance of synchronous discussion to problem-based learning, the increasing importance of and attention to ensuring cohesive connections are made between the type of problem-based learning adopted and the forms of technology and collaboration tools being used. This final chapter also points up the need to hear the perspectives of the students more clearly. While the authors here have evaluated and taken account of the students there does seem to be a virtual void in terms of what it is students are doing, what their perception of PBLonline is and whether, in fact, they believe it contains or uncontains their learning in ways that are enabling.

10

Digital support for a constructivist approach to education: the case of a problem-based psychology curriculum

Wilco te Winkel, Remy Rikers and Henk Schmidt

Introduction

The rise of the world wide web has created high expectations in terms of its potential to renew education. The ability to store and deliver high-quality content, in addition to the possibilities of supporting communication and collaboration, has inspired educationalists to upgrade their educational approaches or even to develop entirely new ones (Mioduser and Nachmias, 2002). Many of these educational approaches support students in taking on an active role in constructing personally meaningful knowledge, often in collaboration with peers.

Unfortunately, the domain of web-based teaching and learning has scarcely benefited from the large body of prior research that might help advance educational practice (Hannafin and Kim, 2003). Mioduser *et al.* (2000) analysed 436 educational websites and reached a disappointing conclusion. Many educators, they discovered, favoured pedagogical approaches requiring students' active involvement and interaction with peers and experts, essentially a constructivistic approach. Yet, they actually implemented educational websites that removed learner control from the students and reduced learning to information retrieval. Mioduser *et al.* summarised their findings as 'one step ahead for technology, two steps back for pedagogy' (Mioduser *et al.*, 2000: 73). Much of the current educational practice tacitly assumes either that prior research does not exist or that it is of little relevance. Consequently little is known about what works, for whom, how or when (Hannafin and Kim, 2003).

With these considerations in mind, the psychology department at the Erasmus University Rotterdam (EUR) developed PsyWeb. PsyWeb builds on research findings in educational psychology, cognitive psychology, and instructional design, and is specifically aimed at supporting student learning activities during self-study. PsyWeb is a learning content management system that manages all curricular content. Its development was inspired by Hannafin's description of open learning environments (Hannafin *et al.*,

1999) and was based on the principled approach to the innovation of education described by Koschmann *et al.* (1996). Prior to actually innovating educational practice, Koschmann *et al.* recommend:

1 explicating the learning model, together with its underlying instructional goals, of a specific educational organisation
2 analysing educational practice to determine whether it meets the theoretical learning model
3 specifying requirements to improve educational practice based on the outcomes of this analysis within the boundaries of the learning model.

This approach reduces the chances that instructional needs are met with solutions that are technology driven or that solutions are offered without any instructional need at all.

Problem-based learning and its underlying principles

Problem-based learning, as implemented at the EUR, is primarily used as a collaborative form of learning aimed at acquiring and organising subject matter. It is sometimes also referred to as 'cognitive constructivism' or, more specifically, 'information-processing constructivism' (Derry, 1996; Marshall, 1996; Mayer, 1996; Savery and Duffy, 1995; Schmidt and Moust, 2000). Although it was acknowledged that ample time should be made available for the training of important skills, knowledge was put forward as the most important outcome of this curriculum (Van Berkel *et al.*, 1995). Each aspect of this learning process had its specific role in supporting students' learning and applying domain-relevant information. The knowledge construction process was organised around authentic problems. These were expected to challenge students' reasoning and serve as triggers for discussion, and help to contextualise and organise the information that needed to be learned (Barrows, 1985; Schmidt, 1993). The initial group discussion helped to activate and mobilise relevant prior knowledge to meet the demands of the new problem, reducing chances that students treated new information as isolated pieces of knowledge (De Grave *et al.*, 2001; Hamilton, 1989; Norman and Schmidt, 1992; Schmidt, 1993; Schmidt *et al.*, 1989). During self-study, students were offered the opportunity to take control of their own learning. Even though the acquisition of subject matter knowledge was of particular importance, texts in which all necessary literature was combined were not given. Rather, students were encouraged to look for relevant resources themselves. This enhanced student control was expected to increase the quality of study behaviour (Van Berkel *et al.*, 1995) and promote divergent thinking, problem solving and critical thinking (Hannafin and Land, 1997). It was also expected to result in more active and autonomous students (Arts *et al.*, 2002). During the second meeting (the reporting phase) students elaborated on the information they found, and integrated their information with information found by their fellow students (Schmidt, 1993).

At the end of every course, students undertook a course test. This test served to inform students how well they had understood the contents of the course. However, to avoid students studying for the test, often postponing their studying efforts until a few days before the exam and memorising small details and facts, their test mark did not contribute to their study credits since the test was formative. Instead, students attained study credits through their success on the progress test. This test was a longitudinal examination that sampled knowledge across all disciplines and content areas that were considered relevant for a psychology degree. Students passed the examination when their individual knowledge growth was consistent with that of their year group. Through its repetitive and longitudinal setup, the progress test encouraged students to spread their study efforts more evenly over the year. Also, rather than assessing specific knowledge over the short term, the progress test aimed at assessing broad and long-term retention of knowledge, thereby allowing students more freedom to determine the contents of their study (Van Berkel *et al.*, 1995; Van Der Vleuten *et al.*, 1996).

Analysis of the educational practice

Despite the many theoretical opportunities for students to learn and apply their knowledge successfully, educational practice tends to reduce some of them. One of the problems is the so-called 'polling problem', that is, the phenomenon that the opinion of a student changes depending on the moment his or her opinion is asked (Koschmann *et al.*, 1996). Contributions of students later in group discussion may be suppressed or contaminated by the opinions of students who contributed earlier, thereby reducing the richness of viewpoints that are expressed and the possibilities for tutors and students to become aware of any misconceptions or omissions. The polling problem is considered to be a weakness that is inherent in any teaching method that depends on group interactions. A further practical problem is the time constraint on the reporting phase (Ronteltap and Eurelings, 2002). During this phase, only a limited amount of time is available for a group of 10 students to report and integrate all of the information they discovered during hours of individual self-study. Only a few students get the opportunity to speak about their work and only a small amount of time remains available for feedback on their learning process. A solution that might solve these problems could be a digital tool that allows students to work individually on a problem without the traditional restrictions of time and place. The specifications of this tool should be consistent with the specific pedagogical approach it aims to support (Koschmann *et al.*, 1996). It should therefore organise the learning processes around problems, support elaboration of knowledge, facilitate the construction of new knowledge, empower students to make personal choices about what to study and emphasise long-term retention of already acquired knowledge.

Previous enhancements of problem-based learning with technology

Over the past decade a number of electronic tools have been developed to support and enhance problem-based learning curricula. In the following section a number of these tools are described together with some considerations about their applicability within a cognitive constructivistic approach to education.

The Collaborative Learning Laboratory

The Collaborative Learning Laboratory (CLL) is a special physical facility, built to enhance regular problem-based learning meetings (Koschmann *et al.*, 1996). Guided by their principled approach (see also Chapters 11 and 12), Koschmann *et al.* evaluated the educational practice at their institute to conclude that there was an explicit need to enhance the physical group discussions. To improve educational practice, students should have access to authentic videocases, an unlimited amount of resources and a tool that would enable them to share their resources and notes freely with their peers in addition to keeping a retrievable record of their group's deliberations. Students should also be offered more individual guidance to improve the chance of locating misconceptions and stimulating the diversity of opinions in their group. In the CLL, every student has access to a personal computer that is connected to a local area network. Through the network, students can access selected videocases of real patients and learning resources in their library as well as on the internet. Students can also view the contents of their screen on a projection system that is visible to all other group members. The projection screen also serves as a whiteboard onto which all students can post their individual notes and which can be accessed and modified by all other group members. The group's deliberations can be accessed within and outside the face-to-face meetings. To facilitate the assessment of students' understanding, and to encourage them to express their personal opinions uncontaminated by the opinion of others, tutors can ask open-ended questions and ask students to respond individually. Even though the CLL is fully in accordance with the principles underlying a cognitive constructivistic curriculum and could actually enrich educational practice, the CLL does not meet all the requirements. It is largely limited to the support of group meetings in a dedicated room at a particular time. An analysis of educational practice at the EUR indicated that a solution was desired that would allow students to work individually on a problem, irrespective of time or place considerations.

POLARIS

Starting from the same principled approach as Koschmann *et al.* (1996), Ronteltap and Eurelings (2002) evaluated several educational practices at Maastricht University. Despite the similarities between their curricula and the educational programmes described by Koschmann (Koschmann *et al.*, 1996), Ronteltap and Eurelings found a different set of problems. A continuously increasing number of students starting their studies at this university year on year led to students reporting a decreasing number of opportunities to meet and discuss their learning issues and an increasing distance between students and tutors. Based on these findings, Ronteltap and Eurelings (2002) built POLARIS (problem-oriented learning and retrieval information system) to offer students an asynchronous communication tool that could extend discussions with tutors and peer students and a shared work environment to submit written reports related to their learning issues. Despite its added value, POLARIS falls short of supporting a cognitive constructivistic approach to education. In these curricula, collaboration is mostly limited to the physical meetings and acquisition and organisation of primary subject matter are put forward as the most important goals. Since POLARIS has no means of organising or delivering primary content or of supporting students in making their personal studying choices, it cannot meet these requirements.

eSTEP

eSTEP (secondary teacher education project) is a web-based course consisting of a Knowledge Web and a problem-based learning support system (Derry, 2005). The Knowledge Web is an online resource library, consisting of a 'hypertextbook' with numerous theories on learning sciences and multiple videocases depicting stories of actual teaching situations. The design of the Knowledge Web is explicitly based on the belief that the ill structuredness of conceptual knowledge in professional practice should be reflected in the organisation of the resources. Tutors are therefore encouraged to change their educational programme to stimulate students to explore the conceptual landscape reflectively, study multiple cases that illustrate instantiations of a single theory and view individual cases through multiple conceptual lenses. The problem-based learning support system can be set up in different ways, but it typically supports a phase of individual study and preparation, a phase of small group design work and a phase of individual reflection. These phases break down into a larger number of steps that students need to pass successively. Despite eSTEP's merits, its adoption would necessitate a number of serious changes in the educational approach described in this chapter.

Central to the design of eSTEP is its claim about the organisation of resources and the way in which students need to learn. All problems and content should be changed to emphasise the complex interactions among central concepts and to combine multiple course ideas in multiple problems. Although it is acknowledged that students should learn about important concepts in a cognitively flexible way (Spiro *et al.*, 1995), it is still an issue of debate whether a hypertext-based approach to learning is the best instructional format (Dillon and Gabbard, 1998; Tergan, 1997). Another important design decision of eSTEP is its organisation of the self-study phase. Whereas students should be encouraged to take increasingly more owner-ship, eSTEP explicitly reduces these opportunities by organising the self-study phase into a number of small steps that need to be satisfied one after the other. Finally, eSTEP requires students to create a group product collaboratively during their self-study. This might not always be from a peda-gogical perspective. At a practical level, an educational organisation should include much more human support for the evaluation of all these products, something Derry admits is a drawback of this web course (Derry, 2002).

Creative open cooperative distributed learning environment

CROCODILE (CReative Open COoperative DIstributed Learning Environ-ment) is a virtual environment to support distributed problem-based learn-ing (Miao, 2000). The core module of this virtual problem-based learning environment is designed as a virtual institute. Students can navigate from one place to another to find specific tools and actors at different places. CROCODILE also includes three problem-based learning modules: PBL-net, PBL-protocol and PBL-plan. PBL-net guides the collaborative problem learning process by enabling students to explore, negotiate and elucidate their shared knowledge. PBL-protocol represents how learners, tutors and experts are expected to behave during the learning process. An initiated PBL-protocol can force learners and tutors to behave appropriately by restricting which behaviours are allowed. Finally, PBL-plan enables students to define collaboratively their own learning plan by specifying actions and relations between these actions. Even though CROCODILE might provide a good solution in a context where students work collaboratively without any possibility of physically meeting each other, it is difficult to see how this tool might integrate with a cognitive constructivist curriculum. CROCODILE introduces metaphors (for example, the virtual institute, its tools and its actors) and possibilities to organise the learning process (for example, PBL-protocol or PBL-plan) that might be suitable for a distributed learning approach, but that would cause some serious changes in the principles and practice of the currently described educational approach. It is also difficult to see how this solution could support the individual knowledge construc-tion process, since every individual student depends on his peer students to co-determine the course of the self-study phase.

Other support systems like McBAGEL (Guzdial *et al.*, 1996), CaMILE

(Hmelo *et al.*, 1995), Web-SMILE (Guzdial *et al.*, 1997), CALE (Mahling, 1995) and CoMMIT (Lautenbacher *et al.*, 1997) are all worth mentioning here as well. These systems were specifically developed to support the collaborative learning aspects of problem-based learning and were aimed at enabling groups of students to work together to solve problems. These tools often consist of an asynchronous discussion board and a shared whiteboard to keep everyone on track at times when the group is not physically together. However, as with POLARIS, the curriculum described here emphasises the cognitive constructivistic approach to education, rather than the social constructivist approach. Even though these tools might provide for a valuable extension of ICT support, they do not meet the main curricular instructional needs of our curriculum.

Specifications of PsyWeb; a tool to support individual knowledge construction

PsyWeb is a learning content management system that aims to extend students' opportunities for individual knowledge construction during self-study. The system manages thousands of learning resources from the entire 4-year psychology curriculum. Rather than treating all resources alike, 10 different categories of learning resources are identified: articles, book chapters, lectures, problems, videos, internet sites, e-chapters, electronic presentations, animations and interactive experiments. Integrated into the system is a set of instructional techniques to assist and enhance student learning activities. These techniques will be described in detail within the context of the problem-based learning model.

Problems as context

As has been outlined in previous chapters, problems are an important aspect of problem-based learning. They provide a meaningful context and have a strong organising effect on newly acquired information. This context, including students' goals for learning and the adopted group perspective, affects students' ability to retrieve and apply the knowledge subsequently (Brown *et al.*, 1989; Koschmann *et al.*, 1996). Therefore all problems used in the curriculum reoccurred electronically in PsyWeb. Integrated in the presentation of every problem was also an extra bar holding relevant study suggestions (see Figure 10.1) that enabled students to use the problems as their anchor around which they could explore all suggested learning materials (CGTV, 1993; Savery and Duffy, 1995).

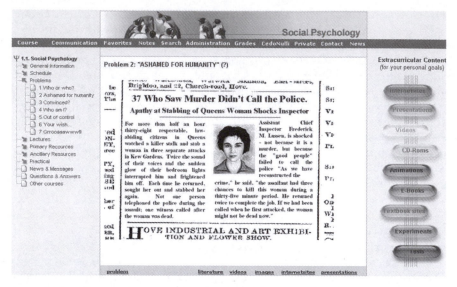

Figure 10.1   The problem ' "ASHAMED FOR HUMANITY"(?)' together with its suggested resources

Elaboration in problem-based learning

A second important aspect of problem-based learning is its emphasis on elaboration during the learning process. In the first and second group meeting as well as during their self-study, students learnt about new concepts by continuously revisiting and elaborating on their prior knowledge. When students had to remember specific information, not all of it came to mind at once; they had to activate bits and pieces of the original information in an attempt to reconstruct the rest. In this reconstruction process, a single mental representation of a concept often proved to be insufficient to recall all the associated information, resulting in a partial or oversimplified reconstruction (Koschmann *et al.*, 1996). Elaboration can help this information reconstruction process. Elaboration can be defined as any enhancement of information that clarifies the relationship between new information and students' prior knowledge or experiences (Hamilton, 1989, 1997). A number of reasons have been offered as to why elaborations might improve the retention of information. They may increase the richness and distinctiveness with which information is stored and/or increase the organisation of already stored information. Multiple representations therefore help students understand and remember information better (Hannafin and Land, 1997; Spiro *et al.*, 1995). Added to the possibilities to elaborate verbally on important concepts, empirical evidence increasingly demonstrates the importance of addressing the different modalities (perception, action and emotion) (Barsalou *et al.*, 2003; Goldstone and Barsalou, 1998; Pecher *et al.*, 2004).

Rather than dissociating conception from perception, treating conceptual knowledge as abstract and modality free, the richness and diversity of information that is available in the naturalistic context should be retained to increase the overlap between the learning context and the context in which the knowledge is applied.

PsyWeb was developed to stimulate the elaboration process by using many, diverse electronic learning resources. These resources could support students not only in remembering the required information more successfully, but also in learning it more easily and applying it more appropriately (Clark and Paivio, 1991; Jacobson and Spiro, 1995; Koschmann *et al.*, 1996; Kozma, 1991; Spiro, 1995; Spiro *et al.*, 1995). Rather than arguing which specific type of learning resource enabled which kind of learning effect (Clark, 1994; Kozma, 1994), it was acknowledged that many of the categories of learning resources served the same learning effect, and that a single category could serve many learning effects (Jonassen *et al.*, 1994). It was left up to the individual student to choose one category over another, based on their individual learning style and specific task requirements (Ayersman and von Minden, 1995; Quealy and Langan-Fox, 1998). Students might choose animations, for example, to study concepts of change (Tversky *et al.*, 2002), videos to acquire a sense of authenticity and relevancy of the learned concepts (Koschmann *et al.*, 1996), experiments to experience the characteristics of a theoretical model (de Jong and van Joolingen, 1998), internet sites to collect multiple perspectives on the same theory or understand how a single theory might apply to different situations (Spiro *et al.*, 1995) and electronic presentations to gain a quick bird's eye overview of a theory or domain. PsyWeb was optimised to offer all these different learning materials to encourage students to continue elaborating on their knowledge and improving the quality of their understanding (Anderson, 1990).

Learner motivation

Another important aspect of problem-based learning is the way in which students are motivated to learn. During the initial discussion, the self-study and the reporting phase students were encouraged to compare, evaluate and integrate information found by themselves or others and to generate explanations for the problems at hand. Learning was perceived as an active, constructive process requiring commitment and cognitive effort on the part of the learner (Marshall, 1996; Savery and Duffy, 1995). Rather than pouring in abstract knowledge that, in principle, could be understood by anyone, students' prior knowledge was considered to play a key role in determining which information was understood and what was remembered. However, possessing the required prior knowledge was an essential, but not a sufficient prerequisite. The instructional context should also explicitly address and activate this, often latently, available prior knowledge before students were able to make adequate use of it (Norman and Schmidt, 1992). By allowing students to construct products individually, they were encouraged to activate their prior knowledge and articulate their current understanding. These learning products could consequently enable students to discover possible inconsistencies or omissions in their reasoning, discuss their ideas and negotiate their understanding with student peers and serve as reminders of earlier learning activities (Hannafin and Land, 1997; Savery and Duffy, 1995). PsyWeb aimed to facilitate this knowledge construction process by a personal favourites folder and a note-taking system. The personal favourites folder enabled students to collect and organise all favourite, or important, learning resources in a single place. Within this folder, students could create, name and delete as many subfolders as they wanted, permitting them to build and organise their own mini-curriculum (see Figure 10.2). Students could move, name and delete any of the learning resources, offering them the possibility to revisit, review and integrate learning materials according to their understanding and goals (Lawless and Kulikowich, 1995). It has often been suggested that this process of organising, reorganising and discovering new relations between the different learning resources can substantially enhance comprehension (Lawless and Brown, 1997; Scardamalia *et al.*, 1989; Wittrock, 1990).

Additionally, students could attach personal notes to all available learning resources. Students were encouraged to review and reuse their private notes, because a copy of every note was made and placed in students' personal notes folder. They could organise their notes in ways similar to their 'personal favourites', so that they were able to change or delete notes made earlier, combine existing notes into new ones, or add new notes starting

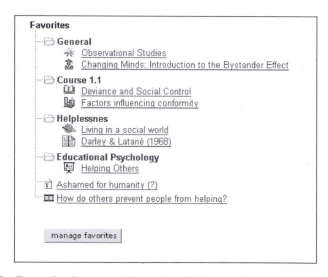

Figure 10.2   Example of a personal favourites folder, in which students can collect and organise all personally relevant learning resources

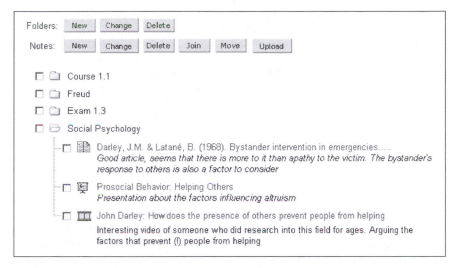

Figure 10.3   Example of a personal note-taking system

entirely from scratch. Students could also share their notes with selected peer students (see Figure 10.3).

To stimulate students to start and sustain attaching notes to all learning resources, this learning activity was explicitly suggested at the top of every listing of learning materials. The hints were different depending on the chosen learning material but they all aimed to encourage students to integrate (parts of) the learning resources into their personal notes. For example, a listing of electronic presentations always starts with: 'Electronic presentations may prove helpful in acquiring an overview of the domain or in constructing a summary. Therefore download the presentations you like best and integrate them in your personal notes.' An extra option was built in to the personal notes folder to enable students to upload and integrate these multimedia notes with their text-based notes.

Student control

The fourth, and final, important aspect of problem-based learning is its emphasis on the students' role during learning. Rather than telling students what to study, when and in what order, they are stimulated to find relevant resources themselves and decide on their own initiative how extensively they should study them. When students have little control over what is taught, they will attempt to accumulate the knowledge they think their tutors will include in the next exam (Van Berkel *et al.*, 1995) and tend to assume less responsibility for their learning (Hannafin and Land, 1997). Many positive outcomes are expected to result from encouraging students to take control over their learning (Arts *et al.*, 2002; Hannafin and Land, 1997; Reigeluth and Stein, 1983; Van Berkel *et al.*, 1995). However, research into students' use of electronic learning environments shows somewhat contradictory findings on this issue. Whereas many studies find positive outcomes of control opportunities for students with much relevant prior knowledge and/or ability, less positive or even negative outcomes are found for students with little prior knowledge and/or metacognitive skills (Dillon and Gabbard, 1998; Kinzie, 1990; Lawless and Kulikowich, 1995, 1996; Shin *et al.*, 1994; Shyu and Brown, 1992, 1995). The last category of students, in particular, seem to experience difficulties in identifying the information that will enhance their understanding, selecting and accessing this information and/or monitoring how far they have progressed in achieving their goals. They also seem more easily seduced by the bells and whistles of an electronic learning environment and consequently allocate a disproportionate amount of time and attention to these special features.

Based on a review of the literature, Lawless and Brown (1997) were able to identify at least three different types of learner. In addition to their so-called 'knowledge seekers' (learners who search for materials needed to enhance comprehension of a specific domain), they also identified 'resource junkies' (learners who spent a disproportionate amount of time interacting with the special effects afforded by computer-based documents), and 'apathetic users' (learners who seem to be unmotivated to engage in any elaborate or meaningful explorations). So, even though more student control seems desirable in general, extra care has to be taken in electronic learning environments to ensure that all learners benefit from its potential. Four different techniques were therefore implemented in PsyWeb to deliver learning content to the students. These techniques offered students successively higher levels of control over their learning process, but they were most often used simultaneously and were complementary to each other.

Techniques in PsyWeb

The first technique was the most tutor-directed technique. Tutors could make selections from all learning materials and present these selections as study suggestions to their students. These lists were often too extensive for individual students to be able to study all the material contained in them. Students therefore had to select those learning resources they thought would be most helpful in meeting their learning goals. Additionally tutors could mark each list as 'primary' or 'ancillary'. Students were advised to restrict themselves to the lists of primary study suggestions when they had only a limited amount of time available. This technique was often used during introductory courses when students still had to familiarise themselves with a particular domain.

The second information delivery technique allowed students to browse through all curricular contents. Depending on the theme of a course, all available learning resources were presented in each category. These listings also included all learning resources that had already been studied on past courses, to remind students of the applicability of already acquired knowledge and to encourage transfer of knowledge over courses (Scardamalia *et al.*, 1989). When this technique was used to complement tutors' lists of study suggestions, PsyWeb presented all learning resources that were not selected by the tutor but that fitted within the theme of the course. These resources were clearly marked as 'extracurricular content', and students were informed that they were for personal learning goals only. While tutors' selections were presented at the left-hand side of the screen, the extracurricular selection was presented at the right-hand side to enable students to stay focused on the selected course while browsing through the extracurricular content (see Figure 10.1).

The third technique used a dedicated search engine to allow students to search through all resources. Whereas browsing enabled students to discover relevant resources without the need of a clear goal definition, students had to rely on the learning environment to guide them during their information search. Searching, however, allowed students to take full control over their learning by allowing them to formulate their own questions (Marchionini, 1995). The search engine was specifically developed to allow students to search bibliographically as well as conceptually. It deliberately searched for learning resources at a curricular level to increase the chances that students stumbled over learning resources they had already studied. In this way, students were reminded of already studied materials and possibly encouraged to review the same materials adopting a new perspective (Koschmann *et al.*, 1996; Spiro *et al.*, 1995). By selecting the appropriate filters, students could be supported in finding the relevant information.

The fourth and final information delivery technique was the most student-centred one. In PsyWeb students were able to upload their personal learning materials and suggestions to the list of study suggestions. These learning materials were treated identically to the selection made by the tutors, the only difference being that students' suggestions were presented under the header 'Student selection'. Students were expected to process information at a deeper level and take more ownership over their learning when they were able to generate and contribute learning materials themselves (Lawless and Brown, 1997; Scardamalia *et al.*, 1989). To ensure relevance and high quality of all suggestions, student peers could rate and review all learning materials (see Figure 10.4).

Conclusion: critical reflections and future research directions

In this chapter, a principled approach to the innovation of education is reported. Based on a reflection of the learning model underlying the problem-based learning programme and an analysis of how well educational

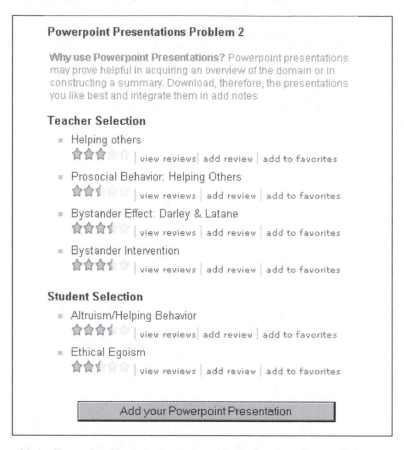

Figure 10.4   Example of how students can add a rating, a review or their own learning materials

practice meets this theoretical model, requirements were formulated for a tool that is currently being implemented to improve educational practice. At present, however, there is only anecdotal evidence that the implemented tool changes educational practice for the better. Little is objectively known about students' acceptance, appreciation or actual use of PsyWeb. Neither is there a crystallised idea about how the tool affects students' studying behaviour. Future research will combine an evaluative and an experimental approach to meet these shortcomings. A survey will be used to gain a clearer picture of students' acceptance, appreciation and use of PsyWeb. This survey is already integrated in the educational programme as part of its quality management system and will be extended with several evaluative questions that specifically address the use of PsyWeb.

An experimental approach will be used to understand the added value of the different components of PsyWeb. Over the past few years much experience has been gained in students' use of the elaborative component of PsyWeb, but little is known about the knowledge construction component. Prior to implementing this component, students will be asked a series of questions about their current study behaviour. After students have undertaken this component these same questions will be asked again, to check whether the completion of this component resulted in any differences in study behaviour. A different type of experimental approach will be used to find out how much student control is desirable. Given the various findings regarding the effects of learner control, more research is needed to determine how much navigational freedom would be beneficial for which group of learners at which time. Of particular interest here is the design and implementation of the search engine. Whereas information seeking is considered to be a vital aspect of problem-based learning, little research has been reported about its implementation in an existing curriculum. Many information-seeking models approach students as experts, who are completely aware of what they are looking for and who can recognise the correct answer amidst of dozens of others. However, there is reason to believe that students who have just started studying a certain domain could better be viewed as novices, who have a general idea about what they are looking for, but still largely depend on the results of their search queries to further refine their search question. The information-seeking model should therefore be recursive in nature, with components later on in this process informing earlier components (Marchionini, 1995). There are also numerous possibilities to support this information-seeking process including conceptual, metacognitive, procedural and strategic scaffolding techniques (Hannafin *et al.*, 1999). Further research is needed to determine what kind of support should be given to which group of learners at any given stage in their learning process.

11

Tools to empower problem-based learning: a principled and empirical approach to the design of problem-based learning online

Frans Ronteltap

Introduction

Although there is increasing use of technology and problem-based learning, questions need to be asked about the role of technology and its impact on problem-based pedagogies. Koschmann *et al.* (1996) introduced the principled approach in analysing the role that technology might have in innovations of problem-based learning. Principles such as interdisciplinarity, self-directed learning and ownership can be used as a framework in the prevention of unwanted consequences of a technology push. Requirements of possible applications and user scenarios are the result of an analysis of the possible gap between principles and daily practice. This is a top-down approach. Innovations in problem-based learning are also possible in a bottom-up approach. Goodyear (2001) made a distinction in the design of networked learning between a pedagogical framework and an educational setting. Interventions in the educational setting, in this case the use of learning technologies, may lead to adaptations of the pedagogical framework and its theoretical foundations.

A design-oriented project (POLARIS: problem-oriented learning and retrieval information system) at the Learning Lab at the University of Maastricht (UM) combined both approaches, starting with the top-down principled approach. After an extensive survey of problem-based learning-in-practice, from the perspective of using technology to overcome barriers in the realisation of specific pedagogical principles, a collaborative learning environment was developed and tested. This first step of the project has resulted in some revisions. User data in educational settings were accumulated for revisions of the tool and thinking about the role of these tools in problem-based learning.

In this iterative process of tool design, development and user tests we came to the conclusion that our vision of problem-based learning was enriched. At the start of the project our vision of problem-based learning was predominantly inspired by pedagogical features, such as self-directed learning and situated learning (Clancey, 1995). The integration of communication technologies enabled us to extend communication facilities between learners, which in turn forced us to link our concept of problem-based learning with theoretical insights and perceptions of social dimensions of knowledge development. This chapter analyses problem-based learning as a dynamic middle-out concept, as a result of theoretical top-down and practical bottom-up input.

A middle-out strategy appeared to be successful in several domains where cross-disciplinary activities are undertaken, for example concept identification in artificial intelligence (López, 1999; Wan and Braspenning, 1995), modelling of biological processes in life sciences (Noble, 2003) and, in our domain, e-learning by development of rich educational scenarios (Schneider *et al.*, 2002). In our middle-out approach the results of design research (bottom up) were linked to top-down results of theoretical analyses and interpretations from the following directions: pedagogical principles of problem-based learning and epistemological considerations and meta-analyses of the consequences of technological developments for working with information and communication. Reeves (2000) suggests that when researchers have development goals they are focused on the dual objective of developing creative approaches to solving human teaching, learning and performance problems, while at the same time constructing a body of design principles that can guide future development efforts. We used this framework shown in Figure 11.1.

Context of the study

Problem-based learning is the main approach in all curricula at UM (medicine, health sciences, economics, law, psychology, cultural sciences, knowledge technology). Although educational practice varies every day, a few basic elements are present in all curricula. Twice a week students meet in small groups (10 to 12 people), coached by a tutor. A characteristic feature of problem-based learning is that students start their learning process with the analysis of a problem. The results of that analysis are expressed in terms of learning issues about which students gather specific information in the context of that problem. Thus, problem-based learning has a reverse relationship between theory and practice as pursued in traditional teaching methods. In traditional teaching methods, students are asked to apply academic knowledge to practice. In problem-based learning however, the study

Figure 11.1   Steps in design research

of information in the context of problem scenarios is concluded with an attempt to solve or manage the problem in question. This approach marks the learning process as doing research. In order to structure this process, students at UM work in the following way when they analyse a problem task in a group meeting:

1 clarification of terms
2 definition of problem(s)
3 analysis of problem (brainstorming)
4 structuring ideas that came up in brainstorming
5 formulate learning issues for the next step
6 collect new information outside tutorial group
7 report and synthesis of information.

In this context the impact of the internet boom, and the use of search engines (for example Yahoo! and Google) for accessing information and facilities such as chat, mail and discussion boards for e-communication was not initially clear. In order to carry out this research a design approach was chosen in which applications would be developed and tested in daily teaching and learning practice.

Design process of a tool to support problem-based learning

The communication tool that was developed was based on an analysis of how people learn in small groups. From the software perspective it looked like a threaded discussion board. However, it was extended with specific functionality, focused on activities in small group learning. The tool supported creative work and continuous improvement of ideas by writing, sharing, discussing, comparing, integrating, reorganising and restructuring of information. It was an answer to the difficulties students experienced in the use of standard tools (newsgroups, discussion boards) in learning. Three phases in the iterative design process will be described here:

1 The start of the project, the *principled approach* phase.
2 The second phase, aimed at *productivity of learning interactions.*
3 The concluding phase in which research of *knowledge building* was an important inspiration for thinking about problem-based learning.

A *principled approach*

In the first step at the start of the project we followed the principled approach that Koschmann *et al.* (1996) suggested; to analyse the requirements of computer support in problem-based learning. Their approach offers a clear structure in managing a project such as this and is also helpful in reporting the results of project activities afterwards (Petrosino and Pfaffman, 1997). The principled approach included a four-step procedure:

1 articulation of desired instructional features
2 analysis of current practice in the light of design goals, the result of step 1
3 development of a specification, based on instructional requirements, the result of step 2, in the context of known capabilities of technology
4 production of an implementation plan and adaptation of instructional practice.

We selected a limited set of key principles for problem-based learning in practice, as were found in basic strategic documents about the innovative mission of UM. These principles were:

- *authentic learning*, situated in the context of practice
- *self-directed learning*, in which students are responsible for their learning process
- *preservation* of complexity
- *multiplicity*, where learners discover that knowledge and problem solving have many perspectives
- *knowledge construction*, differences between information and personal knowledge that is the result in working with that information
- *learning to learn*, meta-knowledge about the process of problem solving.

We specified these principles in a questionnaire, comparable with Kanuka (2002), that contained about 180 items, spread over two main categories in technology: information (search, access, availability) and communication about and with that material, related to detailed aspects of the way in which problem-based learning is organised (group meetings, resources, tutors).

All students and tutors in several of UM's curricula were asked to participate in a comprehensive survey. The outcomes prioritised the use of communication tools because planned face-to-face meetings appeared to be insufficiently supportive of the learning process. This conclusion was reached after the following observations:

- Not all students can discuss their work and get individual feedback in their group meetings.
- The main theme in the discussions is the solution of the problem.
- Not enough time is available for reflection and elaboration of knowledge during group meetings.
- Individual contributions are not compared or integrated.
- It rarely happens that discussions lead to defining new learning issues.
- The way students learn is not discussed in group meetings.
- Students say that they learn from talking about their work in group meetings.
- Students see their participation in group meetings as an informal evaluation of their learning.

Based on these observations a tool for forum discussions, part of the groupware application Lotus Notes, was adopted. Four experiments were carried out with POLARIS. All four experiments, using the same scenario in different curricula and with different classes, gave students access to a group environment in which they worked together in a self-managed manner. In-depth analyses of group interaction patterns and the content of material submitted by the participants illustrated two things:

1 Asynchronous collaborative learning is a complex process that demands specific features and functionality to reduce this complexity.
2 Different, sometimes mutually dependent, entities in the learning situation might contribute to an effective use of the communication tool.

Productive interactions

In the second phase, the characteristics of communication in asynchronous small group learning in relation to specific functional requirements, as well as the design of the learning situation, were explored further.

Figure 11.2 illustrates the logistics of that interaction and the complexity of the support in asynchronous collaboration.

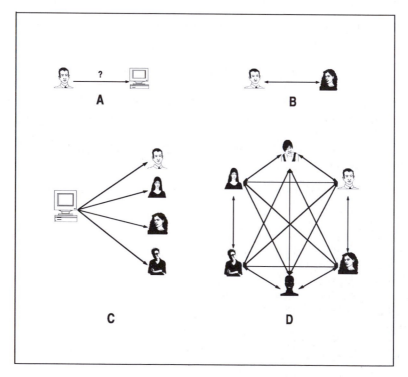

Figure 11.2   Communication patterns

A *The online model:* the interaction between a person and information sources accessible via the network.
B *The email model:* interaction between two persons.
C *The bulletin board model:* one-way traffic, sending information.
D *The conferencing model:* mutual interaction between all persons in a group (Paulsen, 1995).

In the analysis of our first-phase data we found indicators for problems to be solved when general group communication tools were used for collaboration. In summary, the following issues came up:

- *Communication pattern:* The asynchronous character of the interaction between students online often resulted in a wild, sometimes even chaotic pattern. Continuous branching paths, unpredictable moments that learners are logged on and the order of inputs can lead the conversation away from the main topic under discussion.
- *Loss of contact:* During virtual collaboration, learners are often unaware of how and if the submitted information is being used by others. There is a feeling of working alone, despite the fact that individuals are collaborating.
- *A surplus of incoming information:* If a group is active, and generating multiple responses to one another's work, the result is often an explosive growth of information. This desirable situation can be counterproductive if the overview is lost. At that point, not everything is processed and the interaction halts.
- *Thread structure:* The structure of the system (action–reaction–reaction to reaction) in which the individual contributions are placed, makes it sometimes unavoidable that information in different messages, where the content matches closely, becomes separated or even isolated because it is placed in different threads.
- *Transparency:* The process-oriented character of collaborative learning is not visible in a regular discussion board or conferencing tool, which often makes it difficult for the moderator or tutor to maintain supervision.

Some of these difficulties in the practice of asynchronous communication can be related to fundamental shortcomings of the regular threaded discussion boards being used. In a summative evaluation of the effectiveness of threaded discussion tools in knowledge construction, Hewitt (2001) focused on one of the apparent limitations of the medium: the lack of support for convergent processes. Threaded online environments support electronic conversations that expand and branch, but provide few facilities for drawing together discourse in meaningful ways. Hewitt's conclusion therefore is that discussion boards have limited value because ideas are lodged within conversational threads, contributions are unmodifiable, and there is no way of linking ideas in different threads or assimilating them into larger wholes.

The second analysis of the required functionality of the tool was based on

Dillenbourg's model (Dillenbourg, 1999), in which collaborative learning activities were analysed in terms of three main questions:

1 Analysis of learning mechanisms: How can students learn together?
2 Analysis of learning behaviour: What are students doing in a virtual group environment?
3 Analysis of the learning environment in terms of affordances for the purpose of design: What initiates collaborative learning? (See Figure 11.3.)

Learning mechanisms

Research has shown that various situations arise in which people are able to learn via mutual communication. These may include situations such as:

- *Conflict*: We talk of a conflict situation if students are challenged to make statements which contradict one another. Subsequently a debate is held in order to reach a solution. The debate is thus the driving force in creating definitions, and consulting information sources in order to attack or to defend the positions taken up (Baker *et al.*, 2003; Oubenaissa *et al.*, 2002; Sandoval, 1995).
- *Explanation*: A particularly effective form of collaboration is to place

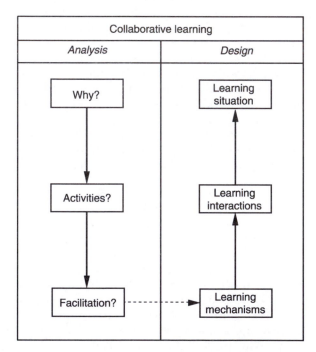

Figure 11.3   Analysis of group learning and design of a learning situation for productive interactions

students in situations in which they explain something to one another. Information is often more deeply processed when written than when read. If people write for one another, all are forced to formulate more clearly (Brown and Palincsar, 1989; Chi *et al.*, 1989; Oshima, 1997; Spivey, 1997).

- *Searching for information*: If students are taught to search for their own information on the basis of questions formulated by themselves, a learning skill is developed that can be used in other situations. Collaboration in this process is stimulating, as during communication large numbers of questions emerge and help students to assess one another's level more effectively than the tutor.
- *Negotiation*: It is useful to introduce students to various sources of information about the same subject. It is difficult in practice to study different sources; however, in a group, agreements can be reached on this question. If a difference of opinion arises, the foundations are laid for a joint harmonisation of terms, necessary in order to be able to continue to communicate with one another (Gunawardena *et al.*, 1997; Moschkovich, 1996).
- *Comparison*: Explicit tasks for comparing information from different sources with one another goes one step further than negotiation, for example, issuing a task to analyse differences and similarities (Barron and Schwartz, 1998).
- *Reflection*: A particular plus point of asynchronous collaboration is that everything remains stored. All communication is reusable in phases of learning when we look back on what has been done.

Learning behaviour

POLARIS contains features and functionality for stimulation of frequency and quality of learning interactions, integrated into the frequently used type of communication tools (discussion boards or fora) that are part of learning management systems.

The following functions were developed and tested, that were tools for:

- *Navigation* and *orientation* enabling the user to simply gain an impression of the nature of the information available and to process that information.
- Making the *learning process transparent*, with a view to offering the tutor an opportunity to improve supervision.
- Limiting the dominance of the thread structure and *reorganising* the content of the group environment according to personal preference.
- Discovering the *common features* between documents, and sharing this insight with others.
- Supporting *decision making* within a group and making visible the *consensus* in collaboration.
- Giving group members insight into who is working with the information made available in order to strengthen *group cohesion*.

- Using the content of the learning environment *once again*, according to personal preference and at an individually chosen moment.
- *Structuring* the contributions from group members such that the interaction is effective for learning.

Learning environment and affordances for productive communication

The following assumption has influenced our design in this phase: situations generate interaction patterns; for their part, interaction patterns trigger learning mechanisms; the learning mechanisms generate desirable learning effects (Goodyear, 2001). The model of affordances shown in Figure 11.4 was developed as part of our design process:

- The *goal* of collaboration between students. Communication is a support process and *process oriented*, so that students are all studying the same subjects, writing about them and issuing one another feedback on the processing of the material studied. Communication is *product oriented* if students collaborate with one another on a text (report), whereby everyone is allocated specific tasks and is responsible for the sub-result, to which others are able to make a contribution.
- The *task* according to which the learning process is directed. Study tasks with an average level of *complexity* in relation to the level of prior

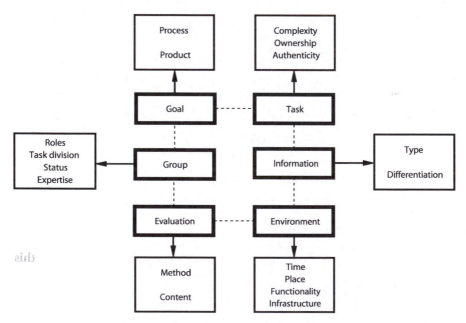

Figure 11.4   Model of affordances for productive learning interactions

knowledge of the student are the ideal basis for interaction. Simple tasks are rapidly concluded and will not inspire the exchange of results. Very complex and difficult tasks do give rise to questioning one another, but the interaction rarely reaches the level of exchange of results. The degree of *independence* in implementing tasks has a major influence on the progress of collaboration. Students solely responsible for studying individual subjects to then feedback to the group tend to negotiate sooner with one another on the structuring of the group learning process, and are more motivated. The degree of *authenticity* of a study task places demands on the capacity to apply theoretical insight in practical considerations. This process elicits interaction, because, on the one hand, students are asked to explicitly take account for their actions, while, on the other, there may be various possible solutions for the same practical problem.

- The composition of the *group* and the organisation of the group process. A *heterogeneous* group with previous knowledge and experience supplemented by the group consciously planning differences in terms of tasks and responsibilities are also guiding factors in communication.

- The *information* used in the learning process. The *form* of the information (text, picture, multimedia) and the *differentiation* of sources inspire mutual communication.

- The *evaluation* and assessment of learning. The choice of *method* and *content* of the evaluation is generally a determining factor for the way in which students work. If in collaborative learning the documents produced play a role in terms of quantity (number of interactions) or quality (content assessment) in the evaluation of the learning results, this will have consequences for the nature of the collaboration.

- The *environment* in which the participants learn, and the tools used. The choice and structuring of this environment, be it physical or virtual, and the coherence between the two in the application of 'blended learning', is the final link that determines the quality and results of collaborative learning. The functions of POLARIS were explicitly developed from the point of view of promoting collaborative learning by placing students in a position where they could actively work with the information they collected and produced themselves.

Learning as knowledge building

As a result of a major change in the technical infrastructure of the learning environment of UM, we were able to redesign the tool and reconsider its basic functions in the light of former conclusions. What was the role of the tool in the learning process? In finding an answer to that question we analysed in detail the database content of previous experiments. We systematically mapped the topics in order to determine if the content of the communication was addressed either to the development of new knowledge or to the application of knowledge to information that was studied in books or other sources. The majority of documents in the different communities were aimed at the exchange of information that was found elsewhere by way of copy and paste or by diversion of summaries of separate sources. Usable information and relevant information was found, but only limited elaboration. In the communication after initial messages we missed new understandings. Critical comparison of different sources of information about the same issue, or reflection and compilation of shared, but separately available, information were only sparsely represented in the learning community (Ronteltap and Eurelings, 2002). The availability of the tool was apparently not sufficient to trigger learning mechanisms such as conflict or negotiation. Two approaches were relevant in this third phase:

1 The decision was made to structure the tool in such a way that specific functions for that purpose became more explicit.
2 Based on the perception that the mere availability of a tool was not enough to fully learning situations, we started to work on the development of pedagogical design patterns to be used in the dissemination of the tool (Ronteltap *et al.*, 2004).

Drawing up the balance in labelling interactions as productive, yet not creative enough, linked us to the view of activity theory, in particular to the theoretical concepts of *knowledge building* (Bereiter, 2002; Scardamelia and Bereiter, 1994). Comparing various trends in activity theory, Paavola *et al.* (2003) characterised the knowledge-building activity as being where the goal of interactions is to develop, evaluate and modify conceptual artefacts collaboratively. Interactions are elements in a process of transforming and developing, in which questioning plays an important role.

In the design of the third version of POLARIS, we had a sharper image of the type of communication that we wanted to realise, in contrast with the communication that is often seen in the use of regular computer-mediated communication with conferencing tools or discussion boards. These standard tools are often used as group mail by which information is exchanged. Interactions are brief and to the point, rapidly written question and reply, in a short-term perspective. For the practice of knowledge building a repository of shared knowledge is needed, supported by specific functions that enable participants to process the content. In Table 11.1, we set out the differences in interaction:

* Short-term interaction has a more temporary and explorative character, in which a group communicates in order to chart out a subject and to reach agreements in collaboration. Given the necessity for everyone to be highly active over a short period of time, in order to establish broad-based support for collaboration, simultaneous collaboration is the best organisational form.
* In long-term interaction objects are studied and the results of these studies are shared and subsequently integrated into individual study. In that process, on the basis of specific objectives, the participants attempt to give

Table 11.1   Interaction differences related to space of time

Interaction	
Short term	*Long term*
Exchange and exploration of ideas	Elaborating ideas including the processing of new information
Linking and ranking points of view and opinions	Comparing, integrating and restructuring information
As many angles of approach as possible (brainstorming)	Specification
Much interaction, everyone takes part	Targeted interaction/feedback to each other
Limited time	No time limits

one another targeted feedback. Learners take time over this process, because comparison and reflection are important elements.

POLARIS contains two components: a group environment *Knowledge Builder* in which information is exchanged, followed by subsequently feedback (Figure 11.5), and the personal environment *Knowledge Manager* (Figure 11.6) in which the products of the collaboration can be manipulated and stored for later access. (Figure 11.7 shows the types of message you can expect to find in POLARIS.)

Table 11.2 gives an overview of functions and purpose of POLARIS.

Reflection

Technology enlarges communication possibilities and enables everyone to access information simply or disperse it to others. Without any doubt we are only at the beginning of great changes in teaching and learning as a consequence of these features. The goal of the project reported here is to facilitate problem-based learning with the use of network technology. For that purpose we developed a new tool for group communication in the context of learning. We introduced problem-based learning as a middle-out educational concept: a concept with many variations in application but with some basic ideas in common. These may change over the years ahead. Top-down change proceeded from theoretical considerations and bottom-up change from reflection on experiences. This chapter presented the results of a design project, in which this middle-out idea was applied.

As a first step we explored the underlying understanding of pedagogical principles of problem-based learning in two faculties at UM. We undertook a large-scale survey among all students and academics and asked them to rate a set of statements about day-to-day activities in their learning situations. The

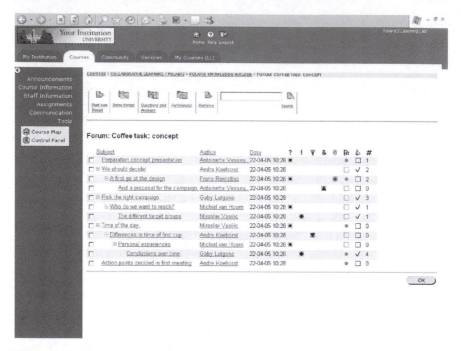

Figure 11.5   Knowledge Builder (group environment)

main conclusion of this study was that everyone would welcome an extension of interactions in the curriculum. In a series of pilot studies, supplementary asynchronous communication was set up that could occur between regular scheduled face-to-face meetings. A standard conferencing tool with some minor moderations was used for this purpose. Analysis of the virtual group environment, combined with focus interviews with all participants afterwards, displayed the complexity of asynchronous communication. By definition effective communication is structured, as is asynchronous interaction, but the sometimes chaotic way in which the content of the communication became initially available sometimes obstructed collaborative problem solving and learning. Learners halted interaction if they had a feeling that they were losing control. An important conclusion of these findings was that conferencing tools needed to be supplemented with functions to enable users to restructure incoming information.

As a second step, we designed a new conferencing tool, based on the observation and analysis of small group learning activities, backed up by an exploration of learning mechanisms that caused these same activities to generate effective learning behaviour. This project was designed to be carried out at different institutes, so for evaluation purposes a model of affordances was developed that could be used in mapping comparable learning situations, in which learning interactions would be essential. The learning environment, including the tool and its functions, were component parts of

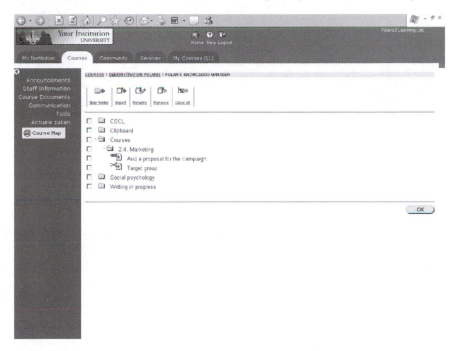

Figure 11.6   Knowledge Manager (personal environment)

this model. With the help of this model we were able to map relationships between the tool and the educational context in which the tool was used. We found a higher level of participation than in the first series of experiments. Content analyses showed us that the tool was predominantly used for the exchange of information and, to a lesser extent, for the development of new insights as a consequence of critical discourse.

In the third phase of the project involving the redesign of the last version, the research perspective of problem-based learning was emphasised. The intention of this was to create learning situations in which participants were tempted to be self-directed and to participate in critical interactions for the development of new knowledge. Desirable learning activities in that perspective were analysis, comparison, debate and integration. A noticeable difference between the second and the third version of the tool was the facilitation of these types of interaction by a new structure and new functions. The application was split up in two parts, a Knowledge Builder (group environment) and a Knowledge Manager (personal environment). In this structure it was more simple and natural to revise, adapt and update information in order to keep the exchange of inputs more productive.

Over the course of this project more and more attention became focused on problem-based learning from the perspective of the distributed development of new knowledge. At first this was by the development and testing of technical facilities in blending asynchronous collaboration with regular

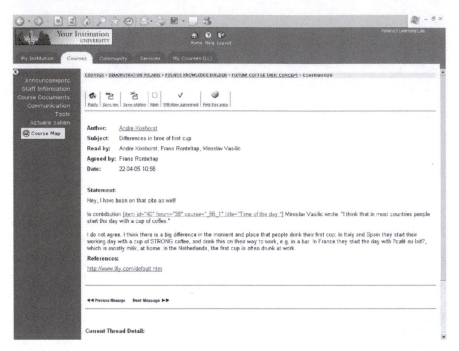

Figure 11.7   Example of message in POLARIS

group meetings. Distributed knowledge development also became a perspective as new theoretical grounded developments were studied, as diffused at CSCL conferences. The enlargement of communication facilities influenced the way we looked at the implementation possibilities of problem-based learning. We improved the way we created learning situations in which we asked learners to work with a research perspective.

As part of our design research we explored fundamental discussions about knowledge and learning and focused on the *knowledge creation* (Paavola *et al.*, 2002, 2004) metaphor. Sfard (1998) made a distinction between an acquisition and a participation metaphor of learning. In the acquisition metaphor the basic goal of learning in the individual mind is to acquire factual or conceptual knowledge. In the participation metaphor, the goal is to learn to participate in those actions and practices that are important in some specific area of expertise, rather than to acquire some specific knowledge. The knowledge creation metaphor is a reaction as well as a supplement to these two. In knowledge creation the goal is to learn collaboratively, with a range of other people, to develop some joint objects of activity and also to develop knowledge and tools for subsequent use (for the learners themselves, or for others); that is to develop mediating artefacts (Paavola *et al.*, 2003). Knowledge creation, a term that is related to constructivism, is introduced as a bridge of the contrasts of both metaphors.

Table 11.2   Functions available in POLARIS

Function	Purpose
Icons	Meta information of function of documents in the discourse. Functions are: Question, Answer, Debate and Supplemental information
Flag	Personal marks, intended as reminders for retrieval at a later point in time
Thumbs up	Positive feedback in knowledge-building process
Number of agreements	Indication for convergence in knowledge building
Overviews: entire thread	Aggregate contents of individual posting in one document that contains a complete conversation. Facilitates learning mechanisms as reflection, negotiation
Overviews: questions and answers	Narrow focus of a complete conversation on questions and answers. Explicates open issues in knowledge building
Overviews: references	Narrow focus of a complete conversation on learning resources referenced by contributors
Save overview	
Search	Free text search on any concept that is used in discourse
Structured form for creating a new posting	Prompts student to explicate role of the posting and references
Knowledge manager	Personal repository of information saved for reference or reuse
Save link, save citation	Make it possible to store postings, and parts of postings in the knowledge manager
Import link, import citation	Build on previous contributions when creating a new posting
Print this page	Support for use of posting in blended scenarios, e.g. use overview as agenda point in physical meeting, use overview in library

Conclusion

Reflecting on the progress that we made in the design of our tool, we experienced a comparable development in our opinions. In the second phase we emphasised the stimulation of participation in building the application in such a way that everybody was enabled to contribute to discourse: becoming productive as an active learner who participated in the community. In the third phase our emphasis shifted to enabling collaborative development of new ideas. We tried to emphasise the research context of problem-based learning in practice, through integrating becoming productive as a knowledge developer with communicating with peers.

Even though problem-based learning is positioned on the side of the participation metaphor, because of its orientation to situated learning through the use of authentic cases, an active role of the learner is not fully guaranteed in this orientation (Hildebrand, 1999). When an authentic case serves as a stepping stone, as merely context for the study of facts triggered by an analysis of the case, we still remain faraway from research and development of new ideas. Our shift of emphasis to knowledge building in this project is linked to different ways of looking at relevant social relationships in the learning process. Salomon and Perkins (1998) made a distinction between active social mediation of individual learning and social mediation as participatory knowledge construction. Active social mediation is characterised as the creation of a better learning system for the primary learner by bringing in a facilitating social agent to help meet the critical conditions of learning.

Looking back on our work, this is what we did in the first two phases of the project. The availability of POLARIS enabled us to create learning situations in which the learner played a more active role than before. It also improved the social process through optimising participation, thus stimulating the development of the problem-based learning research process. After analysing the content of students' work and subsequent interaction patterns, we also integrated a socio-cultural approach in the development of our learning environment. This is characterized by Salomon *et al.* as the creation of an integrated and highly situated system in which interaction serves as the socially shared vehicle of thought. Accordingly, the jointly constructed learning products of this system are distributed over the whole social system rather than being possessed only by the participating individual. Theoretical conceptions such as activity theory (Engeström, 1999), distributed learning (Salomon, 1993) and socio-cognitive conflict (Buchs and Butera, 2004) will be rich sources for inspiration in the further development of problem-based learning.

12

Analysing the use of communication tools for collaboration in PBLonline

Chris Beaumont and Chew Swee Cheng

Introduction

In the 21st century it is becoming increasingly common to work and learn in virtual teams that are globally distributed. Traditional problem-based learning is fundamentally designed around face-to-face team meetings for discussions, sharing of learning and problem solving. Redesigning problem-based learning to incorporate virtual teams (PBLonline) is therefore a logical development that both mirrors real-world practice and merges the e-learning and problem-based learning paradigms. However, these virtual environments create a number of challenges to learning designers to ensure that effective communication is achieved. Indeed, we would argue that this is critical in problem-based learning, since it emphasises social constructivism, rather than the traditional transmission model of teaching and learning.

Virtual teams rely heavily on information and communication technologies (ICT) to define their digital space and facilitate effective communication. There is an ever increasing variety of communication tools and technologies to choose from and it is by no means obvious which technologies are most appropriate for a particular task and whether synergy exists when a digital space that includes a rich set of tools and media is provided.

In traditional face-to-face problem-based learning, students use a range of strategies to develop team trust and complete their tasks. In addition to formal facilitated meetings, the strategies include informal meetings, such as at lunchtimes and coffee breaks, which students report as being important to build team cohesion and also exchange task-related information. There are many subtle aspects of face-to-face communication that can be lost in the use of ICT-enabled communication. We would argue that in order to perform well, PBLonline teams need facilities and tools to enable them to establish equivalent formal and informal communications, and, in particular, to respond to the spontaneity of the latter. We therefore designed a rich environment that provided a multiplicity of communication tools in order to study how PBLonline participants used them in formal and informal ways for social and task-related purposes. We wanted to discover if particular synchronous or asynchronous tools were most useful at particular stages of problem-based learning, and to understand how and why students selected such tools.

This chapter reports on developments from a project sponsored by the British Council and Temasek Polytechnic, Singapore, to explore and analyse how students used ICT to support problem-based learning. The chapter begins by explaining the context and motivation for the study and follows this by a discussion of the research methods used and the results that were obtained. We have chosen to analyse the results both qualitatively and quantitatively and a number of significant points have been identified. Finally, we discuss the relevance of these results to designing environments for distributed or virtual problem-based learning and include some more recent developments in our research.

Context

Successful problem-based learning requires effective communication for a variety of different purposes. These include social and team maintenance, problem solving, constructing understanding related to the problem-based scenario and undertaking tasks or processes related to organisational aspects. Communication is particularly challenging in online forms of problem-based learning as Clark and Brennan (1991: 127) put it, participants, 'have to coordinate on process, they need to update their common ground moment by moment. All collective actions are built on common ground and its accumulation'.

In the last decade, there has been rapid development of communication tools such as SMS text, webcams, ISDN videoconferencing and the integration of some of these into VLEs. Thus, we are faced with a variety of communication tools that can provide a rich environment. The prime motivation for this study was to investigate how such tools could best be used in problem-based learning and if particular tools had specific advantages for the different purposes needed for problem-based learning. While there has been considerable development in VLEs and associated learning technology, none has been specifically designed with problem-based learning in mind. Consequently, in 2001, a purpose-built student-centred learning portal for School of Information Technology (INT-SCL Portal) was launched at Temasek Polytechnic, Singapore. The portal houses instruments and materials that tutors could use in their implementation of problem-based learning programmes. For example, there are collaboration tools such as a forum (allowing threaded postings without attachments) and drop box (a shared repository for files). We envisaged these being used to share research findings and co-construct knowledge through discussion; both being essential components of the problem-based learning process. There were also repositories for resources used by students in their research. These facilities will be familiar to VLE users; however, the portal was designed so that student interaction with it modelled the problem-based learning process. The portal also included specific tools for problem-based learning, including peer and self-assessment instruments.

An international project team was set up in 2002 to investigate the effectiveness of the portal, together with the way in which a wider set of tools could be used for PBLonline. This team comprised tutors from both a UK higher education institution and Temasek Polytechnic, together with student volunteers recruited from those institutions. In order to perform the evaluation, a suitable subject area had to be identified, where there was a reasonable curriculum match and experience of problem-based learning. The research team consisted of subject specialists with experience of problem-based learning in Liverpool, UK, and Singapore, together with a specialist in problem-based learning and staff training from Temasek Polytechnic. The team received funding from the British Council (Singapore) to pilot an 18-month project, designed as two action research cycles.

Boud (2004) suggests that technology can be used in a number of ways. He contrasts the logic of control with the logic of affordances. In the former, the technology can be used to determine student activities; in the latter, the technology provides opportunities for students to explore and learn, with the students being in control. The inclusion of a range of ICT tools for communication, collaboration and sharing enables us to provide a richer learning environment, which gives students the choice to select the most appropriate tool (in their perception) for the particular task.

The researchers regarded it as essential to avoid the logic of control in this project, and to provide a rich set of tools which afford communication and collaboration. An essential part of the project was to determine students' preferred choices of tool. Armed with such an understanding, we believed we could then design more appropriate learning environments to improve task–technology fit for the future.

The problem-based learning model

The study employed a variety of pedagogic and technological strategies in order to develop virtual problem-based learning teams and the requisite common ground needed and to achieve the desired learning outcomes. The technologies used comprised both synchronous and asynchronous tools. Synchronous tools included ISDN videoconferencing, webcam videoconferencing and synchronous chat (Microsoft NetMeeting/Messenger®). The SCL-INT portal provided an asynchronous threaded discussion forum, drop box and peer and self-assessment tools. Each problem-based learning team consisted of four undergraduate information systems students in the UK and four polytechnic students in Singapore. The subteams of UK and Singapore students held local face-to-face meetings in addition to the use of the other communication media. Thus, a form of blended learning was adopted as the problem-based learning model.

The problem-based learning scenario (see Figure 12.1) consisted of a computer network security scenario, involving both theoretical and practical work. Students were required to identify risks and threats for the scenario and design a secure infrastructure. Both UK and Singapore sides of each team also had to construct logically identical demonstration networks using five PCs and associated network software/hardware. The problem-based learning scenario lasted 6 weeks, including one week for preparation and presentation.

Problem-based learning can be modelled as a highly structured process with predefined learning outcomes (see, for example, Steinkuehler *et al.*, 2002: 26). At the other extreme, it can also be designed such that there are no predefined learning outcomes and students negotiate the direction of learning and the resultant outcomes (McConnell, 2002a: 1). Since problem-based learning is aligned with constructivism (see Chapter 7) and the context and prior experience of students is an essential consideration, we believe that it is important to adapt the model to students' experience. Thus, in the subject domain of computing, we have found that novice students benefit from scaffolding and structuring the problem-based learning process. As students gain experience, the degree of scaffolding and structure can be relaxed. In

---

Problem statement

Your company's core business is offshore petroleum drilling, where the floating rigs are located in the North Sea off Scotland. The company has recently designed and tested a new method of drilling that would increase drilling output by 250%; this was documented and stored electronically. The drilling process is still undergoing refinement and its results are documented online with servers located in London. Rival companies are aware of the new innovations from your company and it is rumoured that they will by any means try to obtain information regarding the technologies used.

Your department, Information Systems Security, is tasked to review the current security concerns of each department and the data centre (London). The London HQ has various departments supporting the company functions; all the users have access to the internet from their local ISP. The company has other supporting business partners that supply regular chemicals for its processing site; these companies transact online with your company web application services.

Your team is to provide recommendation(s) to improve various security issues on the WAN, bearing in mind that rival companies have huge resources to conduct electronic espionage or disrupt your company's operations. You are also required to demonstrate a mock-up of WAN security for presentation to the senior management and document the risks and controls you recommend to deal with them. Your CEO will be present in this presentation and he is interested in how it is going to be managed.

Figure 12.1   PBL scenario for first cycle

undergraduate degree courses there are often limited opportunities for negotiated learning outcomes, resulting in a further contextual constraint on the module designers.

In this study, we adopted a problem-based learning model that included explicit learning outcomes. These were expressed in terms that were sufficiently general so that they did not provide direction to students adopting a strategic approach. Some specific deliverables (such as a report, presentation and network topology diagram) were required at specific dates. However, these were limited and students were expected to negotiate their own process. All students were familiar with computing hardware and software, had previously used either WebCT or the SCL-INT portal and were familiar with the asynchronous facilities provided. Most had prior experience of synchronous chat. However, considerable attention was still given to the preparation of students and Salmon's (2000) five-step model also informed the module design.

The main driving force of a problem-based learning process is the problem, with the mechanism that sustains the learning process being collaborative learning. This is in line with the three primary constructivist principles identified by Savery and Duffy (1995: 31) and the constructivist framework that forms the pedagogic backbone of problem-based learning, which includes:

1 understanding comes from our interactions with our environment
2 cognitive conflict stimulates learning
3 knowledge evolves through social negotiation and evaluation of the viability of individual understandings.

A series of papers published in *Distance Education* (23 (1)) in May 2002 described case studies in which a networked environment was used to facilitate problem-based learning curricula. In particular, attention was paid to how ICT tools could support collaborative, problem-solving activities online. Two important considerations were highlighted in these studies, which we shall call technical and social.

In the technical consideration, a VLE must be able to satisfy the following:

1 support discussions and enable participants of these discussions to archive the online dialogues for future reference and reflections
2 support the different stages of the inquiry process.

In the social consideration, a VLE must be used in such a way as to allow participants to establish trust and maintain a group identity. From the start, the researchers were very concerned about what Moore (2002) calls 'dispositional and situational characteristics'. By these he means such factors as 'lack of confidence, fear of failure, lack of access and/or time, and lack of experience with learning in groups when learning activities are group based', which have all been found 'to translate into learner dissatisfaction' (Moore, 2002: 61). Throughout the design process of the study described in this chapter the module developers sought to address Moore's characteristics, by adopting learner-friendly strategies to help students to get the most out of the online module, while remaining faithful to the pedagogic framework that had been adopted. These learner-friendly strategies focused on three factors: a learning environment that encompassed a rich set of tools for communication and collaboration; the usability of the technology; and the induction process for students.

We describe the learning environment as 'rich' because it comprised a wide range of tools: synchronous, asynchronous and face-to-face meetings. Some may argue that this is not a 'pure' PBLonline model; however, Collins and Berge (1994: 5) assert that 'responsible use of CMC means using it in addition to other media, not as a replacement'. Moreover, Levin *et al.* argued that modern interactive media should be used in addition to the current types of media, so that 'teachers and learners will be able to choose the instructional medium that best accomplishes goals within the constraints of a given setting' (Levin *et al.*, 1999: 257). As Palloff and Pratt (1999: 153) state: 'When the content is delivered in multiple ways, it also addresses different student learning styles and creates a more interesting course overall' and tutors fully agreed that 'it is pedagogy and not technology that is critical to the success of an online course'.

The second strategy concerned the usability of the technology. Thus the INT-SCL portal was designed taking account of 'technological minimalism' (Collins and Berge, 1994). This is when minimum levels of technology are carefully chosen with precise attention to their advantages and limitations and used without apology in support of well defined instructional objectives. To this end, the INT-SCL portal was designed by problem-based learning students. The end result was a user-friendly interface with features that were simple to use and appropriate to problem-based learning.

The third strategy concerned students' induction. The researchers in this study felt that it was vital for tutors and students to be prepared for the online programmes. Skills learnt during the induction training period by both tutors and students served as tools for mediation in the module proper. Indeed, the results of the study highlight the importance of thorough preparation for participants in a virtual team. The students from both countries underwent separate induction workshops to acquaint them with techniques for collaborative learning and interacting with each other (giving and receiving feedback and conducting peer assessment).

Research design

This study focused on how information and communication technology enabled participants in their collaborative work in a PBLonline environment. We sought to understand how participants would use the tools to co-construct meaning and achieve their learning goals, in order to enable us to construct more effective and integrated communications environments for future students. The research objectives were to understand:

1 What influences the participants' choice of communication tools in accomplishing the stages of the problem-based learning cycle.
2 How participants use the different communication tools to achieve collaboration with other members of the problem-based learning team.

The choice of tool was largely under the control of the students, the only constraints being relatively restricted access to ISDN videoconferences.

Research method and design decisions

Cohen *et al.* (2000: 226) defined action research as a 'small-scale intervention in the functioning of the real world and a close examination of the effects of such an intervention'. In short, action research involves one or more individuals conducting a self-reflective inquiry in order to understand and improve their own practices. Problem-based learning is a resource-intensive methodology (Steinkuehler *et al.*, 2002). One of the researchers' concerns was whether the use of ICT could help alleviate the problem of constraints on resources and if students would find the ICT tools useful in their collaborations and learning. This study involved the researchers/tutors making a systematic inquiry into how well students learn in a virtual problem-based learning environment, in order to improve the features afforded by the VLE and the online programme.

The project ran in two action research cycles. The first cycle (September–October 2002) provided an opportunity to collect and analyse data from students undertaking the problem-based learning scenario. The scenario for the first cycle (Figure 12.1) required students to analyse risks, and investigate possible solutions to a computer security scenario. The researchers used a variety of methods to analyse the use of the tools and the perceptions of the students. The results from this analysis and evaluation were used to inform the second cycle, where a further 16 students undertook a very similar problem-based learning scenario in September–October 2003. In this second cycle, the data analysis tools were refined and some lessons learned were applied to the communication tools.

Both qualitative and quantitative data were collected and analysed. In this study, the quantitative data was collected by means of a questionnaire that served as a preliminary stage to the analysis of the other, richer qualitative data. Qualitative data was collected in a variety of forms. Use of qualitative methods in the study of computer-supported collaborative learning (CSCL) is something of a tradition (see Andreassen, 2000; Björck, 2002; McConnell, 2002a). The students saved synchronous chat logs and the portal provided a wealth of asynchronous postings, suitably time-stamped. Some ISDN video-conferences were recorded. Students also completed questionnaires and we conducted individual semi-structured interviews, which were video-recorded to enable us to explore in depth their perceptions and motivations for particular actions.

Analysis of results and discussion

Initial quantitative analysis: use of communication media

The first stage of analysis was simply to collect students' opinions about the communication tools. Students were asked to rate the effectiveness of the available communication tools for each of the problem-based learning activities (Table 12.1) using a zero–five-point scale. Team maintenance is an integral activity within problem-based learning whereas the other activities constitute distinct stages.

The results are shown in Figures 12.2, 12.3 and 12.4 which have been separated purely for clarity. The y-axis is a simple summation of the responses, with a possible maximum of 75.

The students rated the synchronous chat, portal forum and drop box as being highly effective for clarifying and understanding the problem statement and identifying and prioritising learning issues, with the chat scoring slightly higher than the portal forum and drop box. In terms of the distribution of learning issues for research and learning by team members, students rated the portal forum and drop box higher than the synchronous chat. Interviews confirmed that they had found that in these areas the asynchronous tools offered them flexible timing, in that they had time to reflect on what had been posted before making their contributions to the discussion.

Most students quickly rejected the WebCam video, as the quality was poor. Audio was also rejected in favour of chat, since differences in English accents between the Singaporean and British students impeded understanding. One team persisted with these tools as an aid to team maintenance and light relief from the substance of the problem-based learning scenario. When the researchers analysed the forum postings and chat logs, it appeared as though participation by some team members was extremely low and this issue was raised with the students early in the project. However, it was discovered that both the Singaporean and the British halves of the teams read the postings and chose to hold face-to-face meetings before posting their contributions,

Table 12.1   Problem-based learning activities

Clarification and understanding of the problem
Identification and prioritisation of learning issues
Distribution of learning issues for research and learning
Individual learning and research
Sharing of learning and teaching with the rest of the team
Application of learning – solving the problem
Reflection
Team maintenance/social
Peer assessment

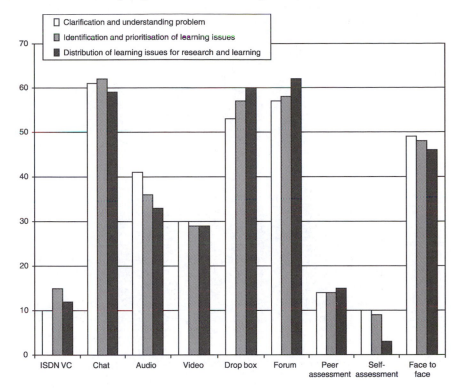

Figure 12.2 Tool preferences in early stages of problem-based learning cycle

thus effectively reducing the online contributions to two sets instead of eight. This is important since one serious problem with asynchronous learning networks is that where the number of participants is large (Goodyear, for example, argued that the ideal group size is four (Goodyear, 2001: 82)) there is a tendency for information overload; sometimes the messages are repetitive or irrelevant, causing a lot of frustration. This frustration was indeed reported by one team in the 2003–2004 cohort, as they chose to conduct most synchronous chat as individuals from their home locations. One slightly curious result apparent in Figure 12.2 concerned the usefulness of the peer assessment instrument for early stages of problem-based learning. Although the numerical scores were low, we had expected zeros. When students were questioned about this, they explained that they had considered the tool as being useful in identifying issues in their own learning, i.e. at a metacognitive level.

The results in Figure 12.3 show that for sharing of learning and application of learning, the asynchronous modes of the portal forum and drop box were considered most effective. The students used the forum mainly to inform members about what they had deposited in the drop box, clarify issues raised by others or give additional information about the postings. The

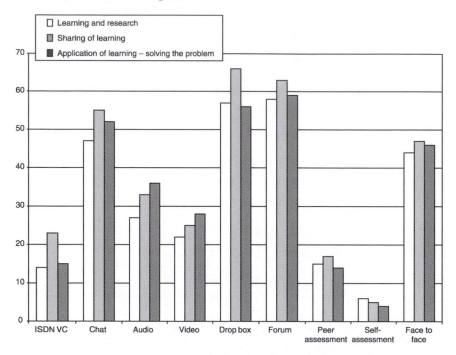

Figure 12.3   Tool preferences in later stages of problem-based learning cycle (1)

drop box was designed in such a way that files deposited can be of any type and size. The work posted was only visible to members of the same team, a trusted environment that ensured the comfort of the contributors.

In terms of reflection, students rated ISDN videoconference (41), the peer assessment instrument (36) and the forum (35) as the media that had encouraged them to do self-reflection. One of the videoconference sessions was scheduled as a group reflection, which provided the explanation for the relatively high rating in that category. It is perhaps interesting that these constituted a variety of tools: a synchronous group discussion tool (video-conference), a group asynchronous discussion tool and a group-to-individual feedback tool. These results provided some initial insight into the use of the tools and helped raise issues and questions to be followed up in the qualitative phase, thus providing further focus for the research. At the next level of analysis the question of how the participants used these media in their collaboration to accomplish their tasks was examined.

Analysis of discussion threads

This next stage of analysis involved creating a timeline and positioning the chat sessions, videoconferences, forum posting and drop box entries within

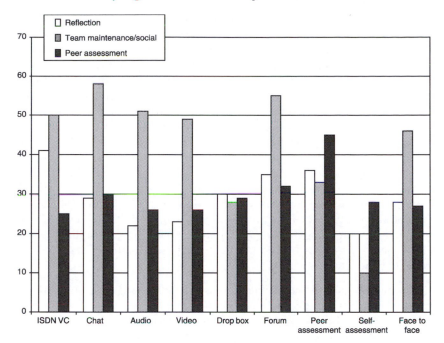

Figure 12.4 Tool preferences in later stages of problem-based learning cycle (2)

this timeline. This allowed us to see the sequence of events. We were then able to identify the start of a particular discussion thread on a specific topic and to follow this through the different media used. For example, the posting of a proposed topology diagram by a Singaporean subteam on the drop box spawned five threads related to specific queries, challenges and requests for research on aspects of the topology. One thread relating to a router could be traced through five forum postings, a NetMeeting, a face-to-face session and two drop box postings. We called this a semantic thread. These threads often split into subtopics, and sometimes introduced new topics, which became new threads. We also coded the dialogue in the threads, using methods adopted from grounded theory. Validation within the context of the project was provided by the four researchers.

In the first phase of the project we were able to identify a number of semantic threads of dialogue which integrated a range of the communication media. These dialogues also displayed distinct milestones (McConnell, 2002a: 74) and we established some patterns of use, which led to some recommendations. Three distinct stages were identified in students' collaborative efforts, corresponding to stages of the problem-based learning cycle.

Stage 1: negotiating direction and goals
As in any problem-based learning programme, the participants began by negotiating the issues to be investigated. Here they discussed possible alter-

natives for the network topology, challenged each other's suggestions and clarified their own. As students explored the learning issues in which they were particularly interested, they kept each international side of the team updated. They also clarified preliminary issues about equipment given and technical terms used. At this stage, the forum was used more frequently than the other tools, since it offered flexibility in terms of students being able to take time to ponder and reflect, on both an individual and group basis, on what had been discussed thus far. The drop box was used primarily to upload files so that the discussion had some focus for students. It is important to note that the four members on each side negotiated their own learning goals and issues and then posted their conclusions in the drop box. The discussion between the two groups was more focused in the sense that they only needed to refer to two possible versions. Finalisation of the negotiation of the goals indicated the beginning of the next level of collaboration, the beginning of a period of research and gathering information. Whether or not the group was able to move on to this higher level of collaboration depended to a large extent on two factors:

1 If the members had established a sense of belonging to a learning community which depended on collaboration.
2 If the goals and learning issues had been negotiated by all the members and that they were clear about what each had to do.

Stage 2: distribution of work and individual research
At this stage, the use of media shifted from mainly the forum to the drop box as the group members began conducting self-directed learning, discussing their findings with members from the same country in face-to-face meetings and posting them in the drop box for the other group to comment on. There were also scheduled synchronous chats. The students used this tool primarily for decision making and to seek agreement on issues that needed clarification. In one meeting they also used an electronic whiteboard to clarify issues related to the setup of the network system. This took place after a good deal of independent research.

Stage 3: preparation of deliverables for submission
At various points of the programme, the programme developers scheduled a number of specific deliverables (such as a network topology diagram, presentation and report template of assets, security risks and controls). These corresponded to real-world project deadlines or milestones and provided focus for the teams. Towards the end of stage two, during the synchronous chats, there was a gradual change in the focus of discussion from the concepts and the sharing of research outcomes towards the specific requirements of the project deliverables.

Having a shared goal (in this case, accomplishing the final version of the network topology diagram) provided the motivation for the team to move their collaborative process forward. It is important to have such 'checkpoints' for students, so that both they and the tutors had a feel of the progress made by the team. The team in this study focused on the process of collaboration, as evidenced by the way they went about seeking clarification and agreement from each other. They regarded consensus as essential prior to moving further forward in the task. The students' reflective journal entries reinforced the researchers' conclusions that the students had been able to use the communication tools effectively to develop trust within the team and had attended successfully to the social and affective dimensions of teamwork.

Analysis of the programme using activity theory

Activity theory has been used in the study of human–computer interactions (Nardi, 1996), and more recently in the study of student collaborative patterns in their use of a virtual platform that supported a total of 19 tools, including those for navigation, production and communication (Andreassen, 2000), and distributed learning (Russell, 2002). Russell (2002: 65) pointed out that if learning in a CSCL environment is social and cultural, then there is a need to understand how the participants in that environment make use of the tools to learn through interactions with the other members. This, in essence, is the research focus of the study described here. In the current study, activity theory has been used to help the researchers understand the collaborative process that the students engaged in, by addressing such questions as: how did the participants set up their own rules for collaboration, how did they divide the workload for individual attention before coming together to share the results, and how did they manage and resolve the contradictions that arose? Three activity systems can be discerned in this problem-based learning programme.

Induction workshop as an activity system

In its simplest form, Engeström's (1999) extended model of an activity system has the subjects, in this case the students of the Singapore group from Team Two, interacting with each other, with the mediating tools such as the artefacts afforded by the workshop context (information resources, discussion, role play cards and so on), and with the other participants in the programme (see Figure 12.5). The subjects then act on an object, in this case the induction course, to achieve the intended outcome of acquiring collaboration techniques and other team skills such as conflict resolution skills. The subjects belong to a community and were governed by rules and norms set up by themselves. Because a VLE was used in this study, the VLE had also, by virtue of its setup, rules that both afforded and constrained the subjects. The processes in an activity system are dynamic and this system did not exist on its own, but was interlinked with other systems such as that which involved the UK students from Team Two.

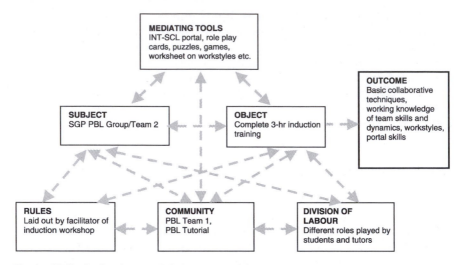

Figure 12.5 Induction workshop as an activity system

The main purpose of the induction workshop was to equip the students with the skills to use the portal effectively and to collaborate in their teams in problem solving. These skills then became one of the mediating tools in the second activity system.

Initial meeting as an activity system

Sometimes, in an activity system, contradictions may arise. These are described by Russell (2002: 65) as points, 'when people are at cross-purposes'. Contradictions can emerge between any two or more elements of an activity system and they act as change catalysts which, through their successful resolution, can enable the community to move closer towards the intended outcomes.

In this system the first contradiction appeared in relation to the initial meeting. The intended conferencing facility was not set up in time due to technical problems and the students had to resort to using the Microsoft NetMeeting® tools. Due to the poor video and audio quality, compounded by the linguistic accents of the students, the initial meeting was not as successful as the participants had hoped it would be. However, instead of complaining, the students switched to chatting online by typing out their messages (see Figure 12.6). Here was the first instance of a conflict resolution and problem-solving model being adopted by the students, which successfully removed the difficulty they experienced.

In this system, the authors distinguished between two outcomes, the intended outcome, which was to establish initial contact between the students

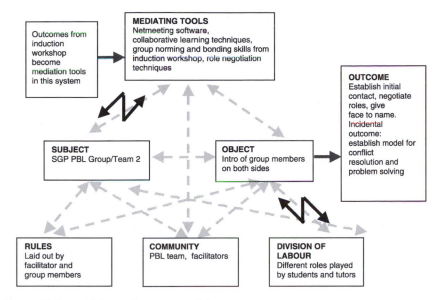

MEDIATING TOOLS
Netmeeting software,
collaborative learning techniques,
group norming and bonding skills from
induction workshop, role negotiation
techniques

Outcomes from
induction
workshop
become
mediation tools
in this system

OUTCOME
Establish initial
contact, negotiate
roles, give
face to name.
Incidental
outcome:
establish model for
conflict
resolution and
problem solving

SUBJECT
SGP PBL Group/Team 2

OBJECT
Intro of group members
on both sides

RULES
Laid out by
facilitator and
group members

COMMUNITY
PBL team, facilitators

**DIVISION OF
LABOUR**
Different roles played
by students and tutors

Figure 12.6   Initial meeting as an activity system

and the incidental outcome, which was the establishment of a problem-solving model, initiated by the students themselves.

Programme as an activity system

When we considered the entire programme as a system, several contradictions were identified (see Figure 12.7). These were: technical, group behaviour and the assignment requirements and conditions. It should be pointed out that the students did not see these contradictions as stumbling blocks to their collaboration. Instead they saw them as something they had to resolve as a group. In other words, the contradictions had become change agents that, through resolution, had helped the group to gel. This reaction to contradictions as a positive stimulus illustrates one of the strengths of problem-based learning. Students were taking control of their own learning, demonstrating initiative.

This is evidence that problem-based learning promotes what Knight and Yorke call learned optimism, rather than learned helplessness (Knight and Yorke, 2003: 18).

Differences in the second cycle

The first cycle provided valuable insights regarding patterns of use of the tools and the purposes for which they were being used. It reinforced our view

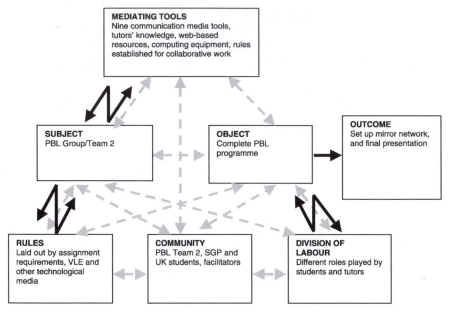

Figure 12.7　Programme as an activity system

that a multiplicity of tools was needed and that a rich learning environment comprising synchronous, asynchronous and face-to-face communication could blend well to enable teams to perform at a high level. Synchronous tools appeared particularly useful for decision making and team maintenance.

The researchers used the results to inform the second cycle in September–October 2003. In this cycle, the students were drawn from the same courses and the conditions were duplicated, with the exception of improved videoconference facilities.

Given the small number of students that were studied, this second stage provided an opportunity to investigate any contextual differences and to gain further information about the validity and reliability of the findings from the first cycle. Most of the results followed the first cycle, but there were some interesting and significant differences:

- First, the usage of synchronous chat using MSN messenger® doubled compared to the first cohort. Moreover, students negotiated in their teams to use the tool in a different way. In the first cycle, students had mostly gathered together in subteams and communicated as two entities. However, the second cohort preferred to meet as individuals, often from their homes, to join the MSN Messenger chat. They stated that they valued the flexibility that it afforded.
- Conversely, the usage of the asynchronous forum and drop box halved. A further apparent feature was that the level and detail of information that

was exchanged and the depth of discussion (as judged by the IT subject experts) were both reduced in the second cohort.

These differences were explored during the interviews, when it became apparent that the Singaporean cohort had much less prior experience of the portal than the previous cohort. However, they were highly proficient users of MSN Messenger® and regarded this tool as sufficient for their needs. They did not have any specific motivation to spend additional time in becoming familiar with the portal. This was therefore a barrier to use. The UK students had similar levels of familiarity with MSN Messenger® which thus very quickly became the default method of communicating.

Conclusion and recommendations

The importance of the rich learning environment consisting of a multiplicity of communication and mediation methods became clear in this project, particularly given the global distribution of the teams. This rich set of tools enabled the students to overcome difficulties. For example, students regarded synchronous discussion as essential for decision making and clarifying issues of understanding. However, WebCam video and audio proved ineffective because of bandwidth, latency and language difficulties, although we expect this technology to improve in the future (Knutsen *et al.*, 2003). The students overcame these issues by using Microsoft NetMeeting® and MSN Messenger® chat. They also demonstrated flexibility in arranging meetings to overcome the 7-hour time difference.

In week two, one of the UK students noted in their reflective journal that: 'Communication with Singapore using NetMeeting has been excellent and it is this method that has enabled the team to discuss differences of opinion and find a compromise needed . . . for the network topology.' Another student, when interviewed, explained 'in that first net meeting, we moved on a hundred paces, rather than the two or three, the real time chats are what got us through it'.

The asynchronous drop box and forum facilities were widely used for complementary tasks such as exchanging research findings in the forum and posting drafts of the deliverables in the drop box. Threaded forums were used to challenge, question and respond to issues (constructing shared understanding), many of which referenced documents in the drop box. However, the inherent delays in the asynchronous tools also caused some frustration, since if students were confused by a posting, they could not clarify it quickly. This was another motivator for using the synchronous tools.

Our analysis showed that the semantic threads incorporated all of these tools in a rational way and this emphasised the need for an integrated set of such tools to encourage the development of high-performing teams. One student commented: 'I am really satisfied with the outcome of this module as I feel all our joint hard work has been justly rewarded and it proves that distance is no object provided the correct technological tools are used.'

Team maintenance is an important aspect of problem-based learning. We analysed discussions (fora and chat) to determine the proportion of utterances devoted to it. In both the cohorts we established that around one-fifth of the total number of interactions in the first two meetings was devoted to this activity. This signalled that students had successfully reached Salmon's (2000) socialisation stage (2). It also demonstrated that the social part was an essential process, being just as important as the problem scenario resolution and problem-solving tasks. In week two, one student observed the social benefits of instant messaging chat for this purpose (NetMeeting): 'Brilliant! The rapport has been building, postings are much more personal, as if we know each other rather than are talking as strangers, and feeling of support and loyalty is definitely developing . . . it does feel like a team.'

It is more difficult to draw conclusions regarding the ISDN videoconference. It provided good-quality audio and video, but technical difficulties restricted its use to one conference at the end of the first phase. It was also the only tool that was not available 'on demand'. However, students found this useful for group reflection and team forming – as one student put it: 'It let you gain more idea of the others . . . to produce a picture and give a sense of working with a team.' In the second phase (September–October 2003) three videoconferences were scheduled, at the start (for team orientation/introductions), middle and end (for group reflection) of the problem-based learning scenario. The teams used the middle conference to resolve team conflict and organisational issues.

Recent work (Beaumont, 2005) investigated the use of videoconferencing as part of a blended-learning problem-based learning approach. In this model, the facilitator was located in Liverpool and students in Blackburn. Students perceived this form of facilitation as significantly different from, and complementary to, face-to-face problem-based learning facilitation. The use of videoconferencing appeared to provide useful elements as part of an effective learning environment, although we believe more work is needed to establish when and how it can be most effective.

A final recommendation concerned the preparation and training of students in the use of the technology. This point was obvious, but often overlooked. Students must become competent in the use of the tools. The differences between the first and second cohorts in the study demonstrated that students will select tools that they are most familiar with, even if they prove to be less than optimally effective. If a contradiction occurs they are likely to seek alternatives. This was consistent with the constructivist view, and emphasised the importance of prior experience and context of the learning.

All the teams involved in this study achieved a high-quality solution that incorporated significant input from both the UK and Singaporean parts of the team. On no occasion did any subteam withdraw to produce their own solution. They successfully demonstrated interdependence and co-construction of knowledge. Students also achieved the learning outcomes at a high grade. As one student reflected:

> PBL . . . forced us to learn more about the subject and enabled us to develop multiple solutions . . . It was not until the presentation that I realised how much we had learned as a group and how the Singaporean side had helped us reach a point of feeling confident about what we had achieved.

Cultural differences caused by the international distribution of students were not investigated in any detail within this project, although it emerged as a factor in selecting communication tools.

One analysis of virtual team effectiveness (Shachaf and Hara, 2002) uses an ecological theoretical framework. The technologies define the digital space in which the virtual (problem-based learning) team operates, enabling the team to define the internal environment and identity of the team. Such an analysis identifies important aspects for successful teams, and is consistent with the view we have presented. The study shows that this model of PBLonline can be successfully implemented.

However, in this study, we have focused on the social dynamics of learning and the learning environment. These alone will not ensure success, but they are essential components in the framework. Peter Goodyear sums it up as follows:

> We are committed to the view that educational outcomes are unlikely to be enhanced through networked learning unless careful attention is paid to the design of learning tasks, the learning environment and the social dynamics of learning. In particular, we believe that designers need to have their eyes firmly on *what the learner will be doing*.
>
> (Goodyear, 2001: 97)

Acknowledgements

We would like to express our thanks for the help and many hours of discussions and contributions from our co-researchers, Seah Chong Poh and Gary Westhead.

Epilogue

The impact of using PBLonline has as yet untold consequences and there remain a number of questions and queries that are still unanswered. For example, throughout this volume a number of authors have documented, critiqued and presented online systems and tools to support problem-based learning. Yet is not entirely clear whether such tools are in fact being used by both tutors and students to contain, control and patrol the learning. Learning management systems such as PsyWeb encourage students to manage information, while POLARIS too encourages students to manage and contain knowledge, as does eSTEP. However, such systems may be seen as progressive compared with conservative VLEs such as WebCT and Blackboard, which remain the most common in use. Certainly Bayne's insightful analysis (Bayne, 2005c) suggests that these conservative VLEs affirm notions of how teaching and learning *should* be. As Cousin (2005: 121) has pointed out too, these VLEs are fraught with images that are deeply problematic, such as 'a little white male professor' that adorns WebCT as its premier logo. These images of scaffolding, structure and safety suggest stability and control. Further, all these systems also encourage students not only to manage knowledge, but also to manage their discussion and possibly even to think and learn in linear ways. The difficulties of designing software for problem-based learning may be in fact because it is, as Land and Bayne suggest, a chaotic and disquieting way of learning. It may be that learning management systems for problem-based learning are actually resulting in the development of more linear models of PBLonline than might be seen in blended approaches or face-to-face problem-based learning.

Thus perhaps some of the questions we should be asking at the close of a volume such as this is what is being managed, by whom and for whose benefit. Indeed, do the screenagers and the mature learners who have lurched into being part of the net generation want to be 'managed' in such a way? Further do VLEs, e-facilitators, scaffolding and a focus on cognition and usage actually close down opportunities for experimentation and innovative approaches to students managing group and individual learning?

Furthermore, does the use of linear, overmoderated and traditionally symbolised VLEs also prevent the creation of disjunction in the minds of the student?

It might be that PBLonline, instead of encouraging students to engage with disjunction, prevents them from being allowed to become uncomfortable and to engage with the complexities of encountering threshold concepts (the idea of a portal that opened up a way of thinking that was previously inaccessible; Meyer and Land, 2003). We suggest that controlling and patrolling learning is at odds with the constructivist nature of problem-based learning and with the vitality of student-centred learning. Yet it could also be suggested that the technology and the tools instead encourage the development of new learning spaces that actually 'uncontain' the learner or even prevent such containment in the first place. Thus what we may come to see instead is not just learning chaos but also a greater degree of oscillation between states and personal transformation, new forms of disjunction and different stages and ways of managing threshold concepts. We may not only see these emerging forms of uncontainment in face-to-face problem-based learning, but also they may become more apparent in types of PBLonline that are supported by face-to-face groups and which use asynchronous discussion that focuses on meta-commenting. Yet with the growth of borderless higher education the future for problem-based learning and PBLonline will no doubt continue to be a place of 'stuckness' that will also bring to the fore new learning spaces (Savin-Baden, 2005).

Glossary

affordance – the potential of a (learning) object for action; the perceived capacity of an object to enable the user to achieve the required outcomes; the perceived and actual fundamental properties that determine how the object may be used to assist the learner.

alternative learning environment – alternative form of education delivery that removes geographical and temporal restrictions on the learner.

asynchronous – two-way communication that occurs with a time delay, thus allowing participants to respond at their own pace and in their own time.

blended problem-based learning – this tends to be used to reflect the idea that students learn through the combination of online and face-to-face instruction (Graham, 2004). For example, students learn through the web-based materials that include text, simulations, videos, demonstrations and resources.

blog (weblog) – personal website consisting of regularly updated entries displayed in reverse chronological order. May be used by learners in PBLonline to evidence their thinking openly to the rest of the team and the e-tutor.

cognitive conflict – cognitive conflict may occur initially when the problem-based learning team attempt to identify and understand the issues generated by the problem scenario and again when trying to integrate the ideas and information that each of them possesses to create (a) solution(s) to the scenario.

cognitive presence – the extent to which online learners are able to construct and confirm meaning through sustained reflection and discourse (Garrison *et al.*, 2001).

commodification – the turning of an object into a commodity, where it has some exchange value, other than the effort taken in its production. With the wider reader audience offered by technology, students find a value for their writing that goes beyond the grade.

community of practice – a group of professionals informally bound to one another through exposure to common problems and common pursuit of solutions thereby generating within themselves a body of 'expert' knowledge.

computer-mediated collaborative problem-based learning (CMCPBL) – this conception of problem-based learning places it pedagogically in a collaborative online environment and focuses on a team-oriented knowledge building discourse. Students work in teams of 8 to 10 on a series of problem scenarios that combine to make a module and are expected to work collaboratively to solve or manage the problem. Students will work in real time or asynchronously, but what is important is that they work *together*.

computer-mediated conferencing (CMC) – use of computers to support human–human communication. CMC ranges from email to group conferencing to 'chatrooms', all of which may be used to support PBLonline.

constructionism – this learning philosophy states that learning is best when the learner is engaged in an active role of designer and constructor especially where the learner is consciously engaged in constructing something that will be shared, for example, with other members of the virtual team (see Papert, 1986).

constructivism – this learning theory is based on the concept that knowledge is created by the learner based on mental activity. Conceptual growth comes from sharing individual constructions and changing perceptions in response to the perceptions of others. Learning is best situated in an environment reflective of real-world contexts (Piaget, 1954).

cyberspace – currently used to describe the whole range of information resources available through computer networks.

distributed problem-based learning (dPBL; DPBL) – problem-based learning that allows the e-tutor (if allocated), the students and the content to be located in different, non-centralised locations and thus allows learning to occur independently of time and place. Involves the use of learning technology.

e-learning – learning facilitated and supported by the use of information and communication technologies. It may take a number of forms from learning support, a blend of online and face-to-face activities to learning that is entirely online. The learning is more important than the technology.

e-learning technology – digital, computerised technology that impacts directly on the learning process through the provision of learning materials, facilitation of communication, assessment and feedback.

e-moderator – online teacher who presides over online meetings or conferences or contributes to online discussion.

e-surveillance – in the PBLonline context, the monitoring or screening of online activity. May include recording of time spent online, websites visited, number and type of contributions to online discussion. Differs from e-moderation or e-tutoring in that the person initiating the surveillance does not engage with the learners or their discussion.

e-tivities – educational online activities, designed to engage and motivate learners. They are usually recyclable and reusable; use other learners and electronic resources and can be used with face-to-face and printed materials (Salmon, 2002).

e-tutor – an online facilitator whose role includes focusing online discussion, asking pertinent questions, responding to students' contributions, assisting in identifying themes from discussion, nurturing online collaboration and who also may be involved in assessment.

flaming – the sending of angry or inflammatory messages by email or group postings. It is considered bad netiquette.

information technology – all forms of technology designed to create, store, exchange and use information in all its various forms (data, voice conversations, still and motion pictures, multimedia presentations and newly developing formats). The term includes telephony and computer technology in the same word.

lurker – a person who reads chatroom discussions, group or message board postings, but does not contribute.

managed learning environment (MLE) – a software system designed to assist teachers in managing online educational programmes. It includes access control, e-learning content, communication tools and the administration of user groups.

mediation – in an online context the computer is the 'intervening' or middle agency through which the students, the learning content and the tutor are connected, allowing learning to occur.

metacognition – the awareness of one's own thoughts, thinking processes and strategies and the ability to reflect on and act in order to modify these; 'thinking about thinking'.

move – speed at which online messages are relayed to the site. Depends on the learner's internet connection, broadband being faster than dial-up.

net generation – the generation that has barely known a world without computers, the world wide web, highly interactive video games and mobile phones. For many of this generation instant messaging, rather than telephone or email, is the primary form of communication.

netspeak – the specialist vocabulary associated with the concept, features and functions of the internet.

platform – a computing platform is a type of software or hardware where applications may run. Operating systems are platforms as are different types of hardware. Specialised platforms included routers and servers.

posting – (verb) to publish a message on an online forum or discussion group; (noun) a message published on an online forum or discussion group.

problem-based learning online – a generic term that captures that vast variety of ways in which problem-based learning is being used synchronously and asynchronously, on campus, or at a distance. It represents the idea that students learn through web-based materials including text, simulations, videos and demonstrations, and resources such as chatrooms, message boards and environments that have been purpose built for problem-based learning.

reusable learning objects – small, reusable components such as video demonstrations, case studies, simulations, assessments that can be used in a variety of contexts to enable students to achieve learning outcomes.

scaffolding – the concept of scaffolding is based on Vygotsky's zone of proximal development. Individualised support designed to facilitate a student's ability to build on prior knowledge and to generate and internalise new knowledge is provided by the tutor or other students. The support is pitched just beyond the current level of the student.

screenager – member of a younger generation of students who have found, through their engagement with new digital technologies, a means of thriving in environments of uncertainty and complexity.

synchronous – two-way communication where there is little or no time delay, allowing participation in real time. In PBLonline times may be set for synchronous discussion between virtual team members and the e-tutor.

telemonitoring – the use of information technology to monitor at a distance. Usually applied to monitoring patient status, but in the context of PBLonline to monitor student progress with the problem scenario.

utterance – individual message made by students or tutors on discussion boards.

virtual learning environment (VLE) – a set of learning and teaching tools, involving online technology, designed to enhance students' learning experience, for example Blackboard, WebCT.

virtual team – group of students working together online, to explore the problem scenario.

WebCast – delivery of live or delayed audio or video recordings using web technologies. The recording is made by conventional equipment, digitised and broadcast (world wide) via a web server.

wikis – server software that allows multiple users to contribute to a website.

References

Albanese, M.A. and Mitchell, S. (1993) Problem-based learning: a review of literature on its outcomes and implementation issues, *Academic Medicine*, 68, 52–81.

Alexander, S. and Boud, D. (2002) Learners still learn from experience when online in J. Stephenson (ed.) *Teaching and Learning Online*. London: Kogan Page.

Alur, P., Fatima, K. and Josheph, R. (2002) Medical teaching websites: do they reflect the learning paradigm? *Medical Teacher*, 24: 422–424.

Anderson, J.R. (1990) *Cognitive Psychology and its Implications*. New York: Freeman.

Andreassen, E.F. (2000) Evaluating how students organise their work in a collaborative telelearning scenario: An activity theoretical perspective. www.ifi.uib.no/docta/dissertations/andreassen/index.htm (accessed 15 June 2003).

Andriessen, J. (in press) Collaboration in computer conferencing in A.M. O'Donnell, C.E. Hmelo-Silver and G. Erkens (eds) *Collaborative Learning, Reasoning, and Technology*. Mahwah, NJ: Lawrence Erlbaum Associates, Inc.

Arbuagh, J.B. and Benbunan-Finch, R. (2005) Contextual factors that influence ALN effectiveness in S.R. Hiltz and R. Goldman (eds) *Learning Together Online: Research on Asynchronous Learning Networks*. Mahwah, NJ: Lawrence Erlbaum Associates, Inc.

Arts, J.A.R., Gijselaers, W.H. and Segers, M.S.R. (2002) Cognitive effects of an authentic computer-supported problem-based learning environment, *Instructional Science*, 30: 465–495.

Ash, C. and Bacsich, P. (2002) The costs of networked learning in C. Steeples and C. Jones (eds) *Networked Learning: Perspectives and Issues*. London: Springer-Verlag.

Atack, L. (2003) Becoming a web-based learner: registered nurses' experiences, *Journal of Advanced Nursing*, 44(3): 289–297.

Atack, L. and Rankin, J. (2002) A descriptive study of registered nurses' experiences with web-based learning, *Journal of Advanced Nursing*, 40: 457–465.

Augar, N., Raitman, R. and Zhou, W. (2004) *Teaching and Learning Online with Wikis*. Perth, Australia: ASCILITE 2004.

Avouris, N., Dimitracopoulou, A. and Komis, V. (2003) On analysis of collaborative problem solving: an object-oriented approach, *Computers in Human Behavior*, 19: 147–167.

Ayersman, D.J. and von Minden, A. (1995) Individual differences, computers, and instruction, *Computers in Human Behavior*, 11(3–4): 371–390.

Bachman, J.A. and Panzarine, S. (1998) Enabling student nurses to use the information superhighway. *Journal of Nursing Education*, 37: 155–161.

Baker, M.J., Lund, K., Quignard, M. and Séjourné, A. (2003) Computer-supported collaborative learning in the space of debate in B. Wasson, S. Ludvigsen and U. Hoppe, *Designing for Change in Networked Learning Environments*. Dordrecht: Kluwer Academic.

Bales, R. (1970) *Personality and Interpersonal Behaviour*. New York: Holt, Rinehart & Winston.

Barab, S.A., Barnett, M., Yamagata-Lynch, L., Squire, K. and Keating, T. (2002) Using activity theory to understand the systemic tensions characterizing a technology-rich introductory astronomy course, *Mind, Culture, and Activity*, 9: 76–107.

Barrett, T. (2005a) Private communication with Ray Land.

Barrett, T. (2005b) Who said learning couldn't be enjoyable, playful and fun? – the voice of PBL students in E. Poikela and S. Poikela (eds) *PBL in Context: Bridging Work and Education*. Tampere, Finland: Tampere University Press.

Barrett, T. (2007) Students talk about problem-based learning in PBL tutorials: illuminative concepts. Unpublished PhD thesis, Coventry University.

Barron, B.J.S. and Schwartz, D.L. (1998) Doing with understanding: lessons from research on problem- and project-based learning, *Journal of the Learning Sciences*, 7(3–4): 271–311.

Barrows, H.S. (1985) *How to Design a Problem-based Curriculum for Preclinical Years*. New York: Springer-Verlag.

Barrows, H.S. (1988) *The Tutorial Process*. Springfield, IL: Southern Illinois University, School of Medicine.

Barrows, H.S. (2000) *Problem-based Learning Applied to Medical Education*. Springfield, IL: Southern Illinois University Press.

Barrows, H.S. (2002) Is it truly possible to have such a thing as dPBL?, *Distance Education*, 23(1): 119–122.

Barrows, H.S. and Tamblyn, R.M. (1980) *Problem-based Learning: An Approach to Medical Education*. New York: Springer-Verlag.

Barsalou, L.W., Simmons, W.K., Barbey, A.K. and Wilson, C.D. (2003) Grounding conceptual knowledge in modality-specific systems, *Trends in Cognitive Sciences*, 7(2): 84–90.

Bassey, M. (1999) *Case Study Research in Educational Settings*. Buckingham: Open University Press.

Bates, A.W. (2000) *Managing Technological Change: Strategies for College and University Leaders*. San Francisco: Jossey-Bass.

Bayne, S. (2005a) Deceit, desire and control: the identities of learners and teachers in cyberspace in R. Land and S. Bayne (eds) *Education in Cyberspace*. Abingdon: RoutledgeFalmer.

Bayne, S. (2005b) Temptation, trash and trust: the authorship and authority of digital texts. Paper presented at ICE2: Ideas in Cyberspace Education, Keswick, February.

Bayne, S, (2005c) Higher education as visual practice: seeing through the virtual learning environment. Paper presented at Society for Research in Higher Education Conference, New Perspectives on Research into Higher Education, Edinburgh, December.

Beaty, L. and Cousin, G. (2002) An action research approach to strategic development in R. Macdonald and H. Eggins (eds) *The Scholarship of Academic Development*. Buckingham: SRHE/Open University Press.

Beaumont, C. (2005) Enhancing the quality of learning through ICT-supported problem-based learning. Paper presented at the 6th Annual Conference of the ICS HE Academy, University of York, 30 August–1 September.

BECTA ICT Research (2003) A review of the research literature on the use of managed learning environments and virtual learning environments in education and a consideration of the implications for schools in the United Kingdom.   www.becta.org.uk/page_documents/research/VLE_report.pdf (accessed 22 July 2005).

Benbunan-Fich, R. and Hiltz, S.R. (1999) Impacts of asynchronous learning networks on individual and group problem solving: a field experiment, *Group Decision and Negotiation*, 8: 409–426.

Bereiter, C. (2002) *Education and Mind in the Knowledge Society*. Mahwah, NJ: Lawrence Erlbaum Associates, Inc.

Berge, Z. (1995) Facilitating computer conferencing: recommendations from the field, *Educational Technology*, 35(1): 22–30.

Bergquist, W.H. (1995) *Quality through Access, Access with Quality: The New Imperative for Higher Education*. San Francisco: Jossey-Bass.

Biggs, J.B. (1999) *Teaching for Quality Learning*. Melbourne, Australia: Australian Council for Educational Research.

Billet, S. (1996) Situated learning: bridging socio-cultural and cognitive theorising, *Learning and Instruction*, 6: 263–280.

Björck, U. (2002) Distributed problem-based learning in social economy – key issues in students' mastery of a structured method for education, *Distance Education*, 23(1): 85–103.

Björck, U. (2004) *Distributed Problem-based Learning. Studies of a Pedagogical Model in Practice*. Göteborg Studies in Educational Sciences 221. Göteborg: Acta Universitatis Gothoburgensis.

Boettcher, J.V. and Conrad, R.M. (1999) *Faculty Guide for Moving Teaching and Learning to the Web*. Mission Viejo, CA: League for Innovation in the Community College.

Bonamy, J., Charlier, B. and Saunders, M. (2002) Issues in the organisational and change context for case study courses in Recre@sup. Final report of the Recre@sup project, Brussels. www.tecfa.unige.ch/proj/recreasup/rapport/WP5.pdf (accessed 1 November 2005).

Bormann, E. (1972) Fantasy and rhetorical vision. The rhetorical criticism of social reality, *Quarterly Journal of Speech*, 58: 396–407.

Boud, D. (2004) Control, influence and beyond: the logics of learning networks. *Proceedings of 4th International Networked Learning Conference*, Lancaster, 5–7 April. www.shef.ac.uk/nlc2004/home.htm (accessed 25 August 2004).

Boud, D. and Feletti, G. (1997) Changing problem-based learning in D. Boud and G. Feletti (eds) *The Challenge of Problem Based Learning*, 2nd edn. London: Kogan Page.

Boys, J. (2002) *Managed Learning Environments, Joined-up Systems and the Problems of Organisational Change*. Bristol: JISC.

Bransford, J.D. and Schwartz, D.L. (1999) Rethinking transfer: a simple proposal with multiple implications, *Review of Research in Education*, 24: 61–100.

Brescia, W., Swartz, J., Pearman, C., Balkin, R. and Williams, D. (2004) Peer teaching in web-based discussions, *Journal of Interactive Online Learning*, 3(2): 1–22.

Britain, S. and Liber, O. (2004) A framework for the pedagogical evaluation of elearning environments. Report to JISC Technology Applications Programme.

www.cetis.ac.uk/members/pedagogy/files/4thMeet_framework/VLEfullReport (accessed 28 July 2004).

Brookfield, S. (2001) Through the lens of learning: how the visceral experience of learning reframes teaching in C. Paechter, R. Edwards, R. Harrison and P. Twining (eds) *Learning, Space and Identity*. London: Paul Chapman/Sage in association with the Open University Press.

Brown, A.L. and Palincsar, A.S. (1989) Guided, cooperative learning and individual knowledge acquisition in L.B. Resnick (ed.) *Knowing, Learning and Instruction: Essays in Honor of Robert Glaser*. Hillsdale, NJ: Lawrence Erlbaum Associates, Inc.

Brown, J.S. (2000) Growing up digital, *Change*, 32(2), March/April.

Brown, J.S., Collins, A. and Duguid, P. (1989) Situated cognition and the culture of learning, *Educational Researcher*, 18(1): 32–42.

Buchs, C. and Butera, F. (2004) Socio-cognitive conflict and the role of student interaction in learning, *New Review of Social Psychology*, 3(1–2): 80–87.

Burns, R.B. (2000) *Introduction to Research Methods*. London: Sage.

Calder, J. and McCollum, A. (1998) *Open and Flexible Learning in Vocational Education and Training*. London: Kogan Page.

Cameron, T., Barrows, H.S. and Crooks, S.M. (1999) Distributed problem-based learning at Southern Illinois University School of Medicine in C. Hoadley and J. Roschelle (eds) *Proceedings of the Computer Supported Collaborative Learning Conference (CSCL)*. Mahwah, NJ: Lawrence Erlbaum Associates, Inc.

Candy, L. (2000) Digital technology in the creative arts: an interdisciplinary research and development context, *Creativity and Cognition Research Studies*, 10 January.

Candy, P.C. (2000) Reaffirming a proud tradition: universities and lifelong learning, *Active Learning in Higher Education*, 1(2): 1–125.

Casey, G. (1996) The curriculum revolution and project 2000: a critical examination. *Nurse Education Today*, 16: 115–120.

CGTV (1993) Anchored instruction and situated cognition revisited, *Educational Technology*, 33(3): 52–69.

Chernobilsky, E., Dacosta, M.C. and Hmelo-Silver, C.E. (2004) Learning to talk the educational psychology talk through a problem-based course, *Instructional Science*, 32(4): 319–356.

Chernobilsky, E., Nagarajan, A. and Hmelo-Silver, C. (2005) Problem-based learning online: multiple perspectives on collaborative knowledge construction in T. Koschmann, D.D. Suthers and T.-W. Chan (eds) *Proceedings of CSCL 2005*. Mahwah, NJ: Lawrence Erlbaum Associates, Inc.

Chi, M.H.T., Bassock, M., Lewis, M.W., Reimann, P. and Glaser, R. (1989) Self-explanations: how students study and use examples in learning to solve problems, *Cognitive Science*, 13: 145–182.

Clancey, W.J. (1995) A tutorial on situated learning in J. Self (ed.) *Proceedings of the International Conference on Computers and Education (Taiwan)*. Charlottesville, VA: AACE.

Clark, H.H. and Brennan, S.E. (1991) Grounding in communication in L. Resnick, J. Levine and S. Teasely (eds) *Perspectives on Socially Shared Cognition*. Washington, DC: American Psychological Association.

Clark, J.M. and Paivio, A. (1991) Dual coding theory and education, *Educational Psychology Review*, 3(3): 149–210.

Clark, R.C. and Mayer, R.E. (2003) *E-learning and the Science of Instruction: Proven Guidelines for Consumers*. San Francisco: Jossey-Bass/Pfeiffer.

Clark, R.E. (1994) Media will never influence learning, *Educational Technology Research and Development*, 42(2): 21–29.

Clarke, A. (2004) *E-Learning Skills*. Basingstoke: Palgrave.

CLaSS Cognitive Learning Strategies for Students (2005) www.uclan.ac.uk/CLaSSProject (accessed 2 December 2005).

Coates, H., James, R. and Baldwin, G. (2005) A critical examination of the effects of learning management systems on university teaching and learning, *Tertiary Education and Management*, 11(1): 19–36.

Cohen, L., Manion, L. and Morrison, K. (2000) *Research Methods in Education*, 5th edn. London: RoutledgeFalmer.

Collins, A., Brown, J.S. and Newman, S.E. (1989) Cognitive apprenticeship: teaching the crafts of reading, writing, and mathematics in L.B. Resnick (ed.) *Knowing, Learning, and Instruction: Essays in Honor of Robert Glaser*. Hillsdale, NJ: Lawrence Erlbaum Associates, Inc.

Collins, M. and Berge, Z. (1994) Guiding design principles for interactive teleconferencing. Paper presented at the Pathways to Change: New Directions for Distance Education and Training Conference, University of Maine at Augusta, 29 September–1 October.

Collins, M.P. and Berge, Z.L. (1997) Moderating discussion in online classrooms. Invited pre-conference workshop. *Conference on Distance Teaching and Learning*, University of Wisconsin-Madison, 6–8 August. www.emoderators.com/mauri/mcvita.shtml (accessed 21 May 2005).

Collis, B. (1997) Pedagogical reengineering: a pedagogical approach to course enrichment and redesign with the WWW, *Educational Technology Review*, 8: 11–15.

Collis, B. and Moonen, J. (2001) *Flexible Learning in a Digital World: Experiences and Expectations*. London: Kogan Page.

Collison, G., Elbaum, B., Haavind, S. and Tinker, R. (2000) *Facilitating Online Learning: Effective Strategies for Moderators*. Madison, WI: Atwood Publishing.

Cook, D. and Dupras, D.M. (2004) Teaching on the web: automated online instruction and assessment of residents in an acute care clinic. *Medical Teacher*, 26(7): 599–603.

Cooke, R. and Sheeran, P. (2004) Moderation of cognition–intention and cognition–behaviour relations: a meta-analysis of properties of variables from the theory of planned behaviour, *British Journal of Social Psychology*, 43: 159–186.

Crooke, C. (1997) Children as computer users: the case of collaborative learning, *Computers and Education*, 30(3/4): 271–247.

Crotty, M. (1998) *The Foundations of Social Research – Meaning and Perspective in the Research Process*. London: Sage.

Cousin, G. (2005) Learning from cyberspace in R. Land and S. Bayne (eds) *Education in Cyberspace*. Abingdon: RoutledgeFalmer.

Cousin, G., Deepwell, F., Land, R. and Ponti, M. (2004) Theorising implementation: variation and commonality in European approaches to e-learning in S. Banks, P. Goodyear, V. Hodgson, C. Jones, V. Lally, D. McConnell and C. Steeples (eds) *4th International Conference on Networked Learning*, Lancaster: University of Lancaster/University of Sheffield.

Coyne, R.J., Lee, J. and Parker, M. (2003) Permeable portals: designing congenial web sites for the e-society. Paper presented at the IADIS International Conference, e-Society, Avila, Spain.

Csikszentmihalyi, M. (1991) *Flow: The Psychology of Optimal Experience*. New York: HarperCollins.

Culler, J. (1983) *On Deconstruction*. London: Routledge & Kegan Paul.

Deepwell, F. (2004) Implementing e-learning at the institutional level in

EQUEL Position Papers. EQUEL project. www.equel.net (accessed 1 November 2005).

Deepwell, F. (2005) Models of institutional support. Paper presented at WebCT Community User Forum, Coventry University, 8 April. www.coventry.ac.uk/ched/webctforum (accessed 1 November 2005).

Deepwell, F. and Beaty, L. (2004) Into uncertain terrain: ensuring quality in implementing online higher education in S. Fallows and R. Bhanot (eds) *Quality Issues in ICT in Higher Education*. London: Kogan Page.

De Grave, W.S., Schmidt, H.G. and Boshuisen, H.P.A. (2001) Effects of problem-based discussion on studying a subsequent text: a randomized trial among first year medical students, *Instructional Science*, 29: 33–44.

de Jong, T. and van Joolingen, W. R. (1998) Scientific discovery learning with computer simulations of conceptual domains, *Review of Educational Research*, 68(2): 179–201.

Deleuze, G. (1992) Postscript on the societies of control, *October*, 59: 3–7.

Dempster, J. and Deepwell, F. (2003) Experiences of national projects in embedding learning technology into institutional practices in UK higher education in J. Seale (ed.) *Learning Technology in Transition: From Individual Enthusiasm to Institution Implementation*. Lisse, The Netherlands: Zwets & Zeitlinger.

Dennis, J. (2003) Problem-based learning in online vs. face-to-face environments, *Education for Health*, 16(2): 198–209.

Department of Health (1999) *Making a Difference: Strengthening the Nursing, Midwifery and Health Visiting Contribution to Health and Health Care*. London: HMSO.

Derrida, J. (1978 [1967]) Structure, sign and play in the discourse of the human sciences (A. Bass, trans.) in J. Derrida (ed.) *Writing and Difference*. Chicago, IL: University of Chicago Press.

Derry, S.J. (1996) Cognitive schema theory in the constructivist debate, *Educational Psychologist*, 31(3): 163–174.

Derry, S.J. (2002) ESTEPWeb.org: a case of theory-based web course design. www.wcer.wisc.edu/estep/images/PDF/TheoryBasedWeb.pdf (accessed 9 June 2005).

Derry, S.J. (2005) STEP as a case of theory-based web course design in A. O'Donnell and C. Hmelo-Silver (eds) *Collaboration, Reasoning and Technology*. Mahwah, NJ: Lawrence Erlbaum Associates, Inc.

Derry, S.J. (in press) ESTEP as a case of theory-based web course design in A.M. O'Donnell, C. Hmelo-Silver and G. Erkens (eds) *Collaborative Reasoning, Learning and Technology*. Mahwah, NJ: Lawrence Erlbaum Associates, Inc.

Derry, S.J. and Hmelo-Silver, C. (2005) Reconceptualizing teacher education: supporting case-based instructional problem solving on the world wide web in L. PytlikZillig, M. Bodvarsson and R. Bruning (eds) *Technology-based Education: Bringing Researchers and Practitioners Together*. Greenwich, CT: Information Age Publishing.

Derry, S.J., Hmelo-Silver, C., Feltovich, J., Nagarajan, A., Chernobilsky, E. and Halfpap, B. (2005) Making a mesh of it: a STELLAR approach to teacher professional development in T. Koschmann, D.D. Suthers and T.-W. Chan (eds) *Proceedings of CSCL 2005*. Mahwah, NJ: Lawrence Erlbaum Associates, Inc.

Dillenbourg, P. (1999) What do you mean by collaborative learning? in P. Dillenbourg (ed.) *Collaborative Learning: Cognitive and Computational Approaches*. Oxford: Elsevier.

Dillenbourg, P., Mendelsohn, P. and Schneider, D. (1994) The distribution of pedagogical roles in a multi-agent learning environment in R. Lewis and P. Mendelsohn (eds) *Lessons from Learning*. Amsterdam: North-Holland.

Dillon, A. and Gabbard, R. (1998) Hypermedia as an educational technology: a review of the quantitative research literature on learner comprehension, control and style, *Review of Educational Research*, 68(3): 322–349.

Dix, A., Finlay, J., Abowd, G.D. and Beale, R. (2004) *Human–Computer Interaction*, 3rd edn. Harlow: Pearson.

Doise, W. and Mugny, G. (1979) Individual and collective conflicts of centrations in cognitive development, *European Journal of Psychology*, 9: 105–198.

Doise, W. and Mugny, G. (1984) *The Social Development of the Intellect*. Oxford: Pergamon Press.

Doise, W., Mugny, G. and Perret-Clermont, A. (1976) Social interaction and cognitive development: further evidence, *European Journal of Social Psychology*, 6: 245–247.

Dolmans, D.H.J.M., De Grave, W., Wolfhagen, I.H.A.P. and Van Der Vleuten, C.P.M. (2005) Problem-based learning: future challenges for educational practice and research, *Medical Education*, 39: 732–741.

Dolmans, D.H.J.M., Gijselaers, W.H., Moust, J.H.C., De Grave, W.S., Wolfhagen, I.H.A.P. and Van Der Vleuten, C.P.M (2002) Trends in research on the tutor in problem-based learning: conclusions and implications for educational practice and research, *Medical Teacher*, 24(2): 173–180.

Donnelly, R. (2004) Investigating the effectiveness of teaching 'on-line learning' in a problem-based learning on-line environment in M. Savin-Baden and K. Wilkie (eds) *Challenging Research in Problem-based Learning*. Maidenhead: SRHE and Open University Press.

Duch, B., Groh, S. and Allen, D. (eds) (2001) *The Power of Problem-based Learning*. Sterling, VA: Stylus.

Dupuis, E.A. (ed.) (2003) *Developing Web-based Instruction*. London: Facet Publishing.

Ede, L. and Lunsford, L. (1990) *Singular Texts/Plural Authors. Perspectives on Collaborative Writing*. Carbondale, IL: Southern Illinois University Press.

Efimova, E. (2005) Not documenting: doing blogging as research. Internet Research 6.0: Internet Generations, Association of Internet Research.

Eklund, J., Kay, M. and Lynch, H. (2003) Emerging issues and key trends: a discussion paper. Australian Flexible Learning Network National Training Authority. www.flexiblelearning.net.au/research/2003/elearning250903final.pdf (accessed 16 May 2005).

Engen, B.K. (2005) Tillit og kommunikasjon I digitale læringsomgivelser. En undersøkelse av IKT-mediert medisinerutdanning [Trust and communication in digital learning environments. A study of ICT-mediated medical education]. Unpublished PhD thesis, University of Oslo.

Engeström, Y. (1999) Activity theory and individual and social transformation in Y. Engström, R. Miettinen and R. Punamaki (eds) *Perspectives on Activity Theory*. New York: Cambridge University Press.

Entwistle, N.J. (1998) Improving teaching through research on student learning in J.J.F. Forest (ed.) *University Teaching: International Perspectives*. New York: Garland.

Entwistle, N., McCune, V. and Hounsell, J. (2002) Approaches to studying and perceptions of university teaching–learning environments: concepts, measures and preliminary findings. Enhancing Teaching–Learning Environments in Undergraduate Courses Project. www.ed.ac.uk/etl (accessed 22 July 2005).

Eva, K.W., Neville, A.J. and Norman, G.R. (1998) Exploring the etiology and content specificity: factors influencing analogic transfer and problem solving, *Academic Medicine*, 73 (10): S1–5.

Evans, C.J., Kirby, J.R. and Fabrigar, L.R. (2003) Approaches to learning, need for cognition, and strategic flexibility among university students, *British Journal of Educational Psychology*, 73, 507–528.

Evensen, D.H. and Hmelo, C.E. (2000) (eds) *Problem-based Learning. A Research Perspective*. Mahwah, NJ: Lawrence Erlbaum Associates, Inc.

Faggiano, E., Roselli, T. and Plantamura, V.L. (2004) Networking technologies to foster mathematical metacognitive processes. *Proceedings of the 4th IEEE International Conference on Advanced Learning Technologies*, California: IEEE.

Feenberg, A. (1989) The written world: on the theory and practice of computer conferencing in R. Mason and A. Kaye (eds) *Mindweave: Communication, Computers and Distance Education*. Elmsford, NY: Pergamon Press.

Fenwick, T.J. (2000) Expanding conceptions of learning: a review of five contemporary perspectives, *Adult Education Quarterly*, 50(4): 243–272.

Foss, S. (1989) *Rhetorical Criticism*. Prospect Heights, IL: Waveland Press, Inc.

Foucault, M. (1988) What is an author? in D. Lodge (ed.) *Modern Criticism and Theory: A Reader*. London: Longman.

Fry, H., Ketteridge, S. and Marshall, S. (2000) *A Handbook for Teaching and Learning in Higher Education*. London: Kogan Page.

Garrison, D.R. (2002) Cognitive presence for effective asynchronous online learning: the role of reflective inquiry, self-direction and metacognition. www.sln.suny. edu/sln/public/original.nsf/dd93a8da0b7ccce0852567b00054e2b6/ 755285ffb5847a4385256c3c006246ea/$FILE/ Learning%20Effectiveness%20paper%20-%20Garrison.doc (accessed 28 August 2005).

Garrison, D.R. and Anderson, T. (2003) *E-Learning in the 21st Century. A Framework for Research and Practice*. London: RoutledgeFalmer.

Garrison, D., Anderson, T. and Archer, W. (2001) Critical thinking, cognitive presence and computer conferencing in distance education, *American Journal of Distance Education*, 15(1): 7–23. www.atl.ualberta.ca/cmc/CTinTextEnvFinal.pdf (accessed 6 December 2004).

Gee, J.P. (2004) *What Videogames have to Teach us about Learning and Literacy*. Basingstoke: Palgrave Macmillan.

Gergen, K. (1991) *The Saturated Self: Dilemmas of Identity in Contemporary Life*. New York: Basic Books.

Glen, S. and Wilkie, K. (eds) (2000) *Problem-based Learning in Nursing: A New Model for a New Context?* Basingstoke: Macmillan.

Goldberg, M. (2000) Message from Murray: student activity tracking, *OTL Newsletter*. www.webct.com/service/viewcontentframe?contentID=2339320 (accessed 20 September 2005).

Goldstone, R.L. and Barsalou, L.W. (1998) Reuniting perception and conception, *Cognition*, 65: 231–262.

Goodyear, P. (2001) *Effective Networked Learning in Higher Education: Notes and Guidelines*. Lancaster University: Centre for Studies in Advanced Learning Technology. www.csalt.lancs.ac.uk/jisc/guidelines_final.doc (accessed 23 April 2004).

Graham, C.R. (2004) Blended learning systems: definition, current trends and future directions in C.J. Bonk and C.R. Graham (eds) *Handbook of Blended Learning: Global Perspectives, Local Designs*. San Francisco: Pfeiffer. www.publicationshare. com/graham_intro.pdf (accessed 22 September 2005).

Gunawardena, C.N., Lowe, C.A. and Anderson, T. (1997) Analysis of a global online debate and the development of an interaction analysis model for examining social construction of knowledge in computer conferencing, *Journal of Educational Computing Research*, 17(4): 395–429.

Guzdial, M., Hmelo, C., Hübscher, R., Nagel, K., Newstetter, W., Puntambekar, S. *et al.* (1997) Integrating and guiding collaboration: lessons learned in computer-supported collaborative learning research at Georgia Tech. Paper presented at the CSCL, Toronto, Ontario, December.

Guzdial, M., Kolodner, J., Hmelo, C., Narayanan, H., Carlson, D., Rappin, N. *et al.* (1996) Computer support for learning through complex problem solving, *Communications of the ACM*, 39(4): 43–45.

Haith-Cooper, M. (2000) Problem-based learning within health professional education: what is the role of the lecturer? A review of the literature, *Nurse Education Today*, 20: 267–272.

Hall, S. (1992) The question of cultural identity in S. Hall, D. Held and T. McGrew (eds) *Modernity and its Futures*. Cambridge: Polity Press.

Hamilton, R. (1989) The effects of learner-generated elaborations on concept learning from prose, *Journal of Experimental Education*, 57: 205–216.

Hamilton, R. (1997) Effects of three types of elaboration on learning from concepts from text, *Contemporary Educational Psychology*, 22: 299–318.

Hannafin, M.J. and Kim, M.C. (2003) In search of a future: a critical analysis of research on web-based teaching and learning, *Instructional Science*, 31: 347–351.

Hannafin, M.J. and Land, S.M. (1997) The foundations and assumptions of technology-enhanced student-centered learning environments, *Instructional Science*, 25: 167–202.

Hannafin, M.J., Land, S. and Oliver, K. (1999) Open learning environments: foundations, methods, and models in C.M. Reigeluth (ed.) *Instructional-Design Theories and Models: A New Paradigm of Instruction Theory*, vol. II. Mahwah, NJ: Lawrence Erlbaum Associates, Inc.

Harasim, L. (1989) On-line education: a new domain in R. Mason and A. Kaye (eds) *Mindweave: Communication, Computers and Distance Education*. Oxford: Pergamon Press.

Harland, T. (2003) Vygotsky's zone of proximal development and problem-based learning: linking a theoretical concept with practice through action research, *Teaching in Higher Education*, 8(2): 263–272.

Hård af Segerstad, H. (2002) Gruppedynamikk og gruppeprosesser [Group dynamics and group processes], in K.H. Lycke (ed.) *Perspektiver på Problembasert Læring* [Perspectives on problem-based learning]. Oslo: Cappelen Akademisk Forlag.

Harvey, J. (1998) Evaluation cookbook, learning technology dissemination initiative. www.icbl.hw.ac.uk/ltdi (accessed 22 July 2005).

Haywood, J., Anderson, C., Day, K., Land, R., Macleod, H. and Haywood, D. (1999) Use of TLTP materials in UK higher education, an HEFCE-commissioned study. Edinburgh: MALTS, University of Edinburgh.

Hewitt, J. (2001) Beyond threaded discourse, *International Journal of Educational Telecommunications*, 7(3): 207–221.

Higher Education Funding Council for England (2003) 'Annex A', Consultation on HEFCE E-Learning Strategy, http://www.hefce.ac.uk/pubs/circlets/2003/c121_03/c121_03a.pdf

Hildebrand, G.M. (1999) Con/testing learning models. Paper presented at the annual conference of the Australian Association for Research in Education (AARE), Melbourne, Australia.

Hmelo-Silver, C.E. (2000) Knowledge recycling: crisscrossing the landscape of educational psychology in a problem-based learning course for preservice teachers, *Journal on Excellence in College Teaching*, 11: 41–56.

Hmelo-Silver, C.E. (2004) Problem-based learning: what and how do students learn?, *Educational Psychology Review*, 16: 235–266.

Hmelo-Silver, C.E. and Barrows, H.S. (2002) Goals and strategies of a constructivist teacher. Paper presented at the American Educational Research Association Annual Meeting, New Orleans, LA, April.

Hmelo-Silver, C.E. and Barrows, H.S. (2003) *Facilitating Collaborative Ways of Knowing*. Manuscript submitted for publication.

Hmelo-Silver, C.E., Derry, S.J., Woods, D., DelMarcelle, M. and Chernobilsky, E. (2005) From parallel play to meshed interaction: the evolution of the eSTEP system in T. Koschmann, D.D. Suthers and T.-W. Chan (eds) *Proceedings of CSCL 2005*. Mahwah, NJ: Lawrence Erlbaum Associates, Inc.

Hmelo, C.E., Guzdial, M. and Turns, J. (1998) Computer support for collaborative learning: learning to support student engagement, *Journal of Interactive Learning Research*, 9: 107–130.

Hmelo-Silver, C.E., Katic, E., Nagarajan, A. and Chernobilsky, E. (in press) Soft leaders, hard artefacts, and the groups we rarely see: using video to understand peer-learning processes in R. Goldman, R. Pea, B. Barron and S. Derry (eds) *Video Research in the Learning Sciences*. Mahwah, NJ: Lawrence Erlbaum Associates, Inc.

Hmelo, C., Vanegas, J.A., Realff, M., Bras, B., Mulholland, H., Shikano, T., *et al.* (1995) Technology support for collaboration in a problem-based curriculum for sustainable technology. Paper presented at the Computer Support for Collaborative Learning, Bloomington, IN, 17–20 October.

Hockings, C. (2004) Practising what we preach? Contradictions between pedagogy and practice in the move to problem-based learning in M. Savin-Baden and K. Wilkie (eds) *Challenging Research in Problem-based Learning*. Maidenhead: SRHE and Open University Press.

Hootstein, E. (2002) Wearing four pairs of shoes: the roles of e-learning facilitators, learning circuits, *ASTD Online Magazine*. www.learningcircuits.org/2002/oct2002/elearn.html (accessed 20 May 2005).

Hung, D. (2002) Situated cognition and problem-based learning: implications for learning and instruction with technology, *Journal of Interactive Learning Research*, 13(4): 393–414.

Hung, D.W.L. and Chen. D.-T. (2001) Situated cognition, Vygotskian thought and learning from the communities of practice perspective: implications for the design of web-based e-learning, *Education Media International*, 38(1): 4–12.

Ingraham, B. (2005) Ambulating with mega-fauna: a scholarly reflection on walking with beasts in R. Land and S. Bayne (eds) *Education in Cyberspace*. Abingdon: RoutledgeFalmer.

IVETTE (2002) European Commission TSER programme. Barcelona, University of Barcelona. www.ub.es/euelearning/ivette/publicdocs.htm (accessed 1 November 2005).

Jacobsen, D.Y. (1997) Tutorial processes in a problem-based learning context: medical students' reception and negotiations. Thesis, Norwegian University of Science and Technology, Trondheim.

Jacobsen, D.Y. (2004) The influence of participants' reception of problem-based learning on problem-based learning tutorials in M. Savin-Baden and K. Wilkie (eds) *Challenging Research in Problem-based Learning*. Maidenhead: SRHE and Open University Press.

Jacobson, M.J. and Spiro, R.J. (1995) Hypertext learning environments, cognitive flexibility, and the transfer of complex knowledge: an empirical investigation, *Journal of Educational Computing Research*, 12(4): 301–333.

Johnson, D.J., Suriya, C., Won Yoon, S., Berrett, J.V. and La Fleur, J. (2002) Team development and group processes of virtual learning teams, *Computers and Education*, 39: 379–393.

Jonassen, D.H. and Grabinger, R.S. (1990) Problems and issues in designing hypertext/hypermedia for learning in D.H. Jonassen and H. Mandl (eds) *Designing Hypermedia for Learning*. Nato Asi Series F, Computer and Systems Sciences, Vol. 67. London: Springer-Verlag.

Jonassen, D.H., Campbell, J.P. and Davidson, M.E. (1994) Learning with media: restructuring the debate, *Educational Technology Research and Development*, 42(2): 31–39.

Kanuka, H. (2002) A principled approach to facilitating distance education: the internet, higher education and higher levels of learning, *Journal of Distance Education*, 17(2): 70–86.

Kaye, A. (1989) Computer-mediated communication and distance education in R. Mason and A. Kaye (eds) *Mindweave: Communication, Computers and Distance Education*. Oxford: Pergamon Press.

Kearsley, G. (1994) Social development theory (L. Vygotsky). Explorations in learning and instruction: the theory into practice database. www.gwu.edu/~tip/vygotsky.html (accessed 22 July 2005).

Kerrey, B., Isakson, J., Abraham, P.S., Arkatov, A., Bailey, G., Bingaman, J., Brown, R.W., Collins, S.R., Enzi, M.B., Fattah, C., Gage, J., Gowen, R.J., King, D.R., McGinn, F., Pfund, N. and Winston, D. (2001) The power of the internet for learning: moving from promise to practice. Report of the Web-based Education Commission to the President and Congress of the United States. Washington DC, Web-Based Education Committee. www.ed.govt/offices/AC/WBEC/Final Report/WBECReport.pdf (accessed November 2005).

Kinzie, M.B. (1990) Requirements and benefits of effective interactive instruction: learner control, self-regulation, and continuing motivation, *Educational Technology Research and Development*, 38(1): 1.

Kitto, S. (2003) Translating an electronic panopticon, *Information, Communication and Society*, 6(1): 1–23.

Klemm, W.R. (1995) Computer conferencing as a cooperative learning environment. Department of Veterinary Anatomy and Public Health, Texas A&M University College Station. www.cvm.tamu.edu/wklemm/cl.html (accessed 28 August 2005).

Kliebard, H.M. (1968) Curricular objectives and evaluation: a reassessment, *The High School Journal*, 241–247.

Knight, P.T. and Yorke, M. (2003) Employability and good learning in higher education, *Teaching in Higher Education*, 8(1): 3–16.

Knowles, M. (1984) *Andragogy in Action: Applying Modern Principles of Adult Learning*. San Francisco: Jossey-Bass.

Knutsen, D., Knutsen, E. and Slazinski, E. (2003) Employing new advances in IP videoconferencing to enhance teaching and learning through the use of a hybrid distance learning course. *Proceedings of the 4th Conference on Information Technology Education,* Lafayette, IN, 16–18 October.

Koschmann, T., Kelson, A.C., Feltovich, P.J. and Barrows, H.S. (1996) Computer-supported problem-based learning: a principled approach to the use of computers in collaborative learning in T.D. Koschmann (ed.) *CSCL: Theory and Practice of an Emerging Paradigm.* Mahwah, NJ: Lawrence Erlbaum Associates, Inc.

Kozma, R.B. (1991) Learning with media, *Review of Educational Research,* 61(2): 179–211.

Kozma, R.B. (1994) Will media influence learning? Reframing the debate, *Educational Technology Research and Development,* 42(2): 7–19.

Kress, G. (2003) *Literacy in the New Media Age.* London: Routledge.

Land, R. (in press) Online learning in the age of 'excellence', *E-Learning.*

Landow, G.P (1997) *Hypertext 2.0. The Convergence of Contemporary Critical Theory and Technology.* Baltimore, MA. Johns Hopkins University Press.

Landow, G. (2004) Is this hypertext any good? *Dichtung-digital,* 2. www.dichtung-digital.com/english.htm (accessed 20 September 2005).

Laurillard, D. (1993) *Rethinking University Teaching. A Framework for the Effective Use of Educational Technology.* London: Routledge.

Laurillard, D. (2002) *Rethinking University Teaching: A Framework for the Effective Use of Educational Technology,* 2nd edn. London: RoutledgeFalmer.

Lautenbacher, G.E., Campbell, J.D., Sorrows, B.B. and Mahling, D.E. (1997) Supporting collaborative, problem-based learning through information system technology. www.fie.engrng.pitt.edu/fie97/papers/1471.pdf (accessed 10 June 2005).

Lave, J. and Wenger, E. (1991) *Situated Learning: Legitimate Peripheral Participation.* Cambridge: Cambridge University Press.

Lawless, K.A. and Brown, S.W. (1997) Multimedia learning environments: issues of learner control and navigation, *Instructional Science,* 25: 117–131.

Lawless, K.A. and Kulikowich, J.M. (1995) Domain knowledge, interest, and hypertext navigation: a study of individual differences. Paper presented at the American Educational Research Association, San Francisco, April.

Lawless, K.A. and Kulikowich, J.M. (1996) Understanding hypertext navigation through cluster analysis, *Journal of Educational Computing Research,* 14(4): 385–399.

Lefebvre, H. (1991) *The Production of Space,* 15th edn. Oxford: Blackwell.

LeJeune, N. (2005) Problem-based learning and the web. University of Colorado at Denver. www.ouray.cudenver.edu-nfljeun/doctoralweb/ (accessed 23 June 2005).

Levin, J. (1995) Organising educational network interactions: steps towards a theory of net-work based learning environments. Paper presented at the Annual Meeting of the American Research Association, San Francisco.

Levin, J., Levin, S.R. and Waddoups, G. (1999) Multiplicity in learning and teaching: a format for developing innovative online education, *Journal of Research on Computing in Education,* 32(2): 256–269.

LoBiondo-Wood, G. and Haber, J. (1994) *Nursing Research,* 3rd edn. St Louis, MO: Mosby.

Lockwood, F. (2003) *Quality Assurance and Evaluation.* Milton Keynes: Open University Press.

López, M. (1999) Overview of methodologies for building ontologies, in V.R. Benjamins, B. Chandrasekaren, A. Gomez Perez, N. Guarino and M. Uschold (eds) *Proceedings of the IJCAI–99 Workshop on Ontologies and Problem-Solving Methods (KRR5),* Stockholm, Sweden.

Lund, A. (2003) The teacher as interface. Teachers of EFL in ICT-rich environments: beliefs, practices, appropriation. Doctorial dissertation, University of Oslo. www.ils.uio.no/forkning/phd-grdrad/doktoravhandlinger/docs/ AndreaaLund-avhandling.pdf (accessed 27 December 2005).

Lycke, K.H. (2002) Inside PBL groups: observations, confirmations and challenges. *Education for Health*, 15(3): 326–334.

Lycke, K.H., Strømsø, H.I. and Grøttum, P. (2002) PBL goes ICT: problem-based learning in face-to-face and distributed groups in medical education at the University of Oslo. Report no. 4, Institute for Educational Research, University of Oslo.

Lyman, P. (1994) Designing the global reference room. Second presentation of the Follet Lecture Series. London, 9 June. Organised by UKOLN on behalf of JISC. www.ukoln.ac.uk/services/papers/follett/lyman/paper.html (accessed 28 October 2005).

Lyotard, J.-F. (1979) *The Postmodern Condition: A Report on Knowledge.* Manchester: Manchester University Press.

McConnell, D. (2000) *Implementing Computer Supported Co-operative Learning*, 2nd edn. London: Kogan Page.

McConnell, D. (2002a) Action research and distributed problem-based learning in continuing professional education, *Distance Education*, 23(1): 59–83.

McConnell, D. (2002b) Negotiation, identity and knowledge in e-learning communities. *Proceedings of the Networked Learning Conference*, University of Sheffield.

Macdonald, D. and Isaacs, G. (2001) Developing a professional identity through problem-based learning, *Teaching Education*, 12(3): 315–333.

McGee, P. (1998) Specialist practitioner in the UK in G. Castledine and P. McGee (eds) *Advanced and Specialist Nurse Practice.* Oxford: Blackwell Scientific.

McLuckie, J. and Topping, K.J. (2004) Transferable skills for online peer learning, *Assessment and Evaluation in Higher Education*, 29(5): 563–584.

Mahling, D.E. (1995) A collaborative environment for semi-structured medical problem based learning. Paper presented at the Computer Support for Collaborative Learning, Bloomington, IN, 17–20 October.

Marchionini, G. (1995) *Information Seeking in Electronic Environments.* London: Cambridge University Press.

Marland, P. (1997) *Towards more Effective Open and Distance Learning.* London: Kogan Page.

Marshall, H.M. (1996) Implications of differentiating and understanding constructivist approaches, *Educational Psychologist*, 31(3): 235–240.

Mason, R. (1998) Models of online courses, *ALN Magazine*, 2(2). www.aln.org/ alnweb/magazine/vol2_issue2/Masonfinal.htm (accessed 22 July 2005).

Mayer, R.E. (1996) Learners as information processors: legacies and limitations of educational psychology's second metaphor, *Educational Psychologist*, 31(3): 151–161.

Mayes, T. (2001) Learning technology and learning relationships in J. Stephenson (ed.) *Teaching and Learning Online.* London: Kogan Page.

Mayes, T., Kibby, M. and Anderson, T. (1990) Learning about hypertext in D.H. Jonassen and H. Mandl (eds) *Designing Hypermedia for Learning.* Nato Asi Series F, Computer and Systems Sciences, Vol. 67. London: Springer-Verlag.

Mentis, M., Ryba, K. and Annan, J. (2001) Creating authentic on-line communities of professional practice. Paper presented at the Australian Association for Research in Education Conference, Fremantle. www.aare.edu.au/01pap/men01511.htm (accessed 28 August 2005).

Mercer, N., Littleton, K. and Wegerif, R. (2004) Methods for studying the processes of interaction and collaborative activity in computer-based educational activities, *Technology, Pedagogy and Education*, 13(2): 195–205.

Meyer, J.H.F. and Land, R. (2003) Threshold concepts and troublesome knowledge (1): linkages to ways of thinking and practising within the disciplines in C. Rust (ed.) *Improving Students Learning: Improving Student Learning Theory and Practice – Ten Years On*. Oxford: OCSLD.

Mezirow, J. (1981) A critical theory of adult learning and education, *Adult Education*, 32: 3–24.

Miao, Y. (2000) *Design and Implementation of a Collaborative Virtual Problem-Based Learning Environment*. Darmstadt: Die Technische Universität Darmstadt.

Miao, Y. (2004) Supporting situated learning for virtual communities of practice: representation and management of situated knowledge. *Proceedings of the 4th IEEE International Conference on Advanced Learning Technologies*, California: IEEE.

Miller, J. and Wallace, L. (2002) An analysis of online access rates and student interaction in distance education courses. Paper presented at NAWeb – the 8th Annual Conference on Web-based Teaching and Learning, University of New Brunswick, Fredericton, 19–22 October.

Mioduser, D. and Nachmias, R. (2002) WWW in education: an overview in H. Adelsberger, B. Collis and M. Pawlowsky (eds) *Handbook on Information Technologies for Education and Training*. Berlin/Heidelberg/New York: Springer-Verlag.

Mioduser, D., Nachmias, R., Lahav, O. and Oren, A. (2000) Web-based learning environments: current pedagogical and technological state, *Journal of Research on Computers in Education*, 33(1): 55–75.

Moore, M.G. (2002) What does research say about learners using computer-mediated communication in distance learning?, *The American Journal of Distance Learning*, 16(2): 61–64.

Moschkovich, J.N. (1996) Moving up and getting steeper: negotiating shared descriptions of linear graphs, *The Journal of the Learning Sciences*, 5(3): 239–277.

Mullen, M. (2002) 'If you're not Mark Mullen, click here': web-based course-ware and the pedagogy of suspicion, *Workplace*, 5.1. www.louisville.edu/journal/workplace/issue5p1/mullen.html (accessed 20 September 2005).

Muukkonen, H., Hakkarainen, K. and Lakkala, M. (1999) Collaborative technology for facilitating progressive inquiry: the future learning environment tools in C. Hoadley and J. Roschelle (eds) *Proceedings of the Computer Support for Collaborative Learning (CSCL) 1999 Conference*. Stanford University, CA.

Nardi, B.A. (ed.) (1996) *Context and Consciousness: Activity Theory and Human–Computer Interaction*. Cambridge, MA: MIT Press.

Nielsen, J. (2002) Top ten guidelines for homepage usability, *Alertbox*. www.useit.com/alertbox (accessed 22 July 2005).

Noble, D.F. (2001) Digital diploma mills: the automation of higher education, *Monthly Review Press*.

Noble, D. (2003) The future: putting Humpty-Dumpty together again, *Biochemical Society Transactions*, 31(1): 156–158.

Norman, G.R. and Schmidt, H.G. (1992) The psychological basis of problem-based learning: a review of the evidence, *Academic Medicine*, 67: 557–565.

Norris, D.M., Mason, J., Robson, R., Lefrere, P. and Collier, G. (2003) A revolution in knowledge sharing, *Educause Review*, 38(5): 15–26. www. educause.edu/ir/ library/pdf/erm0350.pdf (accessed 22 July 2005).

Oblinger, D.G. and Oblinger, J.L. (2005) *Educating the Net Generation*. Boulder, CO: Educause. www.educause.edu/ir/library/pdf/pub7101a.pdf (accessed 28 October 2005).

Ocker, R.J. and Yaverbaum, G.J. (1999) Asynchronous computer-mediated communication versus face-to-face collaboration: results on student learning, quality and satisfaction, *Group Decision and Negotiation*, 8: 427–440.

O'Connor, M.C. and Michaels, S. (1992) Aligning academic task and participation status through revoicing: analysis of a classroom discourse strategy, *Anthropology and Education Quarterly*, 24: 318–335.

Oliffe, J. (2000) Facilitation in PBL – espoused theory versus theory in use. Reflections of a first time user, *Australian Electronic Journal of Nursing Education*, 5(2). www.scu.edu.au/schools/nhcp/aejne/vol5-2/oliffejvol5_2.html (accessed 7 June 2004).

Oliver, M. (2003) Looking backwards, looking forwards: an overview in J. Seale (ed.) *Learning Technology in Transition: From Individual Enthusiasm to Institutional Implementation*. Lisse, The Netherlands: Swets & Zeitlinger.

Oliver, R. (2001) Developing e-learning environments that support knowledge construction in higher education in S. Stoney and J. Burns (eds) *Working for Excellence in the E-conomy*. Perth, Australia: Churchlands.

Oliver, R. and Herrington, J. (2003) Exploring technology-mediated learning from a pedagogical perspective, *Journal of Interactive Learning Environments*, 11(2), 111–126.

Oliver, R. and Omari, A. (1999) Using online technologies to support problem-based learning: learners' responses and suggestions, *Australian Journal of Educational Technology*, 15(1): 58–79.

Oravec, J.A. (2003) Blending by blogging: weblogs in blended learning initiatives, *Journal of Educational Media*, 28(2–3): 225–239.

Orsini-Jones, M. and Davidson, A. (1999) From reflective learners to reflective lecturers via WebCT, *Active Learning*, 10: 32–38.

Orsini-Jones, M. and Davidson, A. (2002) Motivational factors in students' online learning in S. Fallows and R. Bhanot (eds) *Educational Development through Information and Communications Technology*. London: Kogan Page.

Orvis, K.L., Wisher, R.A., Bonk, C.J. and Olson, T.M. (2002) Communication patterns during synchronous web-based military training in problem solving, *Computers in Human Behaviour*, 18: 783–795.

Oshima, J. (1997) Students' construction of scientific explanations in a collaborative hyper-media learning environment. Paper presented at the CSCL Conference, Toronto, December.

Oubenaissa, L., Giardina, M. and Bhattacharya, M. (2002) Designing a framework for the implementation of situated online, collaborative, problem-based activity: operating within a local and multi-cultural learning context, *International Journal on E-Learning*, 1(3): 41–46.

Paavola, S., Ilomäki, L., Lakkala, M. and Hakkarainen, K. (2003) A framework for evaluating virtual learning materials through the three metaphors of learning. Paper presented at the Designing Virtual Learning Material Symposium: The 10th Biennial EARLI (European Association for Research on Learning and Instruction) Conference, Padua, 26–30 August.

Paavola, S., Lipponen, L. and Hakkarainen, K. (2002) Epistemological foundations for CSCL: a comparison of three models of innovative knowledge communities in G. Stahl (ed.) Computer-supported collaborative learning: foundations for a CSCL community. *Proceedings of the Computer-supported Collaborative Learning 2002 Conference.* Hillsdale, NJ: Lawrence Erlbaum Associates, Inc.

Paavola, S., Lipponen, L. and Hakkarainen, K. (2004) Models of innovative knowledge communities and three metaphors of learning, *Review of Educational Research,* 74(4): 557–576.

Palloff, R.M. and Pratt, K. (1999) *Building Learning Communities in Cyberspace: Effective Strategies for the Online Classroom.* San Francisco: Jossey-Bass.

Papert, S. (1986) Constructionism vs instructionism. www.papert.org (accessed December 2005).

Papert, S. (2002) Hard fun Bangor, *Daily News.*

Parker, S. (1997) *Reflective Teaching in the Postmodern World: A Manifesto for Education in Postmodernity.* Buckingham: Open University Press.

Paulsen, M.F. (1995) The online report on pedagogical techniques for computer-mediated communication. www.emoderators.com/moderators/cmcped.html (accessed 28 November 2005).

Paulus, T. (2005) Collaboration or cooperation? Analysing small group interactions in educational environments in T.S. Roberts (ed.) *Computer-Supported Collaborative Learning in Higher Education.* London: Idea Group Publishing.

Pecher, D., Zeelenberg, R. and Barsalou, L.W. (2004) Sensorimotor simulations underlie conceptual representations: modality-specific effects of prior activation, *Psychonomic Bulletin and Review,* 11(1): 164–167.

Pelletier, C. (2005) New technologies, new identities: the university in the informational age in R. Land and S. Bayne (eds) *Education in Cyberspace.* Abingdon: RoutledgeFalmer.

Petrosino, A.J. and Pfaffman, J. (1997) The mission to Mars webliographer: a principled approach to the design of a CSCL tool. *Proceedings of the CSCL Conference,* Toronto, December.

Piaget, J. (1954) *The Construction of Reality in the Child.* New York: Basic Books.

Pilkington, R. (2001) Analysing educational dialogue interaction: towards models that support learning, *International Journal of Artificial Intelligence in Education,* 12: 1–7.

Piskurich, G.M. (1993) *Self-Directed Learning: A Practical Guide to Design, Development and Implementation.* London: Jossey-Bass/Wiley.

Poster, M. (1996) Databases as discourse, or electronic interpellations in D. Lyon and E. Zureik, *Computers, Surveillance, and Privacy.* Minneapolis, MN: University of Minnesota Press.

Prensky, M. (2001) Digital natives, digital immigrants, *On the Horizon,* 9(5). www.marcprensky.com/writing/Prensky%20%20Digital%20Natives%20Digital%-20Immigrants%20-%20Part1.pdf (accessed 20 September 2005).

Price, B. (2000a) Introducing problem-based learning into distance learning in S. Glen and K. Wilkie (eds) *Problem-based Learning in Nursing.* Basingstoke: Macmillan.

Price, B. (2000b) Problem-based learning the distance way: a bridge too far?, *Nurse Education Today,* 20: 98–105.

Privateer, P.M. (1999) Academic technology and the future of higher education, *The Journal of Higher Education,* 70(1): 60–79.

Provenzo, E.F.J. (1992) The electronic panopticon: censorship, control, and indoctrination in post-typographic culture in M.C. Tuman (ed.) *Literacy Online: The*

Promise (and Peril) of Reading and Writing with Computers. Pittsburgh, PA: University of Pittsburgh Press.

Putz, P. and Arnold, P. (2001) Communities of practice: guidelines for the design of online seminars in higher education, *Education, Communication and Information*, 1(2): 181–195.

QAA (2001) *Benchmark Statement: Health Care Programmes, Nursing.* London: HMSO.

Quealy, J. and Langan-Fox, J. (1998) Attributes of delivery media in computer-assisted instruction, *Ergonomics*, 41(3): 257–279.

Race, P. (1994) *The Open Learning Handbook*, 2nd edn. London: Kogan Page.

Ravenscroft, A. (2004) From conditioning to learning communities: implications of 50 years of research in e-learning interaction design, *Association for Learning Technology Journal*, 11(3): 4–18.

Ravenscroft, A. (2005) Towards highly communicative e-learning communities: developing a socio-cultural framework for cognitive change in R. Land and S. Bayne (eds) *Education in Cyberspace.* Abingdon: RoutledgeFalmer.

Reeves, T.C. (2000) Enhancing the worth of instructional technology research through 'design experiments' and other development research strategies. Paper presented at AERA, New Orleans, LA, 1–3 April.

Reeves, T. (2002) Storm clouds on the digital education horizon in A. Williamson, C. Gunn, A. Young and T. Clear (eds) Winds of change in the sea of learning. *Proceedings of the 19th Annual Conference of the Australasian Society for Computers in Learning in Tertiary Education (ASCILITE)*, Auckland: UNITEC Institute of Technology.

Reigeluth, C.M. and Stein, F.S. (1983) The elaboration theory of instruction in C.M. Reigeluth (ed.) *Instructional Design Theories and Models: An Overview of Their Current Status.* Hillsdale, NJ: Lawrence Erlbaum Associates, Inc.

Rendas, A., Pinto, P.R. and Gambosa, T. (1999) A computer simulation designed for problem-based learning, *Medical Education*, 93: 47–54.

Resnick, L.B., Levine, J.M. and Teasley, S.D. (eds) (1991) *Perspectives On Socially Shared Cognition.* Washington, DC: American Psychological Association.

Ritzer, G. (1996) McUniversity in the postmodern consumer society, *Quality in Higher Education*, 2(3): 185–199.

Roald, B. (2000) Videreutvikling av et fleksibelt læringsmiljø for grunnutdanningen I medisin. Pågående og planlagte IKT-prosjekter [Further development of a flexible learning environment for undergraduates. Ongoing and planned ICT-projects]. Policy document to the Board of the Faculty of Medicine, University of Oslo.

Rogerson, E.C.B. and Harden, R.M. (1999) Seven years on: distance learning courses for first level registered nurses and midwives, *Nurse Education Today*, 19: 286–294.

Ronteltap, F. and Eurelings, A. (2002) Activity and interaction of students in an electronic learning environment for problem-based learning, *Distance Education*, 23(1): 11–22.

Ronteltap, F., Goodyear, P. and Bartoluzzi, S. (2004) A pattern language as an instrument in designing for productive learning conversations. Paper presented at Ed-Media, Lugarno, Switzerland, 23–25 June.

Roschelle, J. and Pea, R. (1999) Trajectories from today's WWW to a powerful educational infrastructure, *Educational Researcher*, June–July: 22–25.

Rosenberg, D. and Sillince, J.A.A. (2000) Verbal and non-verbal communication in mediated settings, *International Journal of Artificial Intelligence in Education*, 11(3): 299–319. www.cbl.leeds.ac.uk/ijaied/current.html (accessed 28 September 2005).

Rourke, L. and Anderson, T. (2002) Using peer teams to lead online discussions, *Journal of Interactive Media in Education*, 1.

Rourke, L., Anderson, T., Garrison, D.R. and Archer, W. (2001) Methodological issues in the content analysis of computer conference transcripts, *International Journal of Artificial Intelligence in Education*, 12: 8–22.

Rushkoff, D. (1997) *The Children of Chaos*. London: Flamingo.

Russell, D.R. (2002) Looking beyond the interface: activity theory and distributed learning in R.M. Lea and K. Nicoll (eds) *Distributed Learning: Social and Cultural Approaches to Practice*. London: RoutledgeFalmer.

Ryan, Y. (2001) The provision of learner support services online in G. Farrell (ed.) *The Changing Faces of Virtual Education*. The Commonwealth of Learning. www.col.org/virtualed (accessed 30 November 2005).

Salmon, G. (2000) Learning submarines: raising the periscopes. NETWORKING online conference, 1–14 November. www.flexiblelearning.net.au/NW2000/main/key03.htm.

Salmon, G. (2002) *E-tivities: The Key to Active Online Learning*. London: Kogan Page.

Salmon, G. (2003) *E-Moderating: The Key to Teaching and Learning Online*. London: Kogan Page.

Salomon, G. (ed.) (1993) *Distributed Cognitions. Psychological and Educational Considerations*. Cambridge, MA: Cambridge University Press.

Salomon, G. and Perkins, D. (1998) Individual and social aspects of learning, *Review of Research in Education*, 23: 1–24.

Sandoval, J. (1995) Teaching in subject matter areas: science, *Annual Review of Psychology*, 355–374.

Sauer, I.M., Bialek, D., Efimova, E., Schwartlander, R., Pless, G. and Neuhaus, P. (2005) 'Blogs' and 'wikis' are valuable software tools for communication within research groups, *Artificial Organs*, 29(1): 82–83.

Savery, J.R. and Duffy, T. (1995) Problem-based learning: an instructional model and its constructivist framework, *Educational Technology*, September–October: 31–33.

Savery, J.R. and Duffy, T.M. (2001) Problem-based learning: an instructional model and its constructivist framework. CRLT Technical Report 16–01, Center for Research on Teaching and Technology, Indiana University.

Savin-Baden, M. (2000) *Problem-based Learning in Higher Education: Untold Stories*. Buckingham: SRHE and Open University Press.

Savin-Baden, M. (2003) *Facilitating Problem-Based Learning. Illuminating Perspectives*. Maidenhead: SRHE and Open University Press.

Savin-Baden, M. (2005) Learning spaces, learning bridges and troublesomeness: the power of differentiated approaches to problem-based learning, *Problem-based Learning: New Directions and Approaches*, 1(1): 10–28.

Savin-Baden, M. (2006) Disjunction as a form of troublesome knowledge in problem-based learning in J.H.F. Meyer and R. Land (eds) *Overcoming Barriers to Student Understanding: Threshold Concepts and Troublesome Knowledge*. Abingdon: RoutledgeFalmer.

Savin-Baden, M. and Major, C. (2004) *Foundations of Problem-based Learning*. Maidenhead: Open University Press/SRHE.

Savin-Baden, M. and Wilkie, K. (2004) *Challenging Research in Problem-based Learning*. Maidenhead: SRHE and Open University Press.

Scardemalia, M. and Bereiter, C. (1994) Computer support for knowledge-building communities, *The Journal of the Learning Sciences*, 33: 256–283.

Scardamalia, M., Bereiter, C., McLean, R.S., Swallow, J. and Woodruff, E. (1989) Computer-supported intentional learning environments, *Journal of Educational Computing Research*, 5(1): 51–68.

Schmidt, H.G. (1983) Problem-based learning: rationale and description, *Medical Education*, 17: 11–16.

Schmidt, H.G. (1993) Foundations of problem-based learning: some explanatory notes, *Medical Education*, 27: 422–432.

Schmidt, H.G. and Moust, J.H.C. (1995) What makes a tutor effective? A structural-equation modeling approach to learning in problem-based curricula, *Academic Medicine*, 7(8): 708–714.

Schmidt, H.G. and Moust, J.H.C. (2000) Factors affecting small-group tutorial learning: a review of research in D.H. Evensen and C.E. Hmelo (eds) *Problem-Based Learning. A Research Perspective on Learning Interactions*. Mahwah, NJ: Lawrence Erlbaum Associates, Inc.

Schmidt, H.G., De Volder, M.L., De Grave, W.S., Moust, J.H.C. and Patel, V.L. (1989) Explanatory models in the processing of science text: the role of prior knowledge activation through small-group discussion, *Journal of Educational Psychology*, 81(4): 610–619.

Schmidt, H.G., Machiels-Bongaerts, M., Hermans, H., ten Cate, T.J., Venekamp, R. and Boshuisen, H.P.A. (1996) The development of diagnostic competence: comparison of a problem-based, an integrated, and a conventional medical curriculum, *Academic Medicine*, 71: 658–664.

Schneider, D., Synteta, P. and Frété, C. (2002) Community, content and collaboration management systems in education: a new chance for socio-constructivist scenarios? *Proceedings of the 3rd Congress on Information and Communication Technologies in Education*, Rhodes, Greece, 26–29 September.

Schoenfeld, A.H. (1987) What's all the fuss about metacognition? in A.H. Schoenfeld (ed.) *Cognitive Science and Mathematics Education*. Hillsdale, NJ: Lawrence Erlbaum Associates, Inc.

Sfard, A. (1998) On two metaphors for learning and the dangers of choosing just one, *Educational Researcher*, 27: 4–13.

Shachaf, P. and Hara, N. (2002) Ecological approach to virtual team effectiveness. Working paper WP–02–08, Center for Social Informatics. www.slis.indiana.edu/ CSI/ WP/WP02–08B.html (accessed 1 June 2005).

Shin, E.C., Schallert, D.L. and Savenye, W.C. (1994) Effects of learner control, advisement, and prior knowledge on young students' learning in a hypertext environment, *Educational Technology, Research and Development*, 42(1): 33–46.

Shyu, H.S. and Brown, S.W. (1992) Learner control versus program control in interactive videodisc instruction: what are the effects on procedural learning?, *International Journal of Instructional Media*, 19(2): 217–231.

Shyu, H.S. and Brown, S.W. (1995) Learner-control: the effects on learning a procedural task during computer-based videodisc instruction, *International Journal of Instructional Media*, 22(3): 217–231.

Simpson, O. (2002) *Supporting Students in Online, Open and Distance Learning*, 2nd edn. London: Kogan Page.

Soloman, B.A. and Felder, R. (1991) Index of learning styles. www.ncsu.edu/felder-public/ILSpage.html (accessed 22 July 2005).

Spatariu, A., Hartley, K. and Bendixen, L.D. (2004) Defining and measuring quality in online discussions, *Journal of Interactive Online Learning*, 2(4): 1–15.

Spender, D. (1995) *Nattering on the Net: Women, Power and Cyberspace*. Toronto: Garamond Press.

Spiro, R.J., Feltovich, P.J., Jacobson, M.J. and Coulson, R.L. (1995) Cognitive flexibility, constructivism, and hypertext: random access instruction for advance knowledge acquisition in ill-structured domains in P.S.J. Gale (ed.) *Constructivism in Education*. Hillsdale, NJ: Lawrence Erlbaum Associates, Inc.

Spivey, N.N. (1997) *The Constructivist Metaphor: Reading, Writing, and the Making of Meaning*. San Diego, CA: Academic Press.

Stahl, G. (2002) Contributions to a theoretical framework for CSCL. Paper presented at the Computer Supported Collaborative Learning Conference, Boulder, CO, 7–11 January. www.cis.drexel.edu/faculty/gerry/publications/conference/2002/csc12002/index.html.

Steinkuehler, C.A., Derry, S.J., Hmelo-Silver, C.E. and Delmarcelle, M. (2002) Cracking the resource nut with distributed problem-based learning in secondary teacher education, *Distance Education*, 23(1): 23–39.

Stenhouse, L. (1975) *An Introduction to Curriculum Research and Development*. London: Heinemann.

Stiles, M. and Orsmond, P. (2002) Managing active student learning with a virtual learning environment in S. Fallows and R. Bhanot (eds) *Educational Development through Information and Communications Technology*. London: Kogan Page.

Stoner, G. (1996) A conceptual framework for the integration of learning technology in G. Stoner (ed.) Implementing learning technology. www.icbl.hw.ac.uk/ltdi/implementing-it/ (accessed 30 September 2005).

Strang, W. (1995) Empowering teachers and learners through technology. SEDA Paper 90 2005. www.londonmet.ac.uk/deliberations/seda-publications/strang.cfm (accessed 30 September 2005).

Strijbos, J.-W. (2004) The effect of roles on computer-supported collaborative learning [Het effect van rollen op computerondersteund samenwerkend leren]. www.e-learning.surf.nl/e-learning/onderzoek/2627 (accessed 22 July 2005).

Strømsø, H.I., Grøttum, P. and Lycke, K.H. (2004) Changes in student approaches to learning with the introduction of computer-supported problem-based learning, *Medical Education*, 38: 390–398.

Syson, A. (2005) Talking pages: narrated PowerPoint presentations. www.home.ched.coventry.ac.uk/demo (accessed 30 September 2005).

Swan, K. and Shea, P. (2005) The development of virtual learning communities in S.R. Hiltz and R. Goldman (eds) *Learning Together Online: Research on Asynchronous Learning Networks*. Mahwah, NJ: Lawrence Erlbaum Associates, Inc.

Taylor, P.G. (1999) *Making Sense of Academic Life: Academics, Universities and Change*. Buckingham: SRHE and Open University Press.

Tergan, S.O. (1997) Misleading theoretical assumptions in hypertext/hypermedia research, *Journal of Educational Multimedia and Hypermedia*, 6(3–4): 257–283.

Thomas, T. (2002) Critical thinking and deep cognitive processing by structured discussion board activities. www.celt.lsu.edu/CFD/E-Proceedings/ (accessed 22 July 2005).

Thorpe, M. (2001) Learner support: a new model for online teaching and learning. *Proceedings of the ICDE World Conference on Open Learning and Distance Education*, Dusseldorf, Germany.

Thorpe, M. (2002) Rethinking learner support: the challenge of collaborative online learning, *Open Learning*, 17(2): 105–119.

Trowler, P., Knight, P. and Saunders, M. (2003) *Change Thinking, Change Practices.* York: HE Academy. www.heacademy.ac.uk/resources.asp?process=full_record& section=generic&id=262 (accessed 1 November 2005).

Turkle, S. (1996) *Life on the Screen: Identity in the Age of the Internet.* London: Phoenix.

Tversky, B., Morrison, J.B. and Betrancourt, M. (2002) Animation: can it facilitate?, *International Journal of Human–Computer Studies*, 57: 247–262.

United Kingdom Central Council for Nursing, Midwifery and Health Visiting (1998) *Standards for Specialist Education and Practice.* London: UKCC.

University of Dundee (2005) Evaluation of MSc (practice education) FDL pathway, December.

Van Berkel, H.J.M., Nuy, H.J.P. and Geerligs, T. (1995) The influence of progress tests and block tests on study behaviour, *Instructional Science*, 22: 317–333.

van Boxtel, C., van der Linden, J. and Kanselaar, G. (2000) Collaborative learning tasks and the elaboration of conceptual knowledge, *Learning and Instruction*, 10: 311–330.

Van Der Vleuten, C.P.M., Verwijnen, G.M. and Wijnen, H.F.W. (1996) Fifteen years of experience with progress testing in a problem-based learning curriculum, *Medical Teacher*, 18(2): 103–109.

Vonderwell, S. (2003) An examination of asynchronous communication experiences and perspectives of students in an online course: a case study, *Internet and Higher Education*, 6: 77–90.

von Glasserfeld, E. (1988) Cognition, construction of knowledge and Teaching, Eric Document Reproduction Service No. ED294 754.

Vygotsky, L.S. (1978) *Mind in Society: The Development of Higher Psychological Processes.* Cambridge, MA: Harvard University Press. (Original work published 1930)

Wan, A.D.M. and Braspenning, P.J. (1995) The bifurcation of DAI and adaptivism as synthesis in J.C. Bioch and Y.-H. Tan (eds) *Proceedings of the 7th Dutch Conference on Artificial Intelligence (NAIC95)*, Erasmus University, Rotterdam, 20–22 June.

Watson, G. (2002) Using technology to promote success in PBL courses, *The Technology Source*, May/June. www.technologysource.org/article/using_technology _to_promote_success_in_pbl_-courses/ (accessed 1 November 2005).

Wegerif, R. and Mercer, N. (1996) Computer and reasoning through talk in the classroom, *Language and Education*, 10(1): 47–64.

Wenger, E. (1998) *Communities of Practice: Learning, Meaning and Identity.* Cambridge: Cambridge University Press.

Wenger, E. (2004) Communities of practice: a brief introduction. www.ewenger.com/ theory/communities_of_practice_intro.htm (accessed 22 July 2005).

Wiggins, G. and McTighe, J. (1998) *Understanding by Design.* Alexandria, VA: ASCD.

Wilkersen, L. and Hundert, E.M. (1997) Becoming a problem-based tutor: increasing self-awareness through faculty development in D. Boud and G.I. Feletti (eds) *The Challenge of Problem-based Learning.* London: Kogan Page.

Wilkie, K. (2002) Actions, attitudes and attributes: developing facilitation skills for problem-based learning. Unpublished PhD thesis, Coventry University.

Wilkie, K. (2004) Becoming facilitative: shifts in lecturers' approaches to facilitating problem-based learning in M. Savin-Baden and K. Wilkie (eds) *Challenging Research in Problem-based Learning.* Maidenhead: SRHE and Open University Press.

Winograd, D. (2001) Guidelines for moderating online educational computer conferences. www.emoderators.com/moderators/winograd.html (accessed 20 May 2005).

Wittrock, M.C. (1990) Generative processes of comprehension, *Educational Psychologist*, 24(4): 345–376.

Wood, D. (2001) Scaffolding, contingent tutoring and computer-supported learning, *International Journal of Artificial Intelligence in Education*, 12: 280–292.

Yin, R.K. (1989) *Case Study Research, Design and Methods*. London: Sage.

Yin, R.K. (1994) *Case Study Research – Design and Methods*, 2nd edn. London: Sage.

Zumbach, J. and Reimann, P. (2003) Influence of feedback on distributed problem based learning in B. Wasson, S.R. Ludvigsen and U. Hoppe (eds) Designing for change. *Proceedings of the International Conference on CSCL 2003*. Dordrecht, The Netherlands: Kluwer Academic.

Zumbach, J., Hillers, A. and Reimann, P. (2004) Distributed problem-based learning: the use of feedback mechanisms in online learning in T.S. Roberts (ed.) *Online Collaborative Learning: Theory and Practice*. Hershey, PA: Idea Group, Inc.

Index

Accessibility, 132
Action research, 26, 82, 193, 197
Activity theory
  application, 62–3, 67, 68, 75, 77–8,
    184, 203–5
  definition, 61–2
  tutoring, modelling, fading, 46, 56,
    59–60, 66
Assessment, 161
Asynchronous discussions, 65, 143, 156,
  163, 178–9, 195
Authenticity of online learning, 15–17
Authoring, 8, 13, 16

Backward design model, 68–9
Blackboard, 105, 111–15, 132, 141, 145,
  147, 151, 210
Boundaries, intellectual, 17, 70

Case study research, 85, 195
Cognitive congruence, 47
Collaborative
  learning, 142–4, 148, 160, 164, 180–1,
    195
  working, 41, 89, 90, 107, 110–11, 182–3
  lack of, 55
Communities of practice, 109–11, 148,
  151
Computer-mediated conferencing
  (CMC), 142–4, 150–1, 196
  examples of, 145–7, 148–50
Constructivist stance, 126, 138–9, 142–4,
  155–7, 159, 165, 195
CROCODILE, 164–5
Curriculum design, 135

Dialogic learning, 12, 41, 138
Disciplinary culture, 9, 16, 20, 34, 42,
  141, 151
  Role model, 55
Disjunction, 17–18, 19, 23, 211

Education (as commodity, 25

Education new student market, 33
elearning
  design considerations, 152, 209
  program deficiencies, 84, 136–7
  support models, 34
eStep, 7, 63–7, 71–3, 77–8, 163–4
Espoused theories / theories in use, 46,
  47–8, 58

Facilitation
  essence of, 39–40, 46, 89–90, 97,
    119
  good examples, 69, 70, 75, 76–7, 86–7,
    88, 89
Facilitator
  becoming one, 10–12, 13, 35, 41–3
  Wilkie's 4 approaches, 46, 57–8
Fast click, 'three click', 118, 133–4
Frame factors, 42–3

Higher Education Funding Council for
  England (HEFCE), 9

Implementation
  costs, 32–3, 36
  of technology, 28–9, 29–30, 30–1,
    35–6, 102
  resource restrictions, 30–1,
    40
Infotainment, 101, 134
Interactive media, 126–32

Knowledge
  academic, 17
  acquired by students, 10, 13
  building, 184, 190
  conceptual, professional, 163
  created by students, 5, 9, 11–12, 18,
    137–8, 142, 166, 177, 188
  distributed, 187–8
  ecology of, 17
  hierarchy, 16–17, 18
  managing, 5, 10, 13, 130, 210

Learner
  experience enhancement, 25–6, 106,
    143
  identity, 19–20, 22, 23
  qualities, 22
  styles, 170
  support, 133–4, 159–60
Learning
  active approach by students, 18, 25–9,
    40, 89–90, 107–10, 142, 148, 160,
    167, 190
  context, 130–1, 166–7, 208
  experiential, 110
  face-to-face best, 16, 17, 42, 71, 119
  Management System, 58, 165
  responsibility, 18–19, 76–7, 167,
    169–70
  self-directed, 77, 82–4, 89–90, 112,
    174, 177, 187, 210
  deep level, 117, 171, 209
Lifelong learning, 48, 76, 90

Managed Learning Environment, 31,
  127, 132

Non-verbal /social cues, 11, 15, 43, 47,
  53–4
'Not invented here' syndrome, 26

Open learning environments / spaces,
  40, 159–60
Outcome measure and performance, 9,
  20–1, 25

Pedagogy
  and technology, 6, 8–10, 13, 26, 29, 34,
    99, 136, 174
  lack of, 3
  priorities, 126, 133, 134–6
Performative slide, 25
POLARIS, 163–9, 174, 178, 181
Polling problem, 161
Presence, 15–17
Problem-based learning
  blended, 7, 80–5, 96, 183, 193–4, 208
  built on prior knowledge, 166–8, 170,
    194
  cost issues v onlinePBL, 4, 32
  for critical contestability, 5
  difference to prior learning
    experience, 13, 46, 47, 77
  distributed, 164

  elaboration, 166–7, 177
  online v face-to-face differences, 4,
    12–13, 40–42, 45–8, 51, 191, 208,
    210
  optimal online team size, 40, 121, 199
  or problem-solving?, 5–6, 128, 134
  seven step / jump, 45, 55, 113
PsyWeb, 165–173, 210

Quality assurance, 35–6

Rhetorical criticism, 128, 129

Savin-Baden, M., 5, 7, 13, 17, 19, 23, 39,
  129
Students
  conflict in teams, 12, 109, 110, 180,
    204, 210
  as critical thinkers, 18, 19, 20, 41, 77,
    148, 160, 187
  as dissatisfied consumers, 160, 187
  empowered, 88–9, 160, 168, 205,
    207
  views on poor facilitation, 75
  as independent inquirers, 4, 13, 82,
    128
  induction, 196, 203–4
  learning in teams, 4, 7–8, 11–12, 41,
    134, 138, 147–8, 151, 180–3,
    198–203, 207–9
  losing control, 13, 19–20, 40, 71, 88,
    159, 186
  undervaluing tools provided, 71, 72,
    76, 198, 207
  using tools imaginatively, 72–5, 106,
    155–7, 198–203
Surveillance, 21–2, 32, 40, 72
Symbolic convergence theory, 129
Synchronous facilities, 111–14, 127, 195

Teacher identity, 16, 17, 19
Technology accessible in the hole, 102,
  131–2, 137
Theory-practice gap, 103, 183
Tool descriptions, 162–6, 176–187,
  192–3, 195–7
Tool limitations, 71–4, 118, 198, 204,
  207–9
Tutor role
  communication skills, 88
  e-tutor definition, 81, 84
  learner-centred, 87, 88–9, 93, 106

modelling best practice, 83–4, 86–7,
  89–90, 106
pitfalls to avoid, 95, 119
situation specific, 57, 58, 170
training input, 49, 71, 80–1,
  196
training needs, 41, 58, 59

Virtual learning environment (VLE), 6,
  20–3, 100, 128, 132, 210–11

WebCT, 132, 195, 210

Zone of proximal development, 76, 108,
  111, 150–1

Related books from Open University Press
Purchase from www.openup.co.uk or order through your local bookseller

CHALLENGING RESEARCH IN PROBLEM-BASED LEARNING

Maggi Savin-Baden and Kay Wilkie (eds)

This is a wide ranging, clearly focused, accessible book that engages with the practices and findings of research into problem-based learning ... The book is clear on the problems and the strategies, the debates and the research-based practices which make PBL accessible wherever it is suitable for effective learning.

Professor Gina Wisker, Anglia Polytechnic University

This book punctures the sometimes inflated rhetoric about PBL by exploring some of its inherent difficulties and contradictions, and moves debate on through critical glimpses of the rich and varied practices undertaken under the banner of PBL.

Professor Graham Gibbs, University of Oxford

This book presents international research into Problem-based Learning within a range of subject and vocational disciplines, applications and cultures from a variety of perspectives: student, facilitator, module leader, curriculum designer. It presents a range of findings related to designing, implementing, assessing and evaluating PBL courses.

Challenging Research in Problem-based Learning is key reading for academics and tutors utilising PBL, as well as those studying for teaching qualifications, lecturers involved in teaching for the professions and on continuing professional development courses.

Contributors
Terry Barrett, Brian Bowe, John Cowan, Roisin Donnelly, Erik de Graaff, Chris Hockings, Bill Hutchings, Dan Jacobsen, Peter Kandlbinder, Sharron King, Ranald Macdonald, Claire Howell Major, Yves Maufette, Karen O'Rourke, Betsy Palmer, Maggi Savin-Baden, Charlotte Silén, Alexandre Soucisse, Kay Wilkie.

Contents
Introduction – **Part one: Curricula concerns** – *The problem in Problem-based Learning is the problem* – *The impact of assessment on the Problem-based Learning process* – *Researching the student experience to bring about improvements in Problem-based Learning* – *Investigating the effectiveness of teaching 'online learning' in a Problem-based Learning online environment* – **Part two: Facilitator experiences** – *Practising what we preach?* – *Becoming facilitative* – *Researching the dialogue of Problem-based Learning tutorials* – *The emotional dimension of collaborative change to Problem-based learning* – **Part three: Student Experiences** – *Learning leadership through collaboration* – *The influence of participants' reception of Problem-based Learning on Problem-based Learning tutorials* – *Does Problem-based Learning make students 'Go Meta'?* – **Part four: Comparative issues** – *A comparative evaluation of Problem-based Learning in physics* – *Medical studies to literary studies* – *Exploring the impact of discipline-based pedagogy on Problem-based Learning through interpretive meta ethnography* – *Epilogue* – *Bibliography* – *Index*.

2004   256pp   0 335 21544 0 (Paperback)

E-LEARNING GROUPS AND COMMUNITIES

David McConnell

- How can we design networked e-learning courses to ensure students participate in them and engage in quality learning outcomes?
- What happens in an e-learning course that is designed to foster group work and a sense of 'community'?
- How can we research e-learning practice in ways that will enhance the processes of learning and teaching?

This book outlines approaches to networked e-learning course design that are underpinned by a belief that students learn best in these contexts when they are organised in groups and communities. As such, the book is one of the first to provide a detailed analysis of what goes on in e-learning groups and communities.

But how do students react to working in e-learning groups and communities? What determines their willingness to adopt new forms of learning in order to participate in these new courses? What actually happens in an e-learning community, and what impact does this have on students and tutors? This book examines these key questions through a variety of research approaches aimed at exploring the experience of e-learners as they participate in successful e-groups and communities. It also offers ways in which learning outcomes may be achieved in these communities and outlines the specific skills that students would develop through e-learning.

E-learning Groups and Communities is essential reading for teachers, trainers, managers, researchers and students involved in e-learning courses as well as people interested in improving the quality of the learning experience.

Contents

Acknowledgements – Introduction – Designing for e-groups and communities: theoretical and conceptual issues – Design principles: a model – The experience of e-learning groups and communities – Assessing learning in e-groups and communities – Assessment: the view from inside – Problem-solving and action research in communities of practice – Group dynamics: a view from the inside – Understanding groups, communities and learning technologies – Bibliography – Index.

2006   224pp   0 335 21280 8 (Paperback)   0 335 21281 6 (Hardback)